Marriages and Deaths

from the

Maryland Gazette,

1727-1839

Compiled By

Robert Barnes

CLEARFIELD

FIRST PRINTING 1973
SECOND PRINTING 1976
THIRD PRINTING 1979

Reprinted for
Clearfield Company, Inc. by
Genealogical Publishing Co., Inc.
Baltimore, Maryland
1993, 1994, 1997, 2004

Library of Congress Catalogue Card Number 73-012383
International Standard Book Number: 0-8063-0580-0

Made in the United States of America

INTRODUCTION

The *Maryland Gazette* was first published in Annapolis in 1727 by William Parks. Parks had previously established two newspapers in England: the *Ludlow Post-Man* in 1719 and the *Reading Mercury* in 1723. He came to Annapolis in March 1725/6 and shortly thereafter established the *Maryland Gazette*, which was the first paper to be published south of Pennsylvania. Publication of the *Gazette* was carried on intermittently until 1734.

Parks held the post of Public Printer in the Province of Maryland from 1727 until 1737. In 1730 he established a press in Williamsburg, Virginia and in 1736 became the editor of the *Virginia Gazette*. He was also Public Printer of Virginia until 1750, the year of his death.

The *Maryland Gazette* was re-established in 1745 by Jonas Green, a native of Connecticut and the son of Deacon Timothy Green. Before coming to Maryland Green worked for printers in both Boston and Philadelphia, including Benjamin Franklin and Andrew Bradford. Like William Parks before him, Green, in 1738, was appointed Public Printer of Maryland. He is considered by some to have been one of the best printers in the Colonies. After his death, in April of 1767, his widow, Anna Catherine Green, carried on publication of the paper until her own death in 1775. The paper was thereafter continued by their sons, Frederick and Samuel, and a grandson, Jonas.

The *Gazette* usually consisted of a folded sheet of four pages, with nearly half the space devoted to advertising. News from Europe and from other colonies took up the bulk of the remaining space, with part of one column given over to Annapolis news. Deaths and marriages were sometimes found in this column, but later, when they became a popular feature, they were listed separately under the headings "Marriages" and "Deaths," or as they were waggishly referred to in the early nineteenth century, "The Knot" and "The Knell." The early issues of the paper carried comparatively few marriage and death notices other than those concerning prominent citizens. The inclusion of notices of ordinary citizens was a gradual process.

Publication of the *Gazette* was suspended in 1777 until April 30, 1779. Other gaps in the publication, or in the extant copies of the newspaper, occurred from April 10 to June 12, 1834, from February 14 to March 17, 1836, and from June to December 15, 1836.

Items from the *Maryland Gazette* for the period 1728 to 1800 were compiled by Christopher Johnston and published after his death in Volumes XVII and XVIII of the *Maryland Historical Magazine*. George A. Martin, well known for his transcriptions of marriages and deaths in the Washington, D.C. *National Intelligencer*, published "Biographical Notes from the Maryland Gazette" for the period 1801 to 1821 in Volume XLII of the *Maryland Historical Magazine*.

The marriages and deaths in this present work have been compiled from microfilm copies of the newspaper at the Maryland Historical Society and from original copies of the paper on file at both the Maryland Historical Society in Baltimore and the State Library in Annapolis. The marriages and deaths are alphabetically arranged by the last name of the bridegroom (in the case of marriages) or of the deceased for the whole period from 1727 to 1839, rather than year by year as was done by Messrs. Johnston and Martin. In re-checking the periods for which marriages and deaths had already been published, several new items have been brought to light.

The text consists of newspaper abstracts of approximately 3,000 marriages and deaths of Marylanders—not only from the Annapolis area, but from the entire state. An appendix, the purpose of which is to assist the researcher in locating church records, contains notes on Maryland clergymen mentioned in the text. A surname index to brides, ministers, and others, including parents and relatives, is a guide to an additional 2,000 names.

The author is indebted to Mrs. Mary Meyer of the Maryland Historical Society and to Dr. Michael Tepper of the Genealogical Publishing Company for their invaluable suggestions in preparing this book.

Robert Barnes

TABLE OF CONTENTS

MARRIAGES AND DEATHS FROM THE

MARYLAND GAZETTE, 1727 - 1839

ADAIR, Mr. Robert, one of the representatives for Balto. Co., died
at his house in Balto. Town on Saturday last [Oct. 22].
(Oct. 27, 1768)

ADAMS, Rev. Alexander, died 14th inst., in his 90th year. He had
been rector of Stepney Parish, Som. Co., for 65 years.
(Sept. 28, 1769)

ADAMS, Humphrey, died Sunday last, at Mr. Galloway's; a gentleman
possessed of a large estate in Eng., who came over here this
summer to take his diversion in a tour through the English
colonies on the continent. (Aug. 7, 1755)

ADAMS, President John; obituary notice of. (July 13, 1826)

ADDAMS, Roger, of Dor. Co., having drunk too much at the Proclamation of His present Majesty [George III], laid a wager that
he could drink all the wine left in a decanter at one drought.
He won the wager, but died a few minutes after. (March 5,
1761).

ADDISON, Mrs. Eleanor, died Monday, Jan. 19th, at her house at Oxon-
Hill, on Potowmack River, in her 72nd year; she was the relict
of the late Thomas Addison, Esq. (March 12, 1761)

ADDISON, Mrs. Rachel, wife of Rev. Henry Addison, and second daughter of the late Hon. Daniel Dulany, of this city, died Wed.,
19th inst. (Oct. 27, 1774)

ADDISON, Thomas, Jr., of Potomac, and Rebecca, eldest daughter of
the Hon. Walter Dulany, Esq., of this place, were married
Mon. evening last [Nov. 30]. (Dec. 3, 1767)

ADDISON, Thomas, Esq., died Thurs., 27th ult., at his house on Potomac, in his 56th year; sometime Major of His Majesty's 35th
Regiment of Foot. He left the bulk of his property to his
nephew, Thomas Addison, Esq., of Oxon-Hill. (Dec. 6, 1770)

ADDISON, Thomas, Esq., died Friday last, Sept. 24, at his seat

on Potomac River, leaving a widow and several small children.
(Sept. 29, 1774)

AIRY, Rev. Mr. Thomas, died Friday last [Oct. 25] in Dor. Co.; rector of a parish there. (Oct. 31, 1765)

AIRY, Thomas, was drowned off the schooner Friendship, belonging to
Mathias Traverse, on the 6th inst.; off Bodkin [Point]; aged
about 20 years. A reward is offered for the return of his
body. (Sept. 18, 1788).

AISQUITH, Rev. Henry, rector of St. Margaret's Parish, A. A. Co.,
and Ellen Hodges, of Annap., were married in St. Anne's
Church, the 25th ult., by Rev. Blanchard. (Oct. 2, 1828)

ALDEY, Mr. Perrin, aged 105 years, and Mrs. Anne Tankerly, aged 90,
were married Thurs., 30th ult., in Charlotte Co., Va. It was
the third marriage for both. (Aug. 22, 1805)

ALDRIDGE, Mrs., of P. G. Co., and her two children, were murdered
by a negro slave. (April 1 - April 8, 1729)

ALEXANDER, Mrs. Mary, of this city, died 26th ult., at the residence
of her brother, Dr. Stockett, of Elk Ridge. (Aug. 9, 1827)

ALEXANDER, Thomas S., of Annap., and Priscilla, only daughter of the
late Dr. Ghiselin, were married Tues. evening, 30th ult., at
Brookfield, P. G. Co., by Rev. Mr. Grigg. (Dec. 8, 1830)

ALEXANDER, William, merchant, died in Annap., on Tues. (Oct. 3, 1822)

ALKIN, Rev. Mr., of Q. A. Co., and Miss Ellin Middleton, daughter
of H. S. Middleton, of this city, were married Mon. evening.
(March 5, 1767)

ALKIN, Rev. Mr. Thomas, rector of St. John's Parish, Q. A. Co., died
lately. (April 8, 1773)

ALLEIN, Benjamin, died Sat., 8th inst., in the 47th year of his age.
(Jan. 19, 1814)

ALLEN, John, who lived on the north side of the Severn, about three
weeks ago, was barbarously murdered by one Aggleton, near
Patapsco Ferry, in Balto. Co. (May 13, 1762)

ALLEN, Martin, and Juliet Ann Hess, of Bread Neck, north side of
Severn, were married 25th inst., by the Rev. Nicholas J. Watkins. (Sept. 27, 1827)

AMOS, William, died in Harf. Co., on 26th ult., in the 97th year of
his age, a much revered member of the Society of Friends,

and 76 years a member thereof. (March 24, 1814)

ANDERSON, Major Archibald, died at the Battle of Guilford, on March
15, 1781. [Long eulogy printed] (April 12, 1781)

ANDERSON, Esther, was burned at Chester, Kent Co., for her part in
the murder of her master. (May 20, 1746)

ANDERSON, Mrs. Euphemia, daughter of Mr. Joseph Jefferson, Esq.,
comedian, died in Annap., on Tues. morning last, in her 28th
year. She leaves aged parents, several brothers and sisters,
and two young daughters. (July 15, 1830)

ANDERSON, James, Sr., died on the morning of the 1st inst.; an old
resident of this county, in his 79th year. (Oct. 4, 1804)

ANDERSON, Col. Richard, died suddenly at Philadelphia, on Mon., 22nd
ult., of apoplexy, in his 84th year. He was an officer in
the Maryland Line during the Revolutionary War. He was born
in Maryland on January 16, 1752. In the spring of 1776 he
joined the army. After the war, he settled on his patri-
monial farm in Mont. Co., where he raised a numerous family.
(July 2, 1835)

ANDERTON, Mrs. Amelia, died Mon. last [April 23] at her seat in Dor.
Co. (April 26, 1787)

ANDREWS, Mr. T. P., of the U. S. Army, and Emily R., daughter of the
late Richard Snowden, Esq., were married Tues. evening, 21st
inst., at the seat of Thomas Snowden, Jr., of A. A. Co., by
Rev. Henry Johns. (Oct. 30, 1828)

APPLEBY, William, of Balto. Co., was committed to prison in that
county to stand trial for the murder of his son, aged 12 or
13. (March 30, 1748) Appleby was later acquitted. (June
1, 1748)

ARCHER, John, M. D., died at his seat in Harf. Co., at an advanced
age. (Oct. 10, 1810)

ARCHER, Col. S. B., Inspector-General of the U. S. Army, died at
Philadelphia, on 11th ult. (Dec. 22, 1825)

ARMIGER, Mr. Samuel, and Mrs. Eleanor Gray, both of A. A. Co., were
married in Baltimore, 29th ult., by the Rev. Mr. Valiant.
(Dec. 8, 1825)

ARMISTEAD, Col. George, the gallant defender of Fort McHenry, died.
[Long obit is given]. (April 30, 1818)

ARMSTRONG, Mrs. Catherine, died in Maysville, Ky., Friday, 12th ult., **wife** of John Armstrong, Sr., and daughter of Gen. Thomas Hood, of A. A. Co. (July 2, 1835)

ARMSTRONG, Robert, Esq., died in Cumberland, in his 62nd year. He was Assoc. Judge of the County Court, and was at the time of his death, Judge of the Orphans Court. (July 31, 1828)

ARNEST, Mrs. Juliet S., died at her residence, Nomini Hall, Westmoreland Co., Va., consort of the late Dr. Arnest. She leaves four children. (Feb. 1, 1838)

ARNETT, Mary, of Balto. Co., murdered her bastard child, but died before she could be got to prison. (March 19, 1761)

ARNOLD, Mr. Henry, died Monday morning, July 13, in his 20th year. For a considerable time, he made the Law his principal study. (July 16, 1772)

ASBURY, Francis, died Sun., March 31, 1816, near Fredericksburg, Va., in the 72nd year of his age, bishop of the Methodist Church. (April 18, 1816).

ASHMUN, J., died at New Haven, Mon. last; late Agent for the Colonization Society of Liberia. (Sept. 4, 1828).

ASKEW, Capt. Thomas, commander of the Maryland Merchant, died early Mon. morning last, in Balto. Town. (Nov. 7, 1754) Lancelot Jacques is attorney in fact for the executor. (Nov. 28, 1754)

ATKINSON, Mrs. Elizabeth, died Sun. night last, on South River. (Dec. 5, 1833)

ATKINSON, John, and Ellen Woodward, both of this city, were married in Balto., 27th ult., by the Rev. Mr. Hoskins. (Jan. 4, 1827)

ATKINSON, Miss Leonora, died Sun. night last, at the residence of Mr. C. Jackson, at South River Bridge, in her 19th year. (Dec. 13, 1832)

ATWELL, Joseph, of A. A. Co., and Mary Ann Williams, of Annap., were married Tues. morning last, by Rev. R. S. Vinton. (Dec. 17, 1835)

AYRES, Thomas, died Friday last [May 19], when he accidentally drowned, from his father's boat, off Greenberry [Point]. (May 25, 1769)

BACON, Rev. Thomas, died Tues., 24th ult., at Frederick Town in Fred. Co.; rector of All Saints' Parish in that county; author of laborious and judicious performance entitled "A Complete System of the Revenue of Ireland," published in 1737, by

order of the Chief Commissioners and Governors of the Revenue
in that Kingdom. He also published several other valuable
pieces, and in the decline of life, by several years of intense
labor, compiled "A Compleat Body of the Laws of this Province."
(June 9, 1768)

BADEN, Benjamin, of Md., cadet of West Point, died. Resolutions of
regret by his classmates were published. (Nov. 9, 1837)

BADEN, Mr. John, Sr., died at his residence near Nottingham, P. G.
Co., 30th Sept. last, aged 71 years, 9 mos. and 10 days,
leaving an only son, and a number of grandchildren, and great-
grandchildren to deplore his loss. (Oct. 21, 1824)

BAILEY, Mrs. Mary, died Sat., 18th March, in Dor. Co., in her 39th
year; the wife of Mr. Joseph Bailey, late of Portsmouth, in
New Eng., now resident in Vienna, on the Nanticoke River, in
said county. She was the daughter of John and Rosanna Hodson
of Dor. Co. (April 5, 1749)

BAKER, Henry, died lately in Cecil Co., one of the representatives
of that county. (July 28, 1768)

BALDWIN, Mrs., died on the 27th of last month, at her plantation
near Annap., a widow gentlewoman, aged 99 or 100 years. She
leaves numerous progeny. [Long obit is given.] (Jan. 13,
1748)

BALDWIN, Henry, and Susanna Pearce were married Sun. last, on the
north side of Severn, by the Rev. Mr. Watkins. (Oct. 25, 1827)

BALDWIN, Nicholas, died Mon., Dec. 16, at his residence near this
city. (Dec. 19, 1816)

BALDWIN, Rezin, died Wed., 17th ult. (Feb. 18, 1830)

BALDWIN, Mr. Rezin D., and Miss Charlotte Sullivan, all of this city,
were married Sun. evening [Nov. 15], by the Rev. Mr. Wyatt.
(Nov. 19, 1812)

BALDWIN, Mr. William P., of Easton, Tal. Co., and Miss Caroline
Williams, of New Castle Co., Del., were married in Annap.,
Tues. evening last [Dec. 22], by the Rev. Mr. Guest. (Dec.
24, 1818)

BALLARD, Henry E., Esq., of the U. S. Navy, and Juliana Mackubin,
were married Sun. evening last, on the north side of Severn,
by the Rev. Mr. Dashiell. (June 1, 1815)

BARBER, Mrs. Anne, consort of Mr. John Barber, son of George, died
in Annap., yesterday. (Oct. 9, 1828)

BARBER, Mrs. Catherine, wife of Capt. George Barber, died 23rd inst.,
leaving a husband and children. (April 28, 1823)

BARBER, Charles, died Tues., [July 22], an inhabitant of Annap.
(July 24, 1806)

BARBER, Mrs. Elizabeth, consort of Dr. George A. Barber, of A. A.
Co., died in Annap., Tues. last, at the residence of her
father, Gideon White, Esq. (April 30, 1835)

BARBER, George, of A. A. Co., and Elizabeth White, of Annap., were
married in that city, on Thurs. last, by Dr. Davis. (Nov. 1,
1827)

BARBER, Mr. George, son of John, died Wed. evening, 1st inst., in
his 22nd year. (April 9, 1829)

BARBER, Mr. George W., and Jane Thomas, both of this county, were
married Thurs. evening last, by Rev. Mr. Davis. (Aug. 31,
1826)

BARBER, Dr. Gustavus, and Isabella, second daughter of David Ridgely,
Esq., all of Annap., were married Tues. evening last, by Rev.
Mr. Guest. (Oct. 10, 1839)

BARBER, John, son of George, and Miss Ann R. Hopkins, were married
Thurs. last, by Rev. Mr. Davis. (Nov. 1, 1827)

BARBER, Capt. John T., died Sat. morning last, in his 51st year.
He was buried Sun. evening. (April 11, 1822)

BARBER, John T., and Mary E. Thomas, all of Annap., were married
Thurs. evening last, by Rev. N. J. Watkins. (April 18, 1833)

BARBER, John Thomas, of Annap., and Miss Isabella Reaney, of Balto.,
were married in the latter city, on Thurs. evening, 19th inst.,
by the Rev. Dr. Jennings. (Feb. 26, 1824)

BARBER, Joseph W., died Sat. last, in his 22nd year. (Oct. 1, 1829)

BARBER, Miss Susan Matilda, only daughter of Capt. John T. Barber,
of Annap., died Sat. evening last [Sept. 9], in her 15th
year. (Sept. 14, 1820)

BARCLAY, Mrs., wife of the Rev. Francis Barclay, rector of William
and Mary Parish, St. M. Co., died 9th inst. [Sept.]. (Oct.
4, 1809)

BARKLEY, Thomas, advertises that he and his wife Isabella have con-
sented to live apart. She was formerly married to Richard
Wethered, by whom she had children. (April 7, 1747)

BARNES, Joseph B., died yesterday morning, in Annap., in the 23rd year of his age. (July 25, 1810)

BARNES, Col. Richard, died Sun., 29th April; of St. M. Co. His will declared that all his negroes, amounting to between 300 and 400, are to be free 3 years after his death, if they have behaved themselves well. (May 10, 1804)

BARNEY, Commodore Joshua, a hero of the Revolution, died at Pittsburgh, Penna., on the 1st inst. (Dec. 10, 1818)

BARNEY, William B., and Mary Chase, daughter of the Hon. Judge Chase, all of Balto., were married at Princeton, N.J., on 9th inst., by the Rev. Mr. Comfort. (Sept. 22, 1808)

BARRETT, James, was executed on Wed. last for the murder last Fall of John Cain, in Balto. Co. Barrett admonished the spectators at his execution to avoid drunkenness and passion. He forgave and died in charity with all. (May 3, May 17, 1745)

BARRETT, John, was executed at Joppa for the murder, some time ago, of his wife. He acknowledged the justice of his sentence, and laid the cause of it to his wife's incontinency. (Dec. 6, 1753)

BARRETT, Mr. Joseph, died at the "Half-way House Inn" on the Balto.-Annap. Road, leaving a widow and one child. His death was caused by a shot fired from a gun fired by Mr. William Brown, son of Basil. (Dec. 1, 1825)

BARRY, Commodore John, died at Philadelphia, on 13th inst. He was one of that little band of naval heroes who first hoisted the flag of the American navy in 1775. (Sept. 22, 1803)

BARTON, George, and Eliza Ann, daughter of the late Thomas Rhodes, all of P. G. Co., were married there, Tues., 8th inst., by Rev. Mr. Woodly. (July 17, 1834)

BASIL, Mr. Henry, and Mrs. Ruth Ann Jewell, all of Annap., were married Thurs. evening last by Rev. Mr. Watkins. (Nov. 6, 1834)

BASIL, John, and Miss Lydia Anderson, all of Annap., were married on Tues. evening [Dec. 22], by the Rev. Mr. Guest. (Dec. 24, 1818)

BASIL, Ralph, and Mrs. Mary Russell, were married in this county, Tues. evening last, by Rev. Mr. Hammond. (March 30, 1826)

BASIL, Thomas, died Mon. morning last, in his 18th year. (Sept. 26, 1833)

BASSFORD, Henry, Jr., and Margaret Claggett, were married Thurs.
    evening last, by Rev. Mr. Waters. (July 11, 1833)

BASSFORD, Henry, Sr., died Mon. morning, in his 65th year. [Long
    obit is printed] (Aug. 10, 1837)

BASSFORD, Jacob, and Margaret C. Shephard, all of Annap., were
    married Thurs. evening, by Rev. Mr. Watkins. (Sept. 8, 1825)

BASSFORD, John, died Thurs., 1st inst., at his farm in A. A. Co., in
    his 70th year. (Oct. 8, 1818)

BASSFORD, Thomas, and Mrs. Elizabeth Lusby, all of Annap., were wed
    on Thurs. evening [Oct. 3], by the Rev. Mr. Ryland. (Oct.
    10, 1811)

BATTEE, Dennis H., and Elizabeth Caroline Crandell, only daughter of
    Mrs. Hester Gosnell, were married at West River, Tues., 6th
    inst., by Rev. Mr. Gosnell. (Jan. 15, 1824)

BATTEE, Mrs. Elizabeth, daughter of the Rev. Joshua Jones, of Fred.
    Co., and wife of Rev. Dennis H. Battee, died at the house of
    Col. Richard Harwood, in A. A. Co., on 21st inst., in her
    21st year. (Nov. 28, 1822)

BATTEE, John Osborn, died in Annap., on Sun., 13th inst., in his
    18th year. (Aug. 17, 1820)

BAVIN, Thomas, was executed at the gallows, outside the city gate
    on Friday last, for breaking into the house of Charles Cole.
    (Nov. 6, 1751)

BAXTER, James, died in Caecil [sic] Co., on 24th Feb., past, late
    Sheriff of that county, and formerly one of their magistrates
    and representatives. (March 10, 1763)

BAXTER, John, a sailor, drowned last Wed., in the Choptank [River].
    (April 20, 1748)

BAYARD, James Asheton, expired Sun. evening last [Aug. 6], upon his
    return from the mission at Ghent. The remains of Mr. Bayard
    will be taken to Bohemia, Md., instead of being buried here
    as was contemplated. (from the [Wilmington] Delaware
    Gazette). (Aug. 17, 1815)

BAYLIS, Col. John, was killed in a duel at Dumfries, Va., on Wed.,
    Sept. 4. (Sept. 12, 1765)

BAYLY, Mrs. Leah, died at Cambridge, Mon., 4th inst., consort of
    Josiah Bayly. (Feb. 21, 1805)

BEALE, Mrs. Elizabeth, died Thurs. night last [Nov. 7] at her

plantation near Annap.; she was the widow of the late John
Beale. (Nov. 15, 1753)

BEALL, Col. William Dent, died at his residence in P. G. Co., in his
75th year. He was a worthy and distinguished officer of the
Revolution. (Oct. 29, 1829)

BEALMEAR, Samuel, of A. A. Co., and Miss Anne Janetta, eldest daughter of the late John Brewer, Esq., of Annap., were married
Thurs. evening last, by the Rev. Mr. Dorsey. (Jan. 31, 1831)

BEALMEAR, Mrs. Sarah, died Sat. last, in the 44th year of her age,
wife of Capt. Francis Bealmear of this county. She leaves an
infant child, two weeks old, a mother, mother-in-law, and
step-children. (Feb. 20, 1817)

BEANES, Mr. Colmore, on Sun. evening last [Oct. 24], died of a consumption, at his father's house in P. G. Co.; merchant, late
Sheriff of that county. (Oct. 28, 1762)

BEANES, Mr. William, died last week at his plantation in P. G. Co.,
in his 82nd year. He was born in this Province, and leaves
a widow of nearly his own age, to whom he had been married
for 57 years. (March 7, 1765)

BEANS, Mrs. Henrietta, wife of Col. John H. Beans, died 20th inst.;
of a deep decline, at Mrs. Dent's, near Piscataway, in P. G.
Co. (Aug. 28, 1788)

BEARD, ---, the son of Mr. Beard, of A. A. Co., died 7th inst. of
hydrophobia. (Oct. 21, 1762)

BEARD, John, and Harriett Ann Stewart, all of Annap., were married
Tues. evening last, by the Rev. Mr. Waters. (July 11, 1833)

BEARD, John W., died in Annap., on the 12th inst.; a correct and
worthy man. (Oct. 20, 1825)

BEARD, Miss Mary Eleanor, second daughter of Mr. Stephen Beard, of
A. A. Co., died Thurs., 12th inst., in her 21st year. (May
19, 1825)

BEARD, Stephen, Jr., and Mary S. Collinson, all of A. A. Co., were
married Thurs. evening last, by Rev. Mr. Waters. (Nov. 16,
1837)

BEARD, Mr. Thomas, of A. A. Co., died Sun. last, in his 47th year.
(Dec. 16, 1802)

BEARD, Capt. William C., died at Washington, 28th ult., in his 52nd
year, late of the U. S. Navy (May 11, 1837)

BEAUCHAMP, Mrs. Mary, died a few days ago in Caroline Co., at the
    advanced age of 119 years. (Dec. 31, 1801)

BECK, Thomas, cabin boy in the ship Nisbet, died yesterday in an ex-
    plosion aboard the ship. (Oct. 19, 1758)

BECKLEY, John, died Wed. last, in his 50th year, Clerk of the House
    of Representatives of the United States. (April 16, 1807)

BECRAFT, Mr. William, died at Schoharie, N.Y., on Mon., 18th ult.,
    aged 100 years. He was a native of Conn. (Aug. 4, 1825)

BEDFORD, William Turner, of Balto., and Miss Julia Wisham, of Annap.,
    were married on Sun. evening last [June 9], by the Rev. Mr.
    Duke. (June 13, 1805)

BEEN, Edward Hagthrop, son of Thomas and Catherine Been, died Thurs.
    last in Balto. (Jan. 18, 1830)

BELMEAR, Francis, and Sarah Warfield, were married Thurs. last [Oct.
    10], at the Head of Severn. (Oct. 17, 1811)

BELSER, Michael, from Germany, was killed Sat. afternoon, when a
    gust of wind blew down the barn of his master, Wendel Gilbert,
    four miles from Elizabeth-Town. (May 10, 1798)

BELT, Miss Caroline Anne, youngest daughter of the late Capt. John
    Sprigg Belt, died Friday, 11th inst., at Sandy Hill, in this
    county, in her 23rd year. (Aug. 17, 1826)

BELT, Mrs. Catherine, died 30th ult., in Balto., in her 70th year.
    (June 23, 1831)

BELT, Mr. Edward, of P. G. Co., and Miss Sarah Ann Lane, of Annap.,
    were married Friday last by Rev. Mr. Waters. (April 26, 1832)

BELT, Mr. Joseph, Jr., died Wednesday evening last, at his house
    near Upper Marlborough, aged a little above 40 years. He
    leaves a wife and children. (June 11, 1761). Edward Sprigg
    is his executor. (Sept. 17, 1761)

BELT, Col. Joseph, died Friday night last [June 26] at his planta-
    tion in P. G. Co., aged 86 years. His death is supposed to
    have been occasioned by grief for the death of his son a few
    weeks before. (July 2, 1761) Edward Belt and Humphrey Belt
    are executors. (Sept. 17, 1761)

BELT, Osborne, and Mary Jones, both of A. A. Co., were married on
    Tues. evening last, by Rev. Mr. Waters. (Feb. 23, 1837)

BENGER, Elliott, died a few days ago in Virginia; Sole Deputy-Post-

master-General of all His Majesty's Dominions in America.
(May 22, 1751)

BENNETT, Richard, died 11th inst., at his seat in Q. A. Co., in his
83rd year "supposed to be the richest man in America."
(Oct. 18, 1749). An account of his funeral is given. (Nov.
8, 1749) Edward Lloyd is his executor. (Jan. 10, 1750)

BENSON, Bever'y, of Nanticoke, was drowned last Thurs., while going
up the Bay. (June 5, 1766)

BENSON, Joseph, died Sat., 22nd ult., at the residence of his father,
in the fourth election district, A. A. Co., in his 24th year.
(Oct. 4, 1838)

BENSON, Mr. Perry, died 24 Sept., in Tal. Co.; for many years a magistrate of that county. (Oct. 9, 1751)

BENTON, Mr. Albert, of N. Y., and Mary Barber, eldest daughter of
Capt. George Barber, of Annap., were married Thurs. evening
last, by Rev. Dr. Davis. (July 8, 1824)

BETTS, Mrs. Rebecca, died at Walton, Conn., on 27 Jan.; widow of
Benjamin Betts; aged 100 years, 10 mos., and 9 weeks. She
leaves behind her a daughter of 70, and two sons--one 72,
and the other 74. (March 14, 1805)

BEVANS, George, and Mary, daughter of Benjamin Ogle, Esq., former
Governor of this state, were married in Annap., on Sun. last,
by the Rev. Mr. Duke, rector of St. Anne's Parish. (July 26,
1804)

BEVANS, George, died at Talley's Point, near Annap., on Mon. morning
last. (Aug. 4, 1814)

BICKNELL, Esau, aged 60, and Miss Susanna Rodgers, aged 16, both of
Wash. Co., Md., were married on Wed., 8th inst., by the Rev.
Mr. Bower. (April 16, 1807)

BICKNELL, Thomas, and Mrs. Julia Clarke, both of Annap., were married
on Sun. last, by the Rev. Mr. Ridgely. (Jan. 24, 1805)

BIRDSALL, Major, ___ was murdered by James Hamilton, who has been
sentenced to be executed on 6th Nov. next. (Oct. 22, 1818)

BISCOE, Bennett, formerly of Balto., and Miss Leah Bayly, daughter
of the late Judge Done of Balto., were married at New Orleans
on 21st ult. (Dec. 17, 1835)

BISHOP, William, died in Annap., on Tues. evening last, in his 68th
year. (April 14, 1831)

BISSET, Mr. David, who kept a store at the head of Bush River, in
    Balto. Co., accidentally drowned Friday last [Aug. 6], in a
    mill pond, while bathing. (Aug. 10, 1758) James Bissett and
    John Matthews are administrators. (Sept. 21, 1758)

BLACKBURN, ---, a son of Col. Blackburn, was accidentally drowned
    on 4th inst., in the Potomack River, on the Virginia side.
    (April 16, 1752)

BLACKBURN, Col. Thomas, died 17th inst., at Rippon Lodge, his seat
    in Va.; an old Revolutionary patriot. (July 30, 1807)

BLAIR, John, died Tues. last, in the 83rd year of his age. He had
    discharged the offices of Representative, Auditor, Judge,
    Privy Counsellor, and President of the Colony of Va.
    "Williamsburg - Nov. 7." (Nov. 21, 1771)

BLAKISTONE, Mrs. Mary, consort of Thomas Blakistone, Esq., of St.
    M. Co., died 8th inst., in her 25th year. (Jan. 31, 1810)

BLANCHARD, Rev. John G., rector of St. Anne's, Annap., and Elizabeth
    Philpott, were married Thurs. evening last, by Rev. Mr. Aus-
    tin, in Balto. Co. (Jan. 12, 1826)

BLANCHARD, Rev. John G., died in Balto., 8th inst., for 10 years
    the rector of St. Anne's Parish, Annap., his first and only
    charge since entering the ministry. He was in his 35th
    year, and was a native of Mass. (Oct. 16, 1834; Dec. 3,
    1834)

BLAND, Theodorick, elder son of Chancellor Bland, of Annap., and
    midshipman on board the U. S. S. John Adams, died 13th ult.,
    off Havana. (Oct. 13, 1825)

BLECHER, Mr. Morrison, printer, and Miss Pina Brunner, were married
    in Troy, N.Y. (May 10, 1832)

BLODGET, Capt. John, an officer in the Revolutionary Army, aged 83,
    and Mrs. Hannah Bugbee, aged 77, were married at Brimfield,
    Mass., their combined ages being 160 years. (Jan. 12, 1826)

BLOOMFIELD, Gen. Joseph, died at his residence in the city of Burling-
    ton, N.J., on 3rd inst. (Oct. 9, 1823)

BLUE, Rev. Joel, and Mary Pindell, both of A. A. Co., were married
    Thurs. evening last, by Rev. Thomas McCormick. (Nov. 15,
    1838)

BLUNT, Mrs. Elizabeth, died Mon. morning last, aged between 90 and
    100 years. A native of A. A. Co.. she was long a resident
    of Annap., and was one of the first to join the Methodist

Society in this part of the world. (Oct. 17, 1833)

BOND, Mrs. Alesanna, died on the 13th of last month, in Balto. Co.,
in the 52nd year of her age; wife of John Bond of Fells
Point. She was one of the people called Quakers; she had
been married for 33 years. On the 18th she was interred in
the Quaker's Burying Ground on Bond's Forest. She was the
youngest daughter of John Webster, Sr., deceased, and was
endowed with many good qualities, skilled in medicine and
midwifery, which she administered with freedom and benevolence.
She left 10 children. (Nov. 5, 1767)

BOND, Mr. Benson, died Wed. morning last in Cal. Co.; one of the
representatives for that county. (July 11, 1750)

BOND, Dr. Thomas H., died in Cal. Co., in his 31st year, when lightning struck the house of his uncle, Dr. Duke. (Aug. 23, 1838)

BOND, Uriah, blacksmith, drowned last Sun. se'ennight, when he and
Jonathan Munn, a cabinet-maker, were attempting to cross the
Gunpowder River on ice, and fell in. (Feb. 8, 1749)

BOONE, Capt. Humphrey, died at his plantation on the north side of
Severn, formerly, for many years, one of the magistrates of
this county. (July 3, 1766)

BOONE, James, died on the 20th April, on the north side of Severn;
of the prevailing epidemic. (May 4, 1815)

BOONE, Mr. Robert, died Friday last [Feb. 9] at his plantation near
town, on the north side of Severn, of old age. He was an
honest and industrious planter, who died on the same plantation where he was born in 1690, from which he never went more
than 30 miles in his life. He leaves a widow to whom he had
been married for 57 years. (Feb. 15, 1759)

BOONE, Stephen, died at his residence on the north side of Severn,
on Sat. last. (Feb. 11, 1830)

BOOTH, Mrs., was murdered on Thurs., 7th inst., with her three year
old son, by one of the negroes of her husband, Mr. John
Booth. (April 16, 1754) Her murderer was hanged last week.
(June 11, 1760)

BORDLEY, Mr. Beale, merchant, of this place, and Miss Margaret Chew,
were married Sun. evening last [Oct. 13]. (Oct. 16, 1751)

BORDLEY, John W., and Mrs. Sarah Whittington, all of Annap., were
married Thurs. evening last. (Aug. 31, 1818)

BORDLEY, John W., of Annap., died on Sat., 4th inst., at the resi-

dence of his father, in Kent Co. He had just completed his
23rd year. (Sept. 16, 1819)

BORDLEY, Mr. Matthias, died yesterday morning, in the prime of life
at Charles Town, Cecil Co., Clerk of Cecil Co., and formerly
of Annap. (Sept. 16, 1756)

BORDLEY, Hon. Stephen, Esq., died Thurs. evening last [Dec. 6], at
his house in town, in his 55th year...one of His Lordship's
Council of State, Commissary General of the Province, and one
of the aldermen of this city. He was a gentleman eminent in
the law. He formerly represented this city and county in the
General Assembly, and was Naval Officer of the Province.
His remains were, with great decency, entombed on Tues. last
in the family vault. (Dec. 13, 1764)

BORDLEY, Mr. Stephen, Esq., Attorney-at-Law, died at his house in
Kent Co.; one of the representatives of that county. (Aug.
22, 1771)

BORDLEY, Mr. William, died 11th inst., at night, at his plantation
in Caecil Co.; formerly of Annap. He went to bed well, but
was seized with some violent disorder, and died before morning.
(Feb. 25, 1762)

BOTFIELD, Capt. Meshack, of Tal. Co., was killed about a fortnight
since, when he was flung out of his chaise. His wife was
much hurt, but is recovered. He leaves an elder brother,
Shadrack, and a younger brother Abednego. (Nov. 14, 1750)

BOURKE, Lemuel, and Charlotte Maccubbin, both of A. A. Co., were
married Thurs. evening last, by the Rev. Mr. Dorsey. (Oct.
23, 1830)

BOURNE, Mr. Jesse, a married man with a family, was killed last
week in Cal. Co., when a gust of wind blew a house down.
(May 2, 1799)

BOWEN, Thomas, a married man, with a family, was killed last week
in Cal. Co., when a gust of wind blew a house down. [May
2, 1799)

BOWERS, Edward P., formerly of Annap., and Catherine Lovejoy, of
Leon Co., Fla., where married 22nd ult., at Tallahassee,
Middle Fla., by the Rev. Jacob Singletary. (Sept. 12, 1839)

BOWIE, Mrs. Mary, died at her seat in P. G. Co., on Friday, 15th
inst.; relict of the late Walter Bowie, in her 65th year.
(May 28, 1812)

BOWIE, Mrs. Mary, died Sun. last, at her residence in P. G. Co.,
relict of the late Thos. Bowie, Esq. (Aug. 4, 1825)

BOWIE, Thomas H., and Miss Eliza H. Ray, were married on Sun. morning last, by the Rev. Mr. Higinbothom. (Feb. 6, 1812)

BOWIE, Thomas H., attorney-at-law, and late Register of Chancery, died Tues. night. (Feb. 8, 1821)

BOWIE, Walter, died 24th April, at his residence in P. G. Co., in his 53rd year. (May 9, 1839)

BOWLEY, Daniel, Esq., of Furley, died Thurs., 19th inst. (Nov. 19, 1807)

BOWMAN, Capt. Samuel, died at Wilkes-Barre, Penna., considerably advanced in years. He was from Lexington, Mass., and a patriot in the Revolution. [Long obit gives details of military career.] (July 30, 1818)

BOYCE, Mr. [John], died as a consequence of the great rain on Wed. last. An attorney-at-law, he was on his way home on Friday, from Balto., to his family in Harf. Co., when he drowned attempting to cross a stream swollen after the storm. (Oct. 19, 1786) Roger Boyce will settle the estate. (April 3, 1787 issue of Maryland Journal and Baltimore Advertiser)

BOYD, Dennis, Esq., of A. A. Co., and Amelia F. Whittaker, of P. G. Co., were married Tues., 15 May, by the Rev. Mr. Mackenheimer. (May 17, 1832)

BOYD, Dr. William T., died 9th inst., in his 23rd year, at his father's farm on the Eastern Shore of Md. (Feb. 26, 1835)

BOYLE, Daniel, Esq., Postmaster of Annap., died Sun., 5th inst., in his 66th year. [Long obit is given] (Dec. 26, 1830)

BOYLE, James, Esq., and Miss Susan Maccubbin, were married Tues., 12th inst., at the seat of Gassaway Rawlings, on South River, by the Rev. Mr. Nind. (May 21, 1812)

BOYLE, John H., and Ellen Slemaker, both of A. A. Co., were married Sun., 4th inst., by Rev. Mr. McElhiney. (March 15, 1838)

BOYLE, Mary, only daughter of Col. James Boyle, and student at the School of the Visitation in Georgetown, died in September, 1836. [This belated notice of her death contains a set of memorial verses.] (Jan. 18, 1838)

BOYLES, James, was murdered last Aug., in Fred. Co., by Terence Conner. (Oct. 26, 1752)

BOZMAN, John, Esq., died on Friday last [Sept. 25]; Sheriff of Tal. Co. (Oct. 1, 1767)

BRADESHAW, ---, lately died of the bite of a mad dog, near Fairly
    Creek, in Kent Co.; a lad of about 17 or 18 years of age.
    (May 9, 1754)

BRADFORD, Mrs., of Balto., was drowned Wed. last [July 28], at the
    mouth of Chester River, below Poole's Island. (Aug. 5, 1773)

BRADFORD, Mrs. Mary, consort of Mr. Henry Bradford, of Chas. Co.,
    died suddenly on Wed., the 27th of last month. (May 12, 1763)

BRADY, Mrs., widow of the Rev. John Brady, late rector of William
    and Mary, and St. Andrew, Parishes, in St. M. Co., died Tues.
    evening, 11th March, at the residence of Col. Joseph Harris
    near Leonard-Town. She was the fifth of the same family to
    die within five months. (March 27, 1823)

BRASHEARS, Richard Wells, died 26th ult., at his residence in Upper
    Marlborough, P. G. Co. He leaves a wife and an infant son.
    (Nov. 6, 1806)

BRAWNER, Henry, died in Chas. Co., on the 9th inst., in his 45th
    year. He was Register of Wills and had several times served
    the county in the State Legislature. (Aug. 16, Aug. 23, 1838)

BREASE, Edward, was executed last Friday in Chestertown, for breaking
    open and robbing the store of Capt. Marsh. (May 22, 1755)

BREREWOOD, Thomas, Esq., died Mon., 22nd inst.; late Clerk of Balto.
    Co. He is succeeded in that office by Mr. Talbot Risteau.
    (Dec. 30, 1746)

BREVITT, Miss Matilda, daughter of Dr. J. Brevitt, was killed Mon.
    evening last, when she tried to get out of a carriage pulled
    by a runaway horse. (From the Baltimore Patriot). (Aug. 24,
    1826)

BREWER, Edward, son of John, and Miss Anne Barber, were married Wed.
    morning, in Annap., by Rev. Mr. McElhiney. (Sept. 17, 1835)

BREWER, Edward W., of Annap., and Miss Margaret Ann Abrams, of Balto.,
    were married Thurs. evening last in Balto., by Rev. S. Mc-
    Mullin. (Dec. 14, 1837)

BREWER, Mrs. Elizabeth, consort of Mr. John Brewer, Clerk of the
    House of Delegates, died Sat. night last. (Jan. 6, 1820)

BREWER, George G., of Annap., and Susan Ann Harwood, of Georgetown,
    were married in the latter place on Tues. evening, 1st
    inst., by the Rev. Mr. Addison. (Nov. 10, 1825)

BREWER, Mr. James, and Miss Eliza Rawlings, all of Annap., were married Thurs. evening last, by Rev. T. Riley (May 14, 1829)

BREWER, John, Esq., of Annap., and Miss Ann, daughter of Francis
  Bealmar, Esq., of the county, were married Sun. evening last
  by the Rev. Mr. Murphy, of White Marsh. (May 1, 1823)

BREWER, John, Esq., Register of the Land Office for the Western Shore,
  and Clerk of the Maryland House of Delegates, died in Annap.
  on Sat. last. (Jan. 24, 1827)

BREWER, Joseph, died Mon. evening, 17th inst.; of the Treasury Dept.,
  aged 63. He was a native of Annap., and was for many years
  a citizen of Georgetown. (April 27, 1837)

BREWER, Mrs. Julia, wife of Nicholas Brewer, Jr., Esq., died in
  Annap., on Thurs. night last. (Dec. 21, 1826)

BREWER, Mrs. Mary, consort of George Brewer, died Sat. night last.
  (Dec. 9, 1824)

BREWER, Nicholas, Jr., of Annap., and Catherine M. Medairy, of Balto.,
  were married in that latter city on Thurs. evening last, by
  Rev. Dr. Roberts. (Sept. 13, 1827)

BREWER, Nicholas, died Sun. morning last, in his 68th year. He rep-
  sented Annap., in the State Legislature. (April 18, 1839)

BREWER, Richard Giles, died Sunday afternoon last [9th inst.], in
  this city, of a dropsy supposed to have been contracted in
  the winter campaign of 1793 to quell the Western insurrection.
  A young man, he was buried the following Mon., with the
  honors of war. (June 13, 1799)

BREWER, Mrs. Sarah, wife of Nicholas Brewer, of this city, died Friday evening last. (Dec. 29, 1836)

BREWER, Thomas, died Tues. night last, in his 70th year. He was a
  meritorious soldier in the Revolutionary army. (April 3,
  1823)

BREWER, Thomas, and Ann Purdy, all of Annap., were married Thurs.
  evening last, by Rev. Poisal. (Oct. 8, 1835)

BREWER, William, died at his farm on South River, at an advanced
  age. (July 10, 1811)

BREWER, Dr. William, and Miss Mary Elizabeth Rawlings, all of this
  city, were married Thurs. evening last, by the Rev. Mr.
  McElhiney. (Sept. 28, 1837)

BREWER, William H., and Miss Mary Ann Anglen, were married the eve-

ning of the 27th inst., by the Rev. Job Guest, in Annap.
(Dec. 29, 1831)

BRICE, Mr. Charles C., and Susan Selby, all of A. A. Co., were wed
on Tues., 16th inst., by the Rev. Mr. Waters. (Jan. 25, 1838)

BRICE, Mrs. Charlotte, relict of the late Mr. Edmond Brice, died on
Friday night last. (Jan. 30, 1823)

BRICE, Mr. Edmond, of the north side of Severn, died Sun. evening
in this city. (Nov. 28, 1822)

BRICE, Elizabeth Dulany, third daughter of the late Hon. James Brice,
died Mon. last. (May 21, 1835)

BRICE, Mrs. Frances, died in Annap., on 2nd inst., at the advanced
age of 88 years. (Dec. 8, 1825)

BRICE, James E., American Consular agent at Cape Haytien, and late
of Annap., died at Cape Haytien on Aug. 11th last. (From
the Baltimore American). (Oct. 18, 1827)

BRICE, John, of Annap., died at the house of Mr. Samuel Hanson, in
Chas. Co., yesterday afternoon. He was Chief Justice of the
Province, Alderman of the city, and one of the Judges of
Assize for the Western Shore. He died on the circuit. (Sept.
25, 1766)

BRICE, John, Jr., formerly of Balto., died at Nashville, Tenn., on
the 5th ult., in his 31st year. (Sept. 1, 1825)

BRICE, Mrs. Julianna, relict of James Brice, died. For many years
her husband was the Executive of Maryland. [Long obit is
given.] (Dec. 7, 1837)

BRICE, Mrs. Mary, died in Balto., on Jan. 30th, in her 57th year;
consort of John Brice, of Annap. (Feb. 13, 1806)

BRIGHAM, the Hon. Elijah, died at his lodging in Washington City,
a Representative in Congress from the state of Mass. He was
considerably advanced in age. (Feb. 29, 1816)

BRIGHT, Ignatius, died Thurs., 28th ult., at his residence on the
north side of Severn, in his 53rd year. (Sept. 11, 1823)

BRIGHT, Mr. James H., and Miss Ann Howard, all of Annap., were
married on Sun. evening last, by the Rev. Mr. Smith. (Dec.
15, 1825)

BRIGHT, James H., printer, died Sun. morning last, aged about 30
years. (Jan. 30, 1834)

BRINING, Edward, was drowned last month off Poplar Island. (March
6, 1766)

BRINKS, Jacob, and his family, were lately killed by Indians. (Sept.
27, 1764)

BRISCOE, Brig.-Gen. John Hanson, died Wed., the 7th, at his dwelling
place near Chaptico, St. M. Co., in his 44th year. He leaves
a widow and several small children. (Sept. 15, 1796)

BRISTOL, a Negro man, died here last week, aged 125 years. He said
he was a Man-boy, waiting at dinner behind his master's chair
in Barbadoes, when they received the news that King Charles
[I] had been beheaded. (April 17, 1760)

BRITTEN, Capt. Isaac, of the sloop Philadelphia, died in Annap., on
Mon. last. He leaves a wife and children. (Sept. 27, 1832)

BROGDEN, ---, daughter of the Rev. Mr. Brogden, was accidentally
killed on Mon., 4th inst.; aged 11 or 12. She was rolling
a large hollow log down a declivity, when she fell into a clay
pit, and the log fell on her, killing her. (Feb. 7, 1760)

BROGDEN, David McCulloch, and Miss Margaret Sellman, were married on
Thurs. evening, 11th inst., by the Rev. Dr. Rafferty. (Jan.
17, 1827)

BROGDEN, Miss Mary, only daughter of the late Major William Brogden,
died in the county, on 2nd inst. (Aug. 10, 1826)

BROGDEN, Rev. Mr. William, died Thurs. last [Nov. 1] in his 60th
year; rector of Queen Anne Parish, P. G. Co. He leaves four
sons and one daughter. (Nov. 8, 1770)

BROGDEN, Maj. William, died at his residence in this county, on Sun.
last, aged about 84 years. He served as an officer in the
Revolutionary army, during the glorious struggle of this
country for independence, and was elected to represent the
county in the General Assembly. [Long obit follows] (Sept.
16, 1824)

BROGDEN, William, Esq., of A. A. Co., and Miss Mary Stevenson, of
Balto., were married in that city, 25th ult. (May 22, 1828)

BROME, John, died last week in Cal. Co.; one of the worthy representatives of that county. (Oct. 5, 1748)

BROMWELL, Jacob, died the 15th of last month in a storm off Poplar
Island. (March 6, 1766)

BROOKE, Mrs. Elizabeth, wife of Mr. Thomas Brooke, and the second daughter of Walter Bowie, Esq., died Friday, 17th inst., in the 28th year of her age. (Aug. 29, 1810)

BROOKE, Isaac, Surveyor of Fred. Co., died Thurs. last at his mother's house, in the prime of life. (Nov. 18, 1756). Richard Brooke is the executor. (Feb. 23, 1758)

BROOKE, John J., a distinguished member of the Bar of Cal. Co., died at his residence in that county on Sat., 16th inst. (April 28, 1836)

BROOKE, William, A. M., formerly of P. G. Co., and Mary, daughter of Dr. John Ridgely, late of Annap., were married Tues. morning, 16th ult., by Rev. Joseph Muenscher, at Mt. Vernon, Ohio. (May 2, 1839)

BROOKE, William J., died at the residence of his uncle, E. J. Millard, in Leonard-Town, on 1st inst., in his 22nd year. (July 11, 1822)

BROOKES, Mrs., a widowed gentlewoman, near Upper Marlborough, fell suddenly into the fire, and no assistance being near, perished in the flames. (April 18, 1754)

BROOKES, Mrs. Anne, died 12th inst., the amiable consort of John Smith Brookes, Esq., at his seat near Upper Marlborough. (Dec. 26, 1782)

BROOME, John, died in N.Y., the 8th inst. He was Lieutenant-Governor of that state. (Aug. 15, 1810)

BROUGHTON, Kenelm, and Miss Mary Simmons, all of Annap., were married Thurs. evening last [March 29], by the Rev. Mr. Watkins. (April 5, 1821)

BROWN, Mrs. ---, relict of the late Basil Brown, died Friday last, in A. A. Co. (Feb. 2, 1826)

BROWN, Mrs. Anne, consort of William Brown, of Ben., died in Annap., 2nd inst., in her 32nd year. (April 12, 1832)

BROWN, Basil, died Tues. last [May 2], at his residence at the head of Severn. (May 4, 1815)

BROWN, Mr. Edward, of Kent Island, was found dead on Mon. evening last [July 18], towards evening, on the road near his house, with his skull fractured. He is supposed to have been thrown by his horse. (July 21, 1763). Mary Brown and William Ringgold are administrators. (Oct. 13, 1763)

BROWN, Dr. Gustavus, died suddenly, a few days since at an advanced

age, in Chas. Co.; for a number of years the presiding magistrate of that county. (March 11, 1762)

BROWN, Dr. Gustavus Richard, died on 27th Sept. last, at his seat in
Chas. Co., near Port Tobacco, in his 68th year. (Oct. 18,
1804)

BROWN, Henrietta, second daughter of Dr. John H. Brown, of this county, died Thurs. morning last, in her 17th year. (Aug. 30,
1832)

BROWN, John, was executed for burglary at Annap., on May 16. (June
4, 1753)

BROWN, John B., died in Middlebury, Vermont, on 11th ult., aged 11
years. [Long obit is given] (July 10, 1806)

BROWN, Dr. John H., and Miss Ann Ball, were married on Tues., 17th
inst., at the Head of Severn, by Rev. Mr. Judd. (July 25,
1810)

BROWN, Rev. Richard, of the Balto. Annual Conference, and Matilda
Ridgely Hampton, daughter of the late Major Philip Hammond,
of A. A. Co., were married Thurs., Sept. 24, by Rev. Henry
Slicer, in Alexandria. (Oct. 8, 1835)

BROWN, Robert, and nine of his children were scalped, on Thurs.,
26th ult., at a schoolhouse near Capt. Potter's, in Conoco-
cheague. Two of his children are yet living. (Aug. 9, 1764)

BROWN, Mr. Thomas, of Kent Co., aged about 22 years, was drowned
Wed. last [July 28], at the mouth of Chester River, below
Poole's Island. (Aug. 5, 1773)

BROWN, Wesley Bond, aged 4 years, 10 months, and 14 days, son of
Rev. Richard Brown, of A.A. Co., died Sat., Aug. 24th, at the
residence of Dr. B. F. Steuart, in Westmoreland Co., Va.
(Aug. 29, 1833)

BROWN, William, son of Ben, Examiner-General of this State, and Mrs.
Sarah Gibson, all of Annap., were married Thurs. evening, by
the Rev. Mr. Guest. (Sept. 27, 1832)

BROWN, William, died 24th inst. [June], at the seat of his son in
St. M. Co.; for many years a respectable inhabitant of this
city. (July 7, 1808)

BROWN, William, was drowned on Tues., 20th inst., as he was returning
home from Leonard-Town, in a small boat, which was caught in
a squall. He leaves a widow and an infant child to mourn
his loss. (Sept. 29, 1808)

BROWNE, Charles, Esq., of Q. A. Co., died Thurs., 13th inst. (Nov.
    20, 1766)

BROWNING, The Hon. Louisa, widow, eldest and only surviving daughter
    of Charles Calvert, Lord Baltimore, died Nov. 15, 1821, at
    Horton Lodge, Epsom Parish, Co. Surrey, in her 85th year.
    She leaves one son, Charles Browning. She was buried Sat.,
    Nov. 24th, in the family vault at Epsom Church. (Feb. 7, 1822)

BRUCE, Norman, Sheriff of St. M. Co., and Miss Susannah Gardner Key,
    only daughter of Philip Key, Esq., were married Thurs. last
    [Nov. 19], in St. M. Co. (Nov. 26, 1761)

BRUCE, Col. William, died 26th ult., at his residence in Chas. Co.,
    in his 73rd year, "another soldier of the Revolution gone!"
    [Long obit follows] (Nov. 10, 1825)

BRYAN, Mr. Robert S., and Miss Juliana Mackubin, of Annap., were
    married on the morning of 28th ult., by Rev. James Smith.
    (July 7, 1825)

BRYAN, William, and Mary Jane Shepperd, all of Annap., were married
    Thurs. evening last, by Rev. Watkins. (Sept. 14, 1826)

BRYAN, William, and Rebecca Gassaway, all of Annap., were married
    Thurs. evening last, by the Rev. Mr. Poisal. (March 2, 1837)

BRYAN, Wrightson, merchant, died Sunday last, in Annap., in his 27th
    year. He was a member of the Methodist Episcopal Church.
    (Aug. 22, 1822)

BRYCE, John R., died Sat. morning last [May 4], in his 34th year; a
    resident of Annap. (May 9, 1805)

BUCHAN, Dr. William, died; the author of several useful medical
    books. (May 2, 1805)

BUCHANAN, Dr., died lately at Philadelphia; Collector of that port.
    (July 28, 1808)

BUCHANAN, Mr. Andrew, merchant of Balto. Town, and Miss Susanna Law-
    son, daughter of Mr. Alexander Lawson, were married. (July
    24, 1760)

BUCHANAN, Lieut. Franklin, of the U. S. Navy, and Nancy, daughter
    of the late Gov. Lloyd, of Maryland, were married in Annap.,
    Thurs. evening last, by the Rev. Mr. McElhiney. (Feb. 26,
    1835)

BUCHANAN, Dr. George, died last week in Balto. Co., in his 54th year,
    one of the representatives, and for 20 years a magistrate.
    (May 2, 1750)

BUCHANAN, Mr. Lloyd, and Miss Rachel Lawson, were married a few days ago, in Balto. Town. (July 14, 1757)

BUCHANAN, Samuel, son of Mr. John Buchanan, merchant, died. He left the Province last summer, after a residence of two years. (March 29, 1770)

BUCK, Robert, a servant who belonged to Capt. West, was found drowned in the Dock last Wed. [April 15]. He had been missing for seven days. (April 14, 1747)

BUCKLAND, Benjamin, cabinet-maker, drowned off the mouth of the Mago-thy, Friday last, en route from Annap. to Balto. (Feb. 28, 1793)

BUCKLAND, Mrs. Mary, died in Annap., on Sat. last [Aug. 11], in her 78th year. (Aug. 15, 1810)

BUCKLAY, Robert, died in prison last Mon. He had been confined for stabbing a man in the belly. (Nov. 4, 1756)

BULLEN, John, Esq., died on Mon. last [March 12], of a complication of disorders, at an advanced age; one of the Commissioners of the Paper Currency Office, an Alderman of the city, and formerly for many years, in the Commission of the Peace for this country, and Captain of the City Independent Company. (March 15, 1764)

BUONAPARTE, Mr. Jerome, youngest brother of the First Consul of France, and Miss Elizabeth Patterson, eldest daughter of Mr. William Patterson, of Balto., were married in that city on Sat. evening last, by the Right Rev. Bishop Carroll. (Dec. 29, 1803)

BURDUS, Richard, died last week in Fred. Co., for many years an inhabitant of Annap., and Clerk of the Provincial Court. (May 20, 1756)

BURGESS, Enoch Magruder, merchant, and Miss Sarah Lock Chew Smith, were married on Sun. [Nov. 4], near Pig Point. (May 8, 1806)

BURK, Mrs. ---, of Q. A. Co., was murdered; her husband, John Burk, is to stand trial. (Sept. 13, 1759)

BURROWS, William W., died 6th inst., in the city of Washington, late Colonel Commandant of the Marine Corps. (March 14, 1805)

BUSH, Mr. Mark W., died Mon. night last. (Dec. 7, 1826)

BUTLER, Mr. J. W., printer, of Balto., and Miss Margaret T. Elliott, of Phila., were married on Wed. evening, 20th inst., in the latter city, by Rev. Mr. Janeway. (May 28, 1807)

BUTLER, Capt. Peter, died lately at Fred. Town, "a very useful man in public affairs." (Jan. 19, 1764)

BUTLER, Lieut. William S., of the U. S. Navy, died at the Pass of Christianne (West Fla.), on the 9th inst., after a few days' illness. (Sept. 27, 1809)

BUTTERFIELD, Mrs. ---, wife of William Butterfield, was eating her breakfast on Sun. [March 15], when she was seized with some violent disorder, and died before noon. March 19, 1761)

BUTTON, Mr. George, died Tues., in Annap. (July 30, 1829)

BUTTON, John, and Sarah Wells, daughter of Elijah Wells, were married in Annap., on Thurs. evening, by Rev. Watkins. (Feb. 23, 1826)

BUTTON, Mrs. Sarah, for many years a member of the Methodist Church, died in Annap., Sun. morning last. (April 19, 1832)

BYRN, William, and Mary A., daughter of the late Gideon White, Esq., of Annap., were married Thurs. last, in Balto., by Rev. John Poisal. (April 4, 1839)

BYUS, James, drowned four days ago, when the ice broke on the Furnace Pond at Alexander Lawson's Iron Works in Balto. Co. (Dec. 28, 1752)

C---LEY, Mrs. Catherine, wife of Br. James C---ley, died on Sat., 28th ult., in A. A. Co. (Aug. 9, 1827)

CADLE, Richard H., and Mary E. Jacobs, all of this county, were married on Thurs. evening, 23rd Aug., by the Rev. Thomas G. Waters. (Sept. 6, 1832)

CADWALLADER, John, of Phila., merchant, and Betsy Lloyd, only daughter of the Hon. Edward Lloyd, were married. (Oct. 11, 1768)

CAILE, Hall, Esq., Sheriff of Dor. Co., died. He was in the prime of life, well esteemed and regretted by all his acquaintances. (Feb. 5, 1761)

CAILE, John, died Sun. evening [April 26], Clerk of Dor. Co. This gentleman by a diligent application to business, for many years carried on a very extensive trade, and as a merchant always supported the character of a punctual and strictly upright man. (April 30, 1767)

CAIN, Mr. Alexander, of the New Theatre, died Sun., 12th inst., at Bristol, Penna., where he had gone for the benefit of his

health, in his 28th year. He leaves a wife and two children.
(June 23, 1808)

CALDCLEUGH, Mrs. Rebecca, wife of Robert A. Caldcleugh, died at Phila.,
Thurs. evening, 9th inst., in her 48th year. (Dec. 16, 1830)

CALDCLEUGH, Mr. Robert, late of Balto., was married at Phila., on
Thurs. evening last, by the Right Rev. Bishop White, to Miss
Poyntell, second daughter of Mr. Poyntell of that city. (June
13, 1805)

CALDER, James, died Friday last [April 11], at Chester Town, aged 60
years. He had long practiced the law, and for six years was
a representative in the General Assembly for Kent Co. (April
17, 1755)

CALDWELL, David S., and Miss Sarah D. Lee, were married in Balto.,
on Sun. evening last, by Rev. John Finley. (July 6, 1826)

CALLAHAN, John, died Sat. evening last [Oct. 26], in his 50th year;
Register of the Land Office for the Western Shore of Maryland. (Oct. 27, 1803)

CALLAHAN, Mrs. Mary, died here on Sun. last, March 22, at an advanced
age; for many years an eminent midwife. (March 26, 1761)

CALLAHAN, Miss Mary, died in Annap., on Thurs. evening [April 19]
at an advanced age. (April 26, 1821)

CALLAHAN, Mrs. Sarah, died Tues. morning, in Balto.; relict of the
late John Callahan; formerly of Annap. (June 13, 1839)

CALLAHAN, Thomas, died Thurs., 4th inst., an old and respectable
inhabitant of this city. (July 11, 1816)

CAIMES, Capt. George, died 20th Nov., at his residence immediately
opposite Cumberland, in Hampshire Co., Va.; a soldier of
the Revolution, in his 80th year. (April 23, 1835)

CALVERT, Ariana, youngest daughter of the Hon. Benedict Calvert, died
Mon., 24th ult., at Mount Airy, P. G. Co., in her 21st year.
(June 10, 1784)

CALVERT, Hon. Benedict, Collector of H. M. Customs for Patuxent
District, and Elizabeth, only surviving daughter of the late
Hon. Charles Calvert, deceased (formerly Governor of this
Province), were married Thurs. last. (April 27, 1748)

CALVERT, Hon. Benedict; on Christmas Day morning, his lady was
safely delivered of a daughter. (Dec. 27, 1749)

CALVERT, Cecilius, uncle of the Proprietor of Maryland, died at the beginning of Nov. last, of an apoplectic fit. (Jan. 30, 1766)

CALVERT, Hon. Charles, Governor of Md., died Feb. 2, 1733/4. An elegy on his death is printed. (March 8 - March 15, 1734)

[CALVERT, Charles], LORD BALTIMORE, Proprietor of this Province, died at his seat at Erith, Kent, on April 23, last. He is succeeded in the title and estate by his only son Frederick, now Lord Baltimore, a minor. (July 10, 1751)

CALVERT, Charles, died at Eton, Jan. 30 last, eldest son of the Hon. Benedict Calvert, Esq., of this Province. (April 28, 1774)

CALVERT, George, died Sun., at his residence near Bladensburg, P. G. Co., aged 70. (Feb. 1, 1838)

CAMDEN, Charles C., a citizen of A. A. Co., died Thurs., 27th ult., aged 70 years, less four days, leaving seven children. (Feb. 2, 1837)

CAMDEN, Mrs. Eliza, consort of Thomas M. Camden, and youngest daughter of Caleb Sappington, of A. A. Co., died Sat., 16th inst., in her 23rd year. (Sept. 28, 1837)

CAMDEN, Mr. Joseph, died after a short illness, at the residence of John Claytor, Esq., in A. A. Co., on the 25th inst., at an advanced age. Many years of his life were spent riding through a large district of the country, exhorting the people to piety and religion; but what were his religious tenets was known to few. He was a member of no established church. (March 6, 1823)

CAMPBELL, Miss Frances, died in Annap., Tues. morning, aged about 80 years. (June 13, 1839)

CANN, James, was found dead in the wreck of the sloop Betsy, on March 4. (March 5, 1812)

CANNON, Mrs. Grace, widow, died about 10 days ago, in P. G. Co., in her 105th year. She was born in this county, and within the last year was able to walk 10 or 12 miles in a day. (Feb. 23, 1764)

CARLIN, Mrs. Ann, wife of Daniel Carlin, of Bush River, died Aug. 27 last, from eating mushrooms. (Oct. 10, 1765)

CARLISLE, Rev. Mr., rector of a parish in Balto. Co., died last week. (Aug. 23, 1749)

CARLYLE, Mrs. Sarah, died Jan. 22, in her 33rd year; wife of Col.

John Carlyle, merchant in Alexandria, and daughter of the late Hon. William Fairfax, Esq., President of Virginia. (Feb. 12, 1761)

CARMICHAEL, Richard Bennett, and Miss Kitty Murray, daughter of the late Dr. Murray of Chestertown, Md., were married Sun. evening, 6th inst., by Rev. Mr. Wilmer. (March 17, 1774)

CARNAN, Christopher, and Elizabeth, eldest daughter of Capt. Robert North, were married. (June 19, 1751)

CARNAN, John, merchant, died Tues. last [Dec. 1], in Balto. Town in the prime of life. (Dec. 3, 1761)

CARNAN, Rowland, late of this Province, was lost on his voyage to Eng. Daniel Chamier, and J. Carnan are executors. (May 2, 1754)

CARPENTER, Capt. John, died here yesterday, long a worthy inhabitant of this city, for many years a commander of a ship from London in the tobacco trade. (Nov. 2, 1748). Elizabeth Carpenter is his administratrix. (Jan. 18, 1749)

CARR, Benjamin, of Pig Point, and Miss Kitty Welch, of Portland Manor, were married Sun., 16th inst., near Herring Creek Church, by the Rev. Mr. Compton. (June 27, 1805)

CARR, John, a staymaker, of Annap., drowned a few days since, when he attempted to pass over the Patapsco with his horse. The ice broke, and both were drowned. (Feb. 3, 1747)

CARR, John, went to Eng., in the Richmond, last summer, and returned in almost 11 months. During his wife, by whom he had a nine month old child, had married again. She is now imprisoned in Dor. Co. gaol. (Aug. 18, 1747)

CARR, John, advertises that he repudiates his wife Mary McLaughlin, who "pretends to be his wife." In the same issue, Mary McLaughlin advertises that her marriage to John Carr is registered in St. Anne's Parish Register in Annap. (July 13, 1748)

CARR, Richard F., and Mrs. Elizabeth A. Gardiner, all of A. A. Co., were married Thurs. evening last, by Rev. Waters. (Sept. 19, 1839)

CARROLL, Dr. Charles, died Mon. evening last [Sept. 29] at his house in Annap., aged 64 years, for 40 years a resident in Annap. He followed the practice of physic, and later applied himself to schemes of trade and merchandize. A Roman Catholic, he later renounced the errors of that Church, and became a

Protestant. In 1737 he was chosen to represent the people in the Lower House. (Oct. 2, 1755)

CARROLL, Mrs. Ann, of Annap., died suddenly, on Mon., 20th inst., in Balto. (Sept. 23, 1830)

CARROLL, Charles, Jr., of P. G. Co., and Mary, daughter of Henry Hill, of the same county, were married Sun. last [Feb. 13]. (Feb. 17, 1763)

CARROLL, Charles, Esq., Barrister, of Annap., and Margaret, daughter of Matthew Tilghman, were married Thurs. last [June 23] in Tal. Co. (June 30, 1763)

CARROLL, Charles, Jr., and Miss Mary Darnall, were married Sun. evening, June 5, at his father's house, in Annap. (June 9, 1768)

CARROLL, Charles, of Carrollton, died; a Signer of the Declaration of Independence. [Long obit is given.] (Nov. 22, 1832)

CARROLL, Mr. Daniel, died Wed. last [Feb. 27] at his house in Upper Marlborough. (March 6, 1751)

CARROLL, Mrs. Eleanor, consort of Mr. Daniel Carroll, of Upper Marlborough, died here universally regretted on Tues. [April 12]. (April 28, 1763)

CARROLL, Capt. Henry, of St. M. Co., died Sept. 16. Bred to the sea, he leaves a widow and six children. (Oct. 19, 1775)

CARROLL, Mr. James, died Friday last [June 13] at the house of Charles Carroll, Esq., in this city. (June 17, 1729) Yesterday evening the corps [sic] of Mr. James Carroll was interred at the burial place of that family, near this city, in a decent and handsome manner. (June 24, 1729)

CARROLL, Most Rev. Dr. John, Archbishop of Balto., died yesterday morning in the 80th year of his age. (From the Balto. Telegraph) (Dec. 7, 1815)

CARROLL, Mr. John Henry, died Friday last [Feb. 15] at his father's house in Annap., aged 22, of a confirmed consumption; the youngest son of Dr. Charles Carroll. (Feb. 21, 1754)

CARROLL, Nicholas, died Friday last (May 22), an old inhabitant of this city. (May 28, 1812)

CARTER, Mr. Robert, of Westmoreland, in Va., and Frances, youngest daughter of the Hon. Benjamin Tasker, were married Tues. last [April 2], by Rev. Mr. Malcolm. (April 4, 1754)

CARTY, Enos, was executed in Cecil Co., 14th inst., for being concerned in the murder of his late master, Hugh Mahaffy, Jr.
(March 28, 1750)

CASSELL, Rev. Leonard, pastor of the Methodist Episcopal Church on
Fell's Point, died in Balto., on Mon., 26th ult., in his 24th
year. His remains were interred in the Methodist burying
ground in that city on Tues. (Oct. 6, 1808)

CATON, Miss Susanna, of Annap., died Mon., March 30, at the Annap.
residence of George Keatinge. She was buried in the Presbyterian graveyard. [Long obit is given.] (April 9, 1829)

CAULK, Daniel, and Elizabeth J. Welch, both of Annap., were married
in Balto., on Mon. evening last, by Rev. George G. Cookman.
(Nov. 19, 1835)

CESSFORD, Mr. Thomas, fell from the roof of a house at Upper Marlborough, P. G. Co., on Tues. [Aug. 26], and died the next
morning. (Aug. 28, 1755)

CHALMERS, Rev. Mr. Walter, died Thurs. last [Dec. 27], after a short
illness, on the north side of the Severn. He was rector of
St. Margaret's Westminster Parish. (Jan. 3, 1760) Robert
Swan is administrator. (Feb. 7, 1760)

CHAMBERLAIN, Mr., of St. M. Co., died at Mrs. Simms', in Fred. Co.
(April 24, 1751)

CHAMBERLAIN, Mrs. Rebecca, wife of John Chamberlain, and the oldest
daughter of the late Rezin D. Baldwin, of Annap., died Sat.,
6th inst. (May 11, 1837)

CHAMBERLAINE, Madame, died Tues. se'ennight, in Tal. Co., the wife
of the Hon. Samuel Chamberlaine, Esq. (April 6, 1748)

CHAMBERLAINE, Samuel, died at his house in Tal. Co., for many years
one of the Lord Proprietary's Council of State, and Naval
Officer of the Port of Oxford. (June 10, 1773)

CHAMBERLAINE, Col. Thomas, died Sun. morning last, at his father's
seat, near Oxford, Tal. Co.; eldest son of the Hon. Samuel
Chamberlaine, Esq. He leaves a sorrowful widow, and a young
son. Yesterday, his remains were decently interred. (May
17, 1764)

CHANDLER, Mr. Jehu, editor of the Maryland Republican, died Sun.
night last, in his 38th year. He was a native of the state
of Delaware, but resided in Annap. for the last 13 years
of his life. (Sept. 19, 1822)

CHANEY, Mr. Elijah, died at his residence near South River, A. A.

Co., Thurs., 10th inst., in his 76th year. He leaves a widow
and a large family. (Dec. 24, 1835)

CHANEY, John, and Elizabeth, daughter of Richard Prout, deceased,
all of Cal. Co., were married Thurs., 18th inst., by the Rev.
John Bowen. (July 25, 1833)

CHAPLINE, Capt. Joseph, died lately in Fred. Co., for many years a
representative of that county. (Jan. 12, 1769)

CHAPMAN, Mrs. Eleanor, died 20th ult., in her 29th year, wife of
Major Henley Chapman. She was the youngest daughter of the
late Samuel Hanson. (Aug. 4, 1796)

CHAPMAN, Maj. Henry H., died in Georgetown, a soldier of the Revolution. He had filled various public offices in the State
of Maryland, whence he removed about two years ago. A wife
and nine children survive. (Dec. 13, 1821)

CHAPMAN, Dr. John, died at his house in Port Tobacco, on the 18th
of May, in his 32nd year. He was a tender husband and
parent. (June 10, 1790)

CHAPMAN, John H., died Wed., 2nd inst., in his 13th year, eldest
son of Maj. Henry H. Chapman, of Chas. Co. (March 17, 1814)

CHAPMAN, Capt. Samuel, was found last Sun. evening, lying dead near
a gate on his own plantation near Patuxent. He had been at
Queen Anne [in P. G. Co.], and is supposed to have been
flung by his horse. (Jan. 8, 1767)

CHAPMAN, Mr. William, died Sat. morning last [March 16], at his
house in London Town, after a tedious indisposition, aged
67 years, one of the magistrates of this county. (March 21,
1754)

CHASE, Miss Ann, daughter of Rev. Thomas Chase, former rector of
St. Paul's Parish, Balto., died. (Aug. 26, 1824)

CHASE, Mrs. Hester, consort of the highly respected Judge Jeremiah
T. Chase, died Sat., 22nd inst. [Two obituary notices appear.]
(Nov. 27, 1823)

CHASE, Mr. Jeremiah, of Chas. Co., died 2nd inst., at a gentleman's
house as he was on his way to the Baltimore Assizes. He was
a practitioner of law, and one of the representatives for
St. M. Co. (April 10, 1755) Chase was poisoned. An account
of his poisoner's trial was given. (June 26, 1755)

CHASE, Jeremiah Townley, died Sun., 11th inst., within a few days
of the termination of his 80th year. [A long obit gives

details of his public career in Maryland during the Revolutionary War.] (May 15, 1828)

CHASE, Mary, second daughter of Richard M. Chase, Esq., died in Annap., on Mon., the last of Jan., aged 22 months and 17 days. (Jan. 11, 1827)

CHASE, Mrs. Matilda, relict of the late Thomas Chase, died Thurs., 13th inst. She was the daughter of our late Chief Justice. (Aug. 20, 1829)

CHASE, Mr. Richard, of Balto. Town, died some few days since, in Chas. Co., after a short illness, in the prime of life; a practitioner of law. (Dec. 25, 1757)

CHASE, Richard Halton [Hatton?], died Sat., 17th inst., second son of Richard M. Chase, aged 15 months. (July 29, 1824)

CHASE, Richard M., and Mary Marriott, all of Annap., were married Thurs. evening last [Jan. 28] by the Rev. Mr. Davis. (Feb. 1, 1819)

CHASE, the Hon. Samuel, Associate Judge of the Supreme Court of the United States, and one of the most eminent citizens of this State, died on the 20th. (June 26, 1811)

CHASE, Thomas, of Balto., and Miss Matilda Chase, daughter of the Hon. Jeremiah Townley Chase, were married on Thurs. evening last [Oct. 17], by the Rev. Mr. Davis. (Oct. 24, 1816)

CHASE, Thomas, died 17th inst., in his 49th year. He leaves a widow and three daughters. [A long obit is given] (Feb. 23, 1826)

CHEW, Mr. Benjamin, of Penna., and Mary, daughter of John Galloway, merchant, were married Sat. last [June 13], at West River. (June 16, 1747)

CHEW, Mr. Bennett, a young gentleman of Annap., and Anne, eldest daughter of Col. Edward Tilghman, of Q. A. Co., were married. (Jan. 20, 1763)

CHEW, Mrs. Eliza M., consort of Dr. Samuel Chew, died 26th ult.; she was a resident of Cal. Co. (Oct. 10, 1833)

CHEW, John Walter, of A. A. Co., and Susanna Rebecca, dau. of Samuel Peaco, of Annap., were married Thurs. morning last, by Rev. Mr. Poisal. (Dec. 29, 1836)

CHEW, Leonard H., and Amelia H., eldest daughter of Aquila Beall, all of P. G. Co., were married Thurs. evening, 29th ult., by the Rev. John Swan. (Nov. 19, 1835)

CHEW, Nathaniel, Sr., died at his late residence on West River, on Dec. 22, 1827, in his 80th year. (Jan. 3, 1828)

CHEW, Philemon, of Q. A. Co., died last Sat., March 17, between one and two o'clock. (March 22, 1770)

CHEW, Samuel, of Herring Bay, A. A. Co., former magistrate, died in London, February past, of small pox. (May 10, 1749)

CHEW, Mr. Samuel, of Wells, and Sarah, second daughter of James Weems, Esq., were married Thursday, 3rd inst., in Cal. Co. (Feb. 17, 1763)

CHEW, Mrs. Sarah, died 30th of last month, in Cal. Co., in the full bloom of life; consort of Samuel Chew, and second daughter of James Weems. (Nov. 10, 1763)

CHILD, Mr. Henry, was killed by lightning, Friday last [Sept. 11], at his plantation, part of Anne Arundel Manor. (Sept. 17, 1772)

CHILDS, Benjamin, of Balto., and Miss Elizabeth Munroe, of Annap., were married Sun. evening last [May 12], by the Rev. Guest. (May 14, 1818)

CHILDS, Mr. Benjamin, died in Balto., on Sun., 30th ult.; formerly of Annap. (Aug. 3, 1837)

CHILDS, Henry, of Queen Anne, P. G. Co., and Miss Mary Tootle, of Annap., were married Thurs. evening, 16th inst., at Sotterly, St. M. Co., by the Rev. Mr. Ralph. (Feb. 22, 1809)

CHILDS, Mr. John, and Miss Mary Hyde, all of Annap., were married on Tues. evening last [Feb. 4], by the Rev. Mr. Higinbothom. (Feb. 6, 1812)

CHILDS, Mr. John, died Tues. morning [March 21], in his 25th year. (March 23, 1815)

CHILDS, Mrs. Mary, died in Annap., on Friday morning last [April 14], after a distressing illness. (April 20, 1820)

CHILTON, Capt. William, of the ship Frederick, died of a violent fever, Tues. last [Aug. 14], and was buried at Port Tobacco. His ship was lately arrived in Patuxent from Europe. (Aug. 22, 1750)

CHISHOLM, Archibald, died at West River; formerly of Annap. (Feb. 17, 1810)

CHRISTIE, Charles, Esq., died Thurs. last [March 17], in Balto. Co.;

in the prime of life, after a few days' illness. He was
Sheriff of that county. (March 24, 1757)

CHRISTIE, Gabriel, Esq., Collector of the Port of Baltimore, died in
that city on Friday morning last [April 1], in his 51st year.
(April 7, 1808)

CHRISTIE, Mr. Robert, of Balto. Town, and Miss Polly Lawson, were
married Thurs. (April 19, 1770)

CHRISTOPHER, John, was executed for burglary, 14th inst., in Q. A.
Co. (May 27, 1756)

CLAGGETT, Capt. Charles, died on the last day of Jan., in Cal. Co.,
aged 72 years. (Feb. 17, 1763)

CLAGGETT, Mrs. Elizabeth, relict of the late Mr. William Claggett,
died Sat., Feb. 16th, at her residence on South River, in her
66th year. (Feb. 21, 1833)

CLAGETT, Gustavus A., died Thurs. last [May 17], at Upper Marlboro'.
(May 23, 1810)

CLAGGETT, Rev. Richard, died at the beginning of this week, rector
of a parish in Chas. Co. (Aug. 26, 1756)

CLAGETT, Dr. Thomas John, and Miss Sophia Martin, were married Tues.
evening, 3rd inst., at Rockville, Mont. Co., by the Rev.
Mr. Read. (Dec. 12, 1811)

CLAGGETT, Rev. Thomas John, Bishop of the Protestant Episcopal
Church in Md., died in P. G. Co., on Friday, 2nd inst. (Aug.
15, 1816)

CLAGGETT, Mr. Walter, died Sun. evening last [Sept. 19] at his residence in Annap. (Sept. 23, 1819)

CLAGETT, William, an Associate Judge of the Fifth Judicial District
of the State of Maryland, died at Hagerstown, 25th ult.
(April 4, 1810)

CLAPHAM, John C., died Sun. night, 8th inst., aged 20 years. (From
the Federal Gazette) (July 19, 1821)

CLAPHAM, Jonas, died in Balto. City, 28th inst., in his 75th year.
He was a native of Annap., but for the last 40 years a resident of Balto. (Aug. 31, 1837)

CLARK, Mr. David, died 12th inst., at the seat of Osborn Sprigg,
Esq., P. G. Co., in his 26th year. He leaves a widow and
two children. He was buried the next day in the family
burying ground. (May 17, 1792)

CLARK, Horatio, died Sun., 1st inst., aged 14, eldest son of Joseph
Clark, architect. (Sept. 5, 1793)

CLARK, John, of Kent Co., was killed when struck on the head by
Joseph Helmes, also of Kent Co. (July 21, 1757)

CLARK, Joshua, and Henrietta, eldest daughter of Jeremiah Boyd, formerly of Annap., were married 18th inst., in Q. A. Co., by
Rev. W. H. Bordley. (Dec. 25, 1834)

CLARK, Martha Hall, died in P. G. Co., on Sat. morning, 30th June,
at the seat of James N. L. Weems, Esq.; in the 22nd year of
her age. (July 4, 1810)

CLARK, Mrs. Sarah, was murdered Wed. morning last, by her husband
John Clark. [Long account is given.] (Nov. 27, 1751)

CLARKE, Benjamin Hall, and Miss Nelly Clagett, eldest daughter of
Joseph White Clagett, all of P. G. Co., were married on Tues.
evening, 3rd inst., at Cool Spring Manor, near Queen Anne,
by the Rev. Mr. Scott. (Oct. 11, 1809)

CLARKE, Daniel, Sr., of P. G. Co., died 30th Sept., in his 69th year.
(Oct. 14, 1802)

CLARKE, George, an elderly servant man in Annap., dropp'd down dead
Thurs. last [Jan. 12] as he was sawing of wood. (Jan. 19,
1764)

CLARKE, Mrs. Margaret, aged 39, wife of Daniel Clarke, Esq., of P. G.
Co., died Sun., Sept. 19th, at the residence of her mother,
Mrs. Howard, in A. A. Co. (Oct. 7, 1813)

CLARKE, Lieut. Satterlee and Miss Frances Whetcroft, of Annap., were
married Sun. evening last [Sept. 23], by the Rev. Mr. Judd.
(Sept. 26, 1810)

CLAUDE, Dennis, and Miss Anne Jacob, all of Annap., were married
Tues. evening last [Feb. 13], by the Rev. Mr. Ryland. (Feb.
15, 1816)

CLAUDE, Dennis, Jr., of Annap., and Miss Elizabeth Cotton, of Balto.,
were married in that city, on Sun. morning last, by Rev. Mr.
Bartow. (May 21, 1829)

CLAUDE, Mrs. Elizabeth, died Mon. last [April 29], of Annap. (May 1,
1811)

CLAYTON, Catherine, second daughter of Philip Clayton, of Annap.,
died Sat. evening last, after a short illness. (Aug. 11, 1831)

CLAYTON, Mr. Philip C., and Miss Catherine G. Schwrar, all of Annap.,

were married yesterday morning, by Rev. Robert S. Vinton.
(Nov. 9, 1837)

CLAYTOR, John, died Wed., 13th inst., at Browsley Hall, his late
residence, in his 58th year. (Feb. 21, 1839)

CLEARY, James, died Mon. night last, in his 82nd year. (Oct. 1,
1835)

CLEMENTS, Elizabeth, died Thurs. night last [May 30]; of Annap.
(June 6, 1805)

CLEMENTS, Mr. Francis T., died Mon. morning last, in Annap. (April
3, 1817)

CLEMENTS, Mrs. Sarah, relict of the late Francis T. Clements, Esq.,
died Sun. morning last, at an advanced age. (Feb. 2, 1826)

CLERK, James, Esq., and Margaret Lee, youngest daughter of the late
Hon. Philip Thomas Lee, were lately married, in London.
(Feb. 21, 1793)

CLINTON, George, Jr., Esq., died at New York, Sat., 16th inst., in
his 38th year; late a member of Congress from that city.
(Sept. 27, 1809)

CLINTON, George, Vice President of the United States, died Mon.
morning [April 20] last. (April 23, 1812)

COALE, Edward J., formerly of Balto., died at Washington on Friday.
(Nov. 22, 1832)

COATS, Thomas, of Greenbury's Point, was drowned off the mouth of
the Magothy, Friday last, en route from Annap., to Balto.
(Feb. 28, 1793)

COCHRAN, John J., and Catherine Baumgardner, both of York, were
married, 17th inst. He was junior editor of the York
Republican. (Nov. 7, 1839)

COCKEY, Col. John C., died at his residence in Fred. Co., on Mon.,
4th inst. He was a member of the legislature. (Dec. 14,
1826)

COCKEY, William, a young man, fell from the round-top of a ship at
West River, last Sat., and received so much hurt that he died
soon after. (Sept. 9, 1762)

COE, Alexander B., and Miss Eleanora Thompson, all of Annap., were
married Thurs. evening last, by the Rev. Mr. Watkins. (Jan.
3, 1833)

COE, Mr. Charles, was accidentally drowned on Tues. afternoon last, while angling at the mouth of Carroll's Creek, opposite this city. (Sept. 23, 1824)

COFFIN, William, and Miss Julia Ann Tack, were married in Balto., Thurs. evening last, by the Rev. Mr. Kelsey. (Dec. 29, 1825)

COLBURN, Milton Francis, and Miss Mary Teresa Murdoch, both of Annap., were married Sun. last [April 25], at White Marsh, P. G. Co., by the Rev. Bishop Coleman. (April 29, 1819)

COLE, Mr. Charles, merchant, died here Thurs. last [July 5], at an advanced age. He had resided for upwards of 40 years in Annap.; he had never married. (July 7, 1757)

COLE, Joshua, apprentice to Thomas Jewett, currier, of Balto., died July 12th. (July 29, 1802)

COLE, Mr. Levi, and Elizabeth Simmons, were married Tues. evening last, by the Rev. T. B. Dorsey. (April 8, 1830)

COLEBURN, Mrs. Mary T., consort of Mr. Milton F. Coleburn, and daughter of Mr. Gilbert Murdoch, deceased, died in Balto., on Wed., 22nd inst. She was a member of the Roman Catholic Church for over 25 years. She leaves a husband, and three small children, and an aged mother. (Aug. 30, 1832)

COLLINGS, William, an orderly servant of Mr. Raitt's, accidentally drowned Sun. last [June 3]. (June 6, 1750)

COLLINSON, William, of West River, and Miss Elizabeth Whittington, of Annap., were married Thurs. evening last [Sept. 29], by the Rev. Mr. Wyatt. (Oct. 6, 1808)

COLLINSON, Mr. William, died Sat. last, at his residence in A. A. Co., leaving a widow and eight children. (Sept. 9, 1830)

COLVILL, Col. Thomas, died lately at Clish, near Alexandria, Va., aged 78. He formerly lived at Cecil Co., in this province, and was one of the representatives of that county, for many years. (Oct. 30, 1766)

COMEGYS, Benjamin, died 15th inst., on board the ship Grand Seignor, of Cape Hatteras. He was formerly a merchant of Balto. He was attended on the voyage by his physician, Dr. Cocke, who took the necessary means of preserving the body, and returning it to Kent Co., where the deceased was born. (June 28, 1809)

COMPTON, Mrs., died at her residence, near Tracey's Landing, A. A. Co., aged 66 years. (Jan. 26, 1832)

COMPTON, William J. W., and Caroline Jacob, all of A. A. Co., were married on Tues., 3rd inst., by the Rev. Mr. Chesley. (May 2, 1833)

CONAWAY, Mr. John, of Balto., and Ruth Chaney, of A. A. Co., were married Tues. evening last, by the Rev. Mr. Watkins. (Nov. 28, 1833)

CONKLING, Lieut. Solomon G., of the U. S. Regiment of Artillery, died at Fort McHenry, Balto., 9th inst. (Aug. 15, 1810)

CONN, Rev. Mr. Hugh, on Sun., 28th June last, dropp'd down dead in his pulpit, as he was preaching to a congregation near Bladensburg, P. G. Co.; he was a Presbyterian minister. (July 9, 1752)

CONNER, Nathaniel, a ferryman, drowned while crossing the Bay, when his ferry capsized in a squall yesterday. (March 20, 1751)

CONNER, Terence, was executed Friday last, for the murder of James Boyles, in Fred. Co., in Aug. last. He was born in the Romish persuasion, in Ireland. (Oct. 26, 1752)

CONNOR, Marmaduke W., and Miss Sarah Wessels, all of Annap., were married Sun. evening last [May 14], by the Rev. Mr. Watkins. (May 18, 1820)

CONOWAY, Addison, of P. G. Co., died 20th inst., in his 46th year. (April 26, 1809)

CONTEE, Mr. Alexander, died suddenly, in Chas. Co., Md., at the residence of the Rev. Dr. B. Contee, on the 21st inst., in his 56th year. (March 21, 1810)

CONTEE, John, Esq., and Ann Snowden, daughter of the late Richard Snowden, all of P. G. Co., were married 17th inst., by the Rev. Mr. Tyng. (March 4, 1824)

CONTEE, John, died at his late residence, Pleasant Prospect, P. G. Co., Nov. 15th, aged 45 years. (Nov. 21, 1839)

CONTEE, Mrs. Mary, died at Upper Marlborough, P. G. Co., 11th March, wife of Richard Contee, and eldest daughter of David Craufurd, Esq., aged 19 years. (March 22, 1787)

CONTEE, Philip A. L., of Westmoreland Co., Va., and Miss Ann R. Clerklee, of Chas. Co., Md., were married Thurs., 2nd inst., at Bromont, the seat of James Clerklee, by the Rev. Charles Mann. (July 16, 1818)

CONTEE, Mrs. Sarah, died at Brookfield, P. G. Co., aged 61 years,

the wife of Thomas Contee, Esq., and daughter of the late
Benjamin Fendall, Esq., of Chas. Co. (April 4, 1793)

CONTEE, Mrs. Sarah Russell, wife of the Rev. Dr. Benjamin Contee,
and daughter of the late Philip Thomas Lee, and granddaughter
of the late Richard Lee, of Chas. Co., died Dec. 16, 1810,
in her 44th year. (Jan. 2, 1811)

COOK, Mrs. Alethea, died Thurs. last [Jan. 30], in Cal. Co., of several
wounds and burns she had received; formerly the wife of the
late Walter Smith. Her last marriage was to a man whose
cloth and station in life ought to have rendered him exemplary
for virtue and piety, but his horrid usage and unparallel'd
barbaraity to his wife, which decency forbids even to relate,
is supposed to have been the cause of her death, and he is
now confined in the gaol of that county, in order to be
tried for same. (Feb. 1, 1753) Her husband was indicted for
her murder, but was found not guilty by the jury. (April 26,
1753)

COOK, Rev. James, minister of the Gospel, aged 60 years, and Miss
Rebecca Chambers, aged 16, of Cecil Co., were married Thurs.
evening, 22nd inst., by the Rev. Nicholas Chambers. (Sept.
29, 1808)

COOK, Robert, ropewalker, was found dead, Sun. last, near Newington
Ropewalk. He had been to London Town, and is supposed to
have come by his death by drinking, on his way back, while
he was very hot, too much cold water at the spaw [sic].
(Aug. 14, 1766)

COOLIDGE, Mrs. Mary, died Friday, April 24th, wife of Capt. Judson
Coolidge. (May 7, 1772)

COOMBES, Mr. John, was found drowned in Chas. Co. He had been insane for some time. (Oct. 30, 1766)

COOMES, Dr. Stanislaus, and Miss Maria, daughter of Col. Green,
were married Tues., 14th inst., at the residence of Col.
Green in Chas. Co. (Jan. 23, 1817)

COOPER, Thomas, a young Englishman, was executed at the gallows
just outside the city, for burglary, last Friday. (Oct. 14,
1762)

CORY, Henry, was killed Sat. last, by the premature discharge of
a gun; he was a hand on a vessel. (May 30, 1754)

COSDEN, William Henry, died 9th inst., at Newark, Del., in his 19th
year, the youngest son of Jeremiah Cosden of Elkton. He
committed suicide, rather than apologize to a teacher, which

his father had ordered him to do. (Dec. 29, 1814)

COTTERILL, William, Sr., and his sons William Cotterill, Jr., and
John Cotterill, were executed on Friday last; "Hagerstown,
Feb. 29." (March 9, 1820)

COULTER, Miss Elizabeth, of Annap., died last Tues. morning, in her
21st year. (July 25, 1805)

COULTER, Mrs. Martha, consort of Mr. Henry Coulter, died in Annap.,
yesterday morning. (July 22, 1824)

COURTS, Mr. John, died in Chas. Co., for many years a representative
for that county. He died of the pleurisy after having recovered from the same disorder many times. (Feb. 3, 1748)

COURTS, William, Esq., died 28th ult., at his house Milton-Hill, in
Chas. Co.; aged about 39 years. He leaves a wife and three
children. (Oct. 25, 1792)

COWAN, Alexander, and Miss Susan Coulter, all of Annap., were married
on the evening of Thurs. last, by the Rev. Mr. Wells. (Jan.
8, 1824)

COWAN, John, died this morning, in his seventh year, only son of
Alexander Cowan. (April 20, 1837)

COWELL, William, a native of Boston, and a captain in the Dutch
Navy, died at Batavia, on the 27th of Nov. (April 19, 1809)

COWMAN, Mr. Gerard, of A. A. Co., died Tues. morning. (Feb. 14, 1833)

COWMAN, Capt. Joseph, died yesterday, of the dropsy, aged about 59
years. His remains will be interred on Sat. next, at West
River Meeting House. (Oct. 4, 1753) Joseph Cowman is the
executor. (May 30, 1754)

COWMAN, Joseph, died Wed., 14th inst., at his seat in A. A. Co., in
his 50th year, leaving a wife and four children. (Dec. 22,
1808)

COWMAN, Richard J., Esq., and Harriet Green, were married on Tues.,
by Rev. John G. Blanchard. (June 18, 1829)

COWMAN, Dr. Thomas, of South River, died Thurs. night last. (Jan.
31, 1833)

COWMAN, Dr. Thomas J., and Miss Matilda Battee, were married on
Thurs., 11th inst., by Rev. Mr. Watkins. (May 25, 1826)

COX, Rev. James, rector of St. Paul's Parish, Q. A. Co., died on
Dec. 3. (Dec. 6, 1753)

CRABB, Charles H., and Miss Mary L. Summers, were married at Rockville, Mont. Co., on Thurs. evening, 28th ult., by the Rev. Mr. Read. (Dec. 28, 1811)

CRABB, Richard J., Esq., of Mont. Co., and Miss Catherine Chase, daughter of the Hon. Jeremiah T. Chase, were married Thurs. evening last [Nov. 4], by the Rev. Mr. Nind. (Nov. 11, 1813)

CRAGGS, John, died on Wed. [Nov. 20], at Hammond's Ferry, in his 68th year. (Nov. 28, 1805)

CRAGGS, Mrs. Mary, died Sat., Aug. 5th, at Hammond's Ferry, after a long illness, aged 67 years. (Aug. 17, 1815)

CRAIG, Major Isaac, died 14th ult., at his seat on Montour's Island; formerly a field officer of the Penna. Line, in the American Revolution. (June 1, 1826)

CRAIG, William, died in Annap., Mon. morning last, a delegate to the General Assembly from Cecil Co. (Jan. 2, 1823)

CRANE, Ichabod, and Susanna Hook, were married in Newstead, by the Rev. Mr. Crooks. (Jan. 12, 1826)

CRANWELL, Joseph, servant of Jonathan Mullinix, of Elk Ridge, ran away from his master. (Nov. 27, 1751) A body was found, Mon. last, back of Elk Ridge, supposed to be that of Joseph Cranwell. (March 12, 1752)

CRAUFURD, Mrs. Sarah, consort of David Craufurd, a member of the Assembly, from P. G. Co., died Friday last, 7th inst., in her 32nd year. She was buried Sunday evening. (April 14, 1780).

CRAWFORD, Mr. David, died last week in Upper Marlboro', P. G. Co.; a merchant. (March 15, 1749)

CREAGH, Mr. Patrick, died here, Mon. night last [Dec. 22], after a few days' illness; a merchant, and long an inhabitant of this city. (Dec. 24, 1760) The estate will be settled by Richard Mackubin. (Jan. 15, 1761)

CRESAP, Col. Joseph, died in All. Co., on 20th inst., an officer in the Army of Independence, and at different periods, a member of the Maryland House of Delegates, and Senate. (Jan. 24, 1827)

CRESAP, Thomas, Jr., a widower with two children, was killed by Indians on last St. George's Day. (May 6, 1756)

CROMPTON, Major Thomas, of Cal. Co., died last month. (Jan. 17, 1745)

CROMWELL, Richard, died Sat. last, in Annap.; a member of the House of Delegates of this state, from Wash. Co. His remains were interred the following day. He leaves a disconsolate widow and a large family of children. (Dec. 30, 1802)

CROMWELL, Mrs. Mary, consort of Richard Cromwell, of A. A. Co., died 2nd inst. (Sept. 15, 1831)

CROSS, Miss Elizabeth, aged about 14 years, daughter of the late Mr. John Cross, of Severn, died Thurs. last. (May 5, 1828)

CROSS, Mr. Howerton, of P. G. Co., and Miss Maria Cross, of A. A. Co., were married Sun., 25th May, by Rev. Mr. Watkins. (June 5, 1828)

CROSS, Mrs. Maria, consort of Malverton Cross, of Annap., and daughter of Thomas R. Cross, died Wed., 5th inst., in P. G. Co. (Aug. 13, 1829)

CROSS, Mrs. Rebecca, consort of Walter Cross, of Annap., died Mon. last. (March 31, 1825)

CROSS, Mr. Walter, of Annap., and Miss Sarah Holland, of Mont. Co., were married Tues., 20th inst., by the Rev. Mr. Magruder. (Sept. 29, 1825)

CROUCH, Henry, died here, last month, a carver who was deemed by good judges to be as ingenuous an artist at his business as any in the King's Dominions. (Jan. 7, 1762)

CROUCH, Joseph, died Tues. evening [Jan. 2], of the gun-shot wound received from his "dr--k-n son" on Christmas Day. (Jan. 4, 1753)

CROW, Richard B., of P. G. Co., and Miss Charlotte A. Franklin, of Balto. Town, were married in that town on 12th inst., by Rev. Nevins. (Feb. 23, 1826)

CROWNINSHIELD, Jacob, Esq., died at Washington, from a ruptured blood vessel; one of the Representatives from Mass. in the Congress of the United States. (April 21, 1808)

CUFFEE, a negro, was executed at Annap. last week, pursuant to his sentence. (Sept. 5, 1750)

CULBRETH, Dr. Richard S., of Caroline Co., and Mary Ann Schwrar, of Annap., were married in that city on Tues. last, by Rev. Mr. Vinton. (Nov. 15, 1838)

CULBRETH, Robert Emmet, oldest son of Thomas Culbreth, of Annap., died Sat., 8th inst., in his 26th year. (Sept. 14, 1837)

CULBRETH, Thomas, of Annap., and Martha M. Slade, second daughter of
    of Josiah Slade, of Harf. Co., were married in Washington,
    on the eve of the 4th inst., by Rev. Edmund J. Reis, of Balto.
    (Dec. 13, 1827)

CUMBERFORD, Mrs. Margaret, of Annap., was stabbed to death the evening
    of Tues. last, by a man supposed to be a little intoxicated,
    who went into a house in this city, where rum is sold, and
    insisted on being served some grog, and on being refused,
    pulled out his sword. (Oct. 26, 1769) Michael Mitchell, als.
    Michael Huet was tried and found guilty. (Dec. 21, 1769)

CUMMING, William, Esq., died yesterday morning, of an apoplectic fit,
    near Lower Marlborough, on his return from St. M. Co.; one of
    the alderman of this city, and for many years a practitioner
    of the law in our courts. (March 12, 1752) William Cumming
    is executor. (Aug. 13, 1752)

CUNNINGHAM, Mr. Loudon, a young gentleman, was accidentally shot and
    killed while gunning, a few days ago in Tal. Co. (Nov. 28,
    1771)

CURRAM, Barney, died on Tues. morning [Dec. 17]; a merchant of
    Annap. (Dec. 19, 1816)

CURRAN, Mrs. Mary, died Friday morning last. (Aug. 5, 1824)

CURRAN, Michael, died in Annap., after being thrown from his horse
    on Nov. 2. (Nov. 3, 1808)

CURRAN, Mr. Philip, a native of Ireland, long a respectable teacher,
    and formerly a Professor at St. John's College, drowned in
    the basin of Annap., Sun. last. He leaves a numerous infant
    family. (Oct. 4, 1821)

CURREY, John, on Feb. 27, being at the house of Mr. Matthew Dockery
    in Q. A. Co., fell out of the window, and was so seriously
    injured, his life was despaired of. (March 7, 1750)

CURRIE, Archibald, chief mate of the ship Nisbet, died yesterday in
    an explosion aboard ship. (Oct. 19, 1758)

CURTIS, Capt. William, master of Patrick Creagh's sloop, was murdered
    by John Wright, John Smith, and Toney, who ran away to S. C.,
    where they were captured and brought back to Va. (June 20,
    1754)

DABNEY, John, Esq., Consul General of the United States for the
    Azores, died at Fayel, on Sept. 2nd, of apoplexy. He was a
    native of Boston, and a son of Dr. Dabney, who removed to
    Conn. at the outbreak of the Revolution. Mr. Dabney had

resided at Fayel with his family for over 20 years. (Nov. 2, 1826)

DADDS, Mr. Emanuel, died 6th inst., at the head of South River, at an advanced age. (Feb. 21, 1833)

DADDS, Mr. William, died suddenly, in Annap., on 15th inst. (Dec. 22, 1825)

DADDS, William, and Miss Elizabeth Pearce, all of this city, were married on Thurs. evening last, by the Rev. Mr. Guest. (Oct. 18, 1832)

DAIR, ---, the 18 month old daughter of Mr. Dair, at Herring Bay, was burnt to death Mon. last [March 9], when her clothing caught fire. (March 12, 1752)

DALEY, Francis N., printer, and Julia Ann, second daughter of Elijah Wells, of Annap., were married Thurs. evening last, 16th inst. (May 23, 1839)

DALL, John R., Esq., of Balto., and Miss Meliora O., second daughter of the late Hon. Thomas Buchanan, were married on Tues., 22nd ult., at Woodburn, Wash. Co., by the Rev. Curtis Clay. (March 4, 1819)

DALLAS, Alexander J., died early this morning, after a short illness of 24 hours. (From a Philadelphia paper of Jan. 17) (Jan. 23, 1817)

DALRYMPLE, Mrs. Christiana, consort of James A. D. Dalrymple, a member of the Maryland House of Delegates, died near St. Leonard's, Cal. Co., on Feb. 16th. [Long obit is given] (March 9, 1826)

DALTON, Miss Margaret, died in Mifflin Co. (Penna.), 10th ult., aged 116 years, 3 months, and 10 days, a native of Tyrone, Ireland. (Nov. 14, 1805)

DANCE, Thomas, of Annap., plasterer, died Sat. last, being at work on the inside of the dome of the Stadt-house. He made a false step, and fell to the floor. (Feb. 28, 1793)

DANIEL, negro, was executed on the gallows near Annap., yesterday. (Jan. 24, 1771)

DARBY, John W., of Mont. Co., and Elizabeth Goldsborough, of Annap., were married Tues. evening, by the Rev. Mr. Blanchard. (Nov. 4, 1830)

DARE, Miss Barbara Jane, died at her mother's residence, Cal. Co., aged 19. (Sept. 27, 1832)

DARE, Dr. John, died Sun., 21st May, at his residence in Cal. Co.
He leaves a wife and four children. [Long obit is given.]
(June 1, 1826)

DARNALL, Bennett, died on 23rd ult., at Portland Manor, in his 70th
year. (Feb. 3, 1814)

DARNALL, Mrs. Eleanor, wife of Nicholas Darnall, died Mon., 18th inst.,
in A. A. Co. (May 28, 1835)

DARNALL, Mr. Henry, and Miss Pamelia Dawson, all of Annap., were
married on Sun. last, [Nov. 27], by the Rev. Mr. Wyatt. (Dec.
1, 1814)

DARNALL, John, died Friday night last [Jan. 29], at his house in
Fred. Co.; one of the judges of the Provincial Court. (Feb.
4, 1768)

DARNALL, Philip, died Sun., 17th inst., in A. A. Co. (May 28, 1835)

DARNALL, Mrs. Rachel, died Friday, 24th ult., in her 50th year.
(Sept. 6, 1781)

DASHIEL, Col. George, died 7th inst., in Som. Co.; for many years a
magistrate and a representative. (Nov. 30, 1748)

DASHIELL, Daniel, and Susan R. Maccubbin, all of Annap., were married
on Thurs. evening last, by the Rev. Mr. Blanchard. (Dec. 5,
1833)

DAVID, Davidson, died on the 26th ult., at Elkton; one of the Council
of this state. (Aug. 2, 1804)

DAVIDGE, Mr. John, died last Mon. [April 30], of a consumption;
Deputy Commissary of the county, and Register of the Preroga-
tive Office. His remains were decently interred yesterday.
(May 3, 1764)

DAVIDGE, John, A. M., M. D., Professor of Anatomy at the University
of Maryland, died Sun. evening, Aug. 23, in Balto. He was a
native of Annap. [Long obit is given.] (Sept. 3, 1829)

DAVIDSON, Mrs. Anna Maria L., died Mon. morning last [June 19], of
the prevailing epidemic. (June 22, 1815)

DAVIDSON, Mrs. Eleanor, died on Thurs. night last [Dec. 12], in
Annap., at an advanced age; relict of the late John Davidson.
(Dec. 14, 1815)

DAVIDSON, James, Jr., of Washington City, and Miss Mary Higinbothom,
of Balto., were married at Balto., on Thurs. evening, at

Daniel Delozier's, Esq., by the Rev. Mr. Bend. (Nov. 12, 1807)

DAVIDSON, Dr. James, late Professor in the University of Pennsylvania,
    died at Phila., on the 28th ult., in his 77th year. (July 5,
    1809)

DAVIDSON, John, died in Annap., on 11th inst., in his 57th year. He
    was a tender husband, a good father, the uniform patriot, and
    an honest man. At his sad shrine the poor, the fatherless,
    and the widow, will weep for the loss of their benefactor.
    (Oct. 16, 1794)

DAVIDSON, Gen. John, died in Balto., on Mon. [Feb. 2], an old inhabi-
    tant of this city. His remains were brought here and interred
    with military honors. (Feb. 5, 1807)

DAVIDSON, Lieut. John, of the 11th Regt. of U. S. Artillery, and a
    native of Annap., died at St. Augustine, East Fla., on the
    12th of Nov. last. (Dec. 13, 1821)

DAVIDSON, Mr. John, carpenter and joiner, died Mon. morning last,
    near South River. He had been some time at work on the
    bridge now erecting across that river. (Sept. 19, 1822)

DAVIDSON, Cadet Pinkney, of Annap., Md., died at West Point on the
    17th inst. [Jan.], aged 18 years. (Feb. 1, 1821)

DAVIE, Capt. George, of the ship Frisby, lately from Bristol, died
    Friday last [Aug. 20], in Q. A. Co. (Aug. 25, 1757)

DAVIS, Mrs. Anne, wife of Ebenezer Davis, postmaster of Port Tobacco,
    Chas. Co., died in child-bed on the 23rd ult. (Jan. 10, 1793)

DAVIS, Rev. Benjamin, of the Balto. Conference, and Miss M. Jane,
    eldest daughter of the late Joseph M---- [illegible], of
    Berkeley Co., Va., were married in Va., on Tues., June 14th,
    by the Rev. Richard Brown, also of the Balto. Conference.
    (July 16, 1835)

DAVIS, Charles, died Sun. last, of croup, aged four years, the
    eldest son of Gustavus and Rebecca Davis. (Nov. 22, 1838)

DAVIS, Edward A., and Miss Rebecca Henshaw, all of Annap., were
    married Thurs. evening last. (Dec. 5, 1833)

DAVIS, Rev. Henry L., of Annap., and Miss Jane B. Winter, of Fred.
    Co., were married on Sun. evening, the 22nd inst., at Rich-
    land, the seat of William Campbell, by the Rev. Frederick W.
    Hatch. (Oct. 3, 1816)

DAVIS, John, an overseer, was murdered a few days ago, by two servant

men, of Dr. Parker's, living near Rock Creek in Fred. Co.
(Feb. 11, 1773)

DAVIS, Mary, daughter of the late Naylor Davis, of P. G. Co., died
on the 7th inst., at the house of John Comegys, in Sassafras
Neck, Cecil Co. The deceased was a resident of Annap. (Aug.
30, 1821)

DAVIS, Miss Mary, died Friday last, at an advanced age. (Aug. 24,
1837)

DAVIS, Mr. Robert, Jr., died on Mon. [May 15], of the epidemic,
at Col. Duvall's landing. (May 18, 1815)

DAVIS, Mr. Robert, died in Annap., Friday morning last, of Pulmonary
Consumption, in his 48th year. He leaves a widow and several
children. (May 29, 1823)

DAVIS, Miss Ruth, died Thurs. last. (May 2, 1833)

DAVIS, Rev. Samuel, died in Washington City, after an illness of two
weeks, minister of the Methodist Episcopal Church, aged about
28 years. (Sept. 19, 1822)

DAVIS, Mrs. Sarah, died on Sat. morning last [Oct. 19], in her 86th
year; of South River. (Oct. 24, 1805)

DAVIS, Thomas, and Letitia Orme, were married Thurs. last, in A. A.
Co., by the Rev. Mr. Battee. (Aug. 17, 1826)

DAW, Samuel, and Miss Elizabeth Earl, all of Annap., were married
on Thurs. evening last [May 28], by the Rev. Mr. Wyatt.
(June 4, 1807)

DAWSON, Jonas, died on Sat., 16th inst., near Magothy River, after
a boxing match with William Rodwell. He leaves a wife and
five small children. (Aug. 21, 1760)

DAWSON, the Hon. and Rev. Thomas, died Sat. last [Dec. 3], one of
His Majesty's Honourable Council, Commissary for the Lord
Bishop of London, President of William and Mary College, and
Minister of Bruton Parish; "Williamsburg, Dec. 5." [Long
obit is given.] (Jan. 8, 1761)

DAWSON, the Hon. Dr. and Rev. William, died July 20, one of His
Majesty's Council for the Colony of Virginia; President of
the College of William and Mary, and the Lord Bishop's
Commissary for that colony. (From the Virginia Gazette,
July 24) (Aug. 6, 1752)

DEACON, William, Esq., died lately at his seat in St. M. Co.; one of His Majesty's Collectors of Customs, on Potomac. (Dec. 27, 1759) Ignatius Fenwick is administrator. (Oct. 1, 1761)

DEAL, Mrs. Mary, consort of Capt. James Deal, of Balto., and daughter of Mr. Jacob Franklin, of A. A. Co., died Wed., 25th ult. (April 9, 1812)

DEALE, Capt. James, and Miss Mary Franklin, were married Sun. last [Feb. 17], at West River, by the Rev. Mr. Compton. (Feb. 21, 1805)

DEALE, Capt. James, died at his residence on West River. (Feb. 9, 1837)

DEALE, Mr. James, and Elizabeth, daughter of Capt. Theophilus Norman, were married Thurs. last, at St. James' Church, West River, by Rev. Mr. Chesley. (Aug. 3, 1837)

DEALE, Mr. William, and Arian Auld, were married the evening of 26th ult., in Annap., by the Rev. Mr. Griffith. (July 1, 1824)

DEARBORN, Gen. Henry, died Sat. morning last, at the residence of his son in Roxbury, Mass., aged 78 years, and 3 months. (June 18, 1829)

DE BUTTS, Rev. Mr. Lawrence, died two or three days ago in St. M. Co., rector of William and Mary Parish in that county. (July 9, 1752)

DECKER, John, and Elizabeth, daughter of Henry Thompson, all of Annap., were married Thurs. evening last, by Rev. Dr. Rafferty. (Oct. 28, 1824)

DE L'ALLIE, Mr., long a teacher of the French language at St. John's College, died Sun. last, 1st Aug., after a severe illness. (Aug. 5, 1802)

DELL, Rev. Mr. Thomas, died lately in Dor. Co.; rector of St. Mary's White Chapel Parish in that county. (Oct. 11, 1753)

DE LOZIER, Daniel, died on Sat. [Nov. 6], at his residence on the Western precincts, in his 53rd year; for many years Surveyor of the Port of Balto. (Nov. 11, 1813)

DENNIS, John, died in Phila., on Sun., Aug. 17, in his 35th year; of Som. Co., Md. For many years he was a Representative in the Congress of the United States. (July 28, 1806)

DENNIS, Joseph, editor of the Port-Folio, died in Phila., on 7th inst., in his 45th year. (Jan. 16, 1812)

DENNY, Capt., and his wife, were drowned Sun. last, when their small schooner capsized on the Chester River. (From the Easton Gazette) (Aug. 9, 1838)

DENNY, Mrs. Augusta, formerly of Annap., and relict of the late Robert Denny, Esq., died Sat. night last, at Ellicott's Mills, in her 64th year. (July 24, 1823)

DENNY, Israel, was executed for piracy yesterday (From the Baltimore Patriot, March 14) (April 27, 1820)

DENNY, Dr. John, died in N.Y., on 19th inst., in his 26th year; of the U. S. Navy. (Sept. 24, 1829)

DENNY, Capt. Robert, Auditor General of ths State, and Auditor of the Court of Chancery, died Sat. morning, 23rd inst., in his 65th year. He was one of the soldiers of the Revolution, and at the time of his death, he was Secretary of the [Society of the] Cincinnati of Md. (Oct. 29, 1812)

DENNY, Thomas O., died at his residence at West River, A. A. Co., on Friday evening, 21st ult., in his 36th year. He leaves a wife and two children. (Oct. 4, 1838)

DENNY, Dr. William, of Ellicott's Mills, A. A. Co., and Miss Henrietta Yates, were married in Balto., on the 19th ult., by the Rev. Dr. Wyatt. (June 3, 1825)

DENT, Col. George, died Sun. last [May 12], at his plantation in Chas. Co., at an advanced ago. In his younger years, he was one of the representatives of that county, one of their magistrates, and for three years, sheriff. In 1729, he was appointed one of the Justices of the Provincial Court, and at the time of his death was Chief Justice of the Province. (May 16, 1754)

DENT, Mr. Peter, died Sun. last, in P. G. Co. He had been Deputy Commissary of that county for over 20 years, and at the time of his death was Chief Justice of the county. (Oct. 20, 1757)

DENT, Warren, died 24th inst., at his seat in Chas. Co. (Oct. 30, 1794)

DENTON, Mrs. Anne, widow, died Sun. last [July 14], of the small pox, at the house of her brother Mr. Chief Justice Brice. (July 18, 1765)

DENVER, Mrs. Catherine, died in Annap., on Sat., 12th inst. She leaves a husband and four children. (May 24, 1827)

DICK, Mr. Thomas, merchant, formerly of Annap., and late of Balto.

Town, died 1st inst., on his passage from St. Kitts, on the sloop Somerset, Capt. Eareckson, which arrived here Monday last [May 14]. (May 17, 1764)

DICK, negro, near 80 years old, was found dead on a grass walk in Annap. He was remarkable for his strength of lungs. (Aug. 2, 1753)

DICK, negro, was executed Friday last at Port Tobacco, for house-breaking. (July 10, 1755)

DICKINSON, John, died after a few days illness at Wilmington, Del., on Sun. morning, 13th ult.; formerly President of the Commonwealth of Pennsylvania, and author of the celebrated "Letters of a Pennsylvania Farmer." (Feb. 25, 1808)

DIGGES, Mrs., consort of William Digges, of Potomac, died suddenly Sun. last. (Aug. 18, 1757)

DIGGES, Mr. Charles, of Upper Marlborough, merchant, died 5th inst., after two days illness, at Dumfries, Va. (April 13, 1769)

DIMMOCK, Lieut. Charles, of the U. S. Navy, and Miss Henrietta Johnson, were married yesterday morning by the Rev. Mr. Blanchard. (May 29, 1828)

DISKINS, alias PRICE, William, was executed Friday last at Upper Marlborough, for horse stealing. (Dec. 28, 1748)

DISNEY, Aquila, was drowned some few days ago, near Love Point, when he was knocked overboard by a jibbing boom. (Aug. 1, 1750)

DISNEY, Mr. Edward, of Annap., died Friday last [May 18], after a short illness. (May 24, 1809)

DISNEY, Edward W., and Miss Deborah McLaughlin, of Ellicotts Mills, A. A. Co., were married in Balto., on Tues., 21st inst., by the Rev. Mr. Blanchard. (July 30, 1835)

DISNEY, James, died in A. A. Co., 16th Feb. last, in his 98th year, leaving a widow in her 94th year. He has never been known to be in a court of justice from his birth to his death. He belonged to the Methodist Church. (March 13, 1834)

DISNEY, Miss Jane, died Thurs. last, at the residence of Dr. Walter Wyvill, in Lower Marlborough, in her 78th year. She had been a member of the Methodist Church for about 40 years. (Sept. 30, 1824)

DISNEY, Mr. Joshua, and Miss Edith Malonee, both of A. A. Co., were married Thurs., 6th inst., by the Rev. Mr. Davis. (Dec. 13, 1827)

DOBBINS, Capt. James, died on board the frigate Thames a few days after he left our capes. Communicated from Lisbon by Leonard Brooke, Capt. of the Horatio. (Feb. 27, 1755)

DOBBS, John, a carrier, was found drowned with two stones about his neck on Thurs. morning last [Oct. 4], a suicide. (Oct. 11, 1735)

DOBINSON, Mr. Ralph, accidentally drowned on Sat. night last [June 30]. He was officiating clerk in the Prerogative Office under Mr. Valette. He had resided but four years in this place. (July 4, 1771)

DOBSON, George, on Monday, March 26, was shot and scalped in sight of Fort Bedford. (April 5, 1764)

DODSON, Mrs. Lydia, died in Annap., Sun. morning, in her 92nd year. (Sept. 5, 1822)

DONE, the Hon. John, died Sun. last, in his 84th year. (Oct. 13, 1831)

DONE, Miss Sarah M., eldest daughter of the late Hon. John Done, of Annap., died in New Orleans, at the residence of her brother-in-law, John H. B. Morton, on Jan. 10th, in her 49th year. (Feb. 7, 1833)

DONE, Col. William, of Som. Co., died at the residence of his father, Judge Done, of Annap., on Friday night last, in his 38th year. (Oct. 21, 1830) A long obit is given in a later issue. (Oct. 28, 1830)

DONNAHOE, John, was drowned when the Kent Island ferry capsized. (June 8, 1748)

DORSETT, Samuel H., and Mary Elenor, daughter of John Iglehart, Esq., all of South River, were married Thurs., 18th inst., by the Rev. Mr. Wright. (Dec. 25, 1834)

DORSEY, Mr. Basil, Jr., attorney-at-law, died Tues. evening last [Feb. 17], at his father's house on Elk Ridge; of a confirmed consumption, in his 23rd year. (Feb. 19, 1761)

DORSEY, Capt. Basil, died Sat. last [Aug. 20], at his plantation at Elk Ridge, after a long and tedious indisposition. His funeral is to be attended this day. (Aug. 25, 1763)

DORSEY, Mr. Caleb, Jr., son of Capt. Basil Dorsey, of Elk Ridge, one of the magistrates of this county, last Mon. evening [Feb. 7], was taken in a fit, and died in a few minutes. (Feb. 10, 1763) Thomas Dorsey is administrator. (May 26, 1763)

DORSEY, Caleb, son of Thomas, died Friday, 14th ult., at Alpton, his residence in A. A. Co., in his 90th year. He has left a wife to whom he has been married 65 years. (May 4, 1837)

DORSEY, Caleb, member of the Senior Class at St. John's College, died. Resolutions of sorrow and regret by his classmates are given. (Sept. 13, 1838)

DORSEY, Daniel, and Rachel Wales, were married Thurs. evening last, by Rev. Mr. Watkins. (March 16, 1826)

DORSEY, Daniel, of Annap., and Ann Parrott, of Tal. Co., were married in the latter place on 28th ult., by the Rev. Levi Storks. (April 18, 1833)

DORSEY, Edward, attorney-at-law, and Henrietta Maria Chew, were married Thurs. evening last [Feb. 18]. (Feb. 24, 1748)

DORSEY, Mr. Edward: by the last post from the Northward we have advice of his death. He was an eminent attorney of this city, and a Representative for Fred. Co. This gentleman went from home in Md. for the recovery of his health, had been as far as Boston, and on his return, died at New-Port, R.I., the 20th of March last. (Oct. 9, 1760). Henrietta Maria Dorsey is the executrix. (June 25, 1761)

DORSEY, Essex R., of Balto., and Miss Anne E. Dorsey, of A. A. Co., were married Tues. evening last by the Rev. John G. Blanchard. (Feb. 11, 1830)

DORSEY, Mrs. Henrietta Maria, relict of the late Edward Dorsey, Esq., died in Annap. on Mon. last [May 17], in her 32nd year. (May 20, 1762)

DORSEY, Miss Henrietta Maria, died Sun. last [Oct. 12], in her 10th year, and on Tues. morning was very decently interred. She was the only child of the late Edward Dorsey, Esq., deceased. By her death, her fortune, supposed to be at least £ 30,000, falls to her father's relatives. (Oct. 16, 1766)

DORSEY, Mr. Henry, Jr., of Elk Ridge, died as he was about to mount his horse, Tues. last. He was a young man about 21 years old, in seeming good health. (March 12, 1761)

DORSEY, Mr. James Madison, youngest son of the late Hon. Lloyd Dorsey, died Wed., 5th inst., on Elk Ridge, in his 20th year. (Sept. 20, 1827)

DORSEY, John Henry, aged 20 years, died 18th inst., at the residence of John Hammond, at the Head of Severn. (Sept. 27, 1832)

DORSEY, Lloyd, died at his farm on Elk Ridge, on Tues. morning, 12th inst., in his 49th year; for the last 10 years a member of the Senate of Md. (May 21, 1812)

DORSEY, Nicholas, Esq., of Elk Ridge, was killed Tues. last, 7th inst., by a fall from his horse on his return from Annap. (Oct. 16, 1788)

DORSEY, Mr. Richard, died early Tues. morning last [Sept. 2], at his plantation near the town, of the Gout in his stomach, head and bowels; aged 47; Clerk of the Paper Currency Office for about 20 years past, and a very worthy magistrate of this county. (Sept. 11, 1760)

DORSEY, Mr. Richard, died on Sat. morning last [June 29], at his plantation near this city, in his 39th year. He leaves a a wife and five small children. (Aug. 4, 1808)

DORSEY, Mr. Thomas, and Mrs. Anne Dorsey, all of this county, were married Thurs. evening last by the Rev. Mr. Judd. (May 22, 1811)

DORSEY, the Hon. Walter, died at Philadelphia, on 31st ult., Chief Judge of the Judicial Circuit composed of Balto. and Harf. Counties. (Aug. 7, 1823)

DORSEY, William, a member of the House of Delegates for A. A. Co., died. William Hall, III, was elected to fill the vacancy. (Nov. 25, 1802)

DORSEY, Dr. William R., of A. A. Co., died Sun., 7th inst., at the residence of Mr. Gerard R. Hopkins, at the Head of South River, where he had lately entered the practise of medecine. (Aug. 11, 1825)

DOUGHERTY, Neil, died in Annap., 13th inst.; a native of the county of Donegal, Ireland, and Captain of the Schooner Ann Sophia, of Philadelphia. He leaves a wife and family in the latter city. (Oct. 18, 1832)

DOUGHERTY, Mr. Michael, died at his plantation on Horse Creek, in Scriven Co., Ga., aged 135 years, and one of the first settlers of that state. The day before he died he walked two miles-- the day on which he died, he eat [sic] a hearty dinner, smoked his pipe, and in the two hours after, expired, which was on May 29, 1808. (June 30, 1808)

DOUGHERTY, Thomas, Esq., of Washington, died at Lexington, Ky., for the last eight years, clerk in the House of Representatives. (Aug. 29, 1822)

DOW, Lorenzo, died in Georgetown, D.C. (From the Balto. Chronicle) (Feb. 6, 1834)

DOWELL, Capt., his wife and child, were killed by lightning, on Mon., 13th inst., while travelling in Cal. Co., not far from Prince Frederick. (May 23, 1839)

DOWELL, George W., and Margaret, daughter of Gilbert Ireland, deceased, were married Tues. evening, July 16th, by Rev. John Bowen. (July 25, 1833)

DOWNS, Stephen, was killed in a fire, leaving a wife and five children. (From the Balto. Chronicle, Feb. 26) (March 5, 1835)

DOWSON, Mrs. Elizabeth, of Washington City, died 15th inst., in the 60th year of her age. (Oct. 9, 1816)

DREW, Miss Kitty, of Q. A. Co., Md., was killed recently when she was thrown from her carriage. (April 9, 1807)

DRUMMOND, Mr. Samuel, of the city of Washington, and Miss Zipporah Auld, of Annap., were married on the evening of the 18th inst., by the Rev. Mr. Griffith. (June 24, 1824)

DRURY, Henry C., of Herring Creek, and Miss Eliza Mills, also of Herring Creek, were married May 27th by the Rev. Mr. Compton. (May 29, 1806)

DUBOIS, Edward, Esq., and Rosetta, daughter of the late James Holland, were married Sat. evening last, at St. M. Church, by the Rev. R. D. Woodley. (Aug. 27, 1835)

DUCHART, Valerious, was killed Wed. last in Balto. Co., when a gust of wind blew down a barn on him. One other man was killed also. (May 20, 1756)

DUCKETT, Allen B., Esq., died in P. G. Co., on Wed. last [July 18], one of the Judges of the District Court of Columbia. (July 26, 1809)

DUCKETT, Baruch, died at his seat in P. G. Co., in the 66th year of his age. (Oct. 17, 1810)

DUCKETT, John B., Clerk of the House of Delegates of this State, died 10th April, in P. G. Co. (April 25, 1805)

DUCKETT, Mrs. Margaret, died 3rd inst., in P. G. Co., in the early bloom of youth, wife of Mr. Isaac Duckett, and eldest daughter of Walter Bowie, Esq. (June 22, 1797)

DUCKETT, Richard I., M. D., of P. G. Co., died Nov., 1801, of a long
    inflammatory fever, a member of the board of medical examiners
    for the western shore. (July 1, 1802)

DUCKETT, Sally, daughter of Thomas Duckett, Esq., of Annap., died the
    morning of Sun., the 19th. (Oct. 23, 1834)

DUCKETT, Thomas, one of the Senate of this place, died on Tues. [Dec.
    2]. (Dec. 4, 1806)

DUFF, Mr. Simon, died on Sat. last [Nov. 17], on the north side of
    Severn, of an apoplectic fit, as he was walking in the corn-
    field, aged 59, a carpenter, who formerly, for many years
    was a Common-Council Man, and a useful inhabitant of this
    city. (Nov. 22, 1759) John Campbell is the administrator.
    (Sept. 24, 1761)

DUGAN, Matthew, of Kent Co., was arraigned at the Bar of the Provin-
    cial Court for shooting and killing his wife. He pleaded
    guilty. (Sept. 13, 1759)

DUKE, Capt. James, died about a fortnight ago, at his house on the
    Patuxent River, aged upwards of 60 years, who for above 20
    years past was a worthy magistrate of Cal. Co., and for many
    years past was presiding magistrate. (Feb. 28, 1754)

DULANY, Daniel, Jr., Barrister at law, and Rebecca Tasker, second
    daughter of the Hon. Benjamin Tasker, of Annap., were married
    Sat. last [Sept. 16]. (Sept. 20, 1749)

DULANY, Hon. Daniel, Esq., died yesterday about 10 o'clock in the
    evening, at his house in the city, in the 68th year of his
    age. He was Commissary General of this Province, and one
    of His Lordship's Council of State, and Recorder of this
    city. He resided in Md. for 50 years. (Dec. 6, 1753) An
    account of his funeral is given. (Dec. 13, 1753) Daniel
    Dulany and Walter Dulany are executors. (Sept. 26, 1754)

DULANY, Mrs. Mary, relict of the late Hon. Walter Dulany, died lately
    in Annap., aged 74. (Sept. 17, 1801)

DULANY, the Hon. Walter, died Mon. last [Sept. 20], one of the Lord
    Proprietary's Council of State, and Commissary General for
    this Province. The Hon. William Fitzhugh is appointed Commissary
    General in his place. (Sept. 23, 1773)

DULANY, William A., of Chas. Co., and Matilda, eldest daughter of
    George Mackubin, of Annap., were married Tues. evening last,
    by Rev. Mr. McElhiney. (June 1, 1837)

DULCHER, Mr. James, died in Annap., Mon. last, in his 33rd year.
    (Oct. 21, 1824)

DULEY, Capt. James, formerly of A. A. Co., died in Balto., on 19th
inst. (May 28, 1829)

DUNCAN, Rev. William, rector of Allhallows Parish, A. A. Co., died
on the 3rd inst., at his residence on South River, in his
56th year. (March 11, 1819)

DUNGAN, Benjamin, and Eleanor Griffith, were married Tues. evening,
12th inst., in Annap., by Rev. Mr. Hammond. (May 21, 1812)

DUNLOP, Capt. William, drowned yesterday morning, near Greenbury's
Point. He was supposedly seized with a frenzy and jumped
overboard with his clothes on. (Nov. 12, 1772)

DUNMORE, Lord, formerly Gov. of Va., died in England. (July 19, 1809)

DUNN, Mr. James, of Annap., and Elizabeth Fenix, of Kent Island,
were married at the latter place, on Tues. evening, by the
Rev. Dr. Rafferty. (March 20, 1823)

DUNN, Mr. Patrick, died Mon. evening, at an advanced age. He was
a native of Ireland. (Oct. 16, 1823)

DUNSTER, John, and Mrs. Frances Hephner, were married Sun. last, by
the Rev. Mr. Davis. (March 24, 1815)

DUPRIEST, Capt. William, died Sun. morning last, in the jail of this
city. He was under confinement for being concerned in the
counterfeiting of the Eight Dollar Bills of Credit of this
province. (March 17, 1768)

DUSENBERRY, Lieut. Samuel B., of the U. S. Army, and Mary, daughter
of the late Thomas Hamilton Bowie, of Balto., were married
Tues., 3rd inst., by the Rev. Mr. McElhiney. (March 5, 1835)

DUVALL, Aaron, and Elizabeth Shephard, all of Annap., were married
Thurs. evening last, by the Rev. N. J. Watkins. (Dec. 30,
1830)

DUVALL, Alexander, of Louisville, Ky., and formerly of Annap., and
Anne Elizabeth Elliott, of Lexington, Ky., were married in
the latter city. (Sept. 10, 1835)

DUVALL, Alexander, formerly of Annap., died at Mobile, of yellow
fever. (Oct. 10, 1839)

DUVALL, Edmund B., of P. G. Co., and Miss Augusta M'Causland, the
daughter of Marcus M'Causland, were married in Balto., on
Tues. evening, 6th inst., by the Rev. Mr. Richards. (Jan.
15, 1818)

DUVALL, Edwin, and Elizabeth Parkinson, all of Annap., were married

Sun. evening last, by the Rev. Mr. Guest. (Sept. 19, 1839)

DUVALL, Eli, of A. A. Co., and Sarah E. Thompson, of Annap., were
married on Christmas Eve, by the Rev. Mr. Gere. (Jan. 2,
1834)

DUVALL, Mrs. Elizabeth, consort of Henry Duvall of Severn, died
Mon. morning last. (Nov. 24, 1808)

DUVALL, Ephraim, of Greenbury's Point, died on Sat. night last
[March 27], in his 65th year. (April 2, 1807)

DUVALL, Grafton B., Esq., of A. A. Co., and Elizabeth, daughter of
Richard Duvall, Esq., of P. G. Co., were married in the
latter county, on Thurs. evening, by Rev. Mr. Watkins.
(March 30, 1826)

DUVALL, Henry, died in Annap., Mon. last, in the 43rd year of his
age, one of the Judges of the Orphans Court of A. A. Co.
(July 25, 1822)

DUVALL, Howard, died at his residence near this city, on the 19th
ult., in his 73rd year. (Dec. 11, 1834)

DUVALL, Dr. Howard M., of A. A. Co., and Maria Tuck, of Annap., were
married Thurs. last, by the Rev. Mr. Guest. (April 25, 1833)

DUVALL, Lemuel, Esq., formerly of Annap., and Mary Jane, eldest
daughter of William P. Mills, of Balto., were married in the
latter place on Tues., 9th inst., by Rev. **Dennis R. Battee.**
(April 18, 1833)

DUVALL, Mr. Lewis, died Mon. morning last. He leaves a large family.
(Nov. 26, 1829)

DUVALL, Dr. Mareen, and Harriet Evans, daughter of Henry Evans, of
A. A. Co., were married Friday last, by Rev. Vinton. (April
9, 1829)

DUVALL, Mr. Mareen B., died on Mon. last [May 4], near the Head of
Severn. (May 7, 1812)

DUVALL, Mr. Richard, son of Howard Duvall, Esq., died Sun. morning
last. (July 17, 1829)

DUVALL, Samuel, of Severn, and Miss Mary Duvall, daughter of Mr.
Marden [sic] Duvall, of P. G. Co., Md., were married Thurs.
last [Oct. 25], by the Rev. Mr. Scott. (Oct. 27, 1808)

DUVALL, Samuel E., and Adeline E. Slemaker, all of Annap., were
married Thurs., 23rd inst., by Rev. John A. Gere. (May 30,
1833)

DUVALL, William, and Miss Anne Tucker, were married Sun. [March 15], by the Rev. Mr. Wyatt. (March 19, 1807)

DUVALL, Zachariah, and Miss Mary Powell, all of Annap., were married Thurs. evening last, by the Rev. T. B. Dorsey. (May 13, 1830)

DWIGHT, Rev. Timothy, D. D., President of Yale College, died Sat. morning, in the 65th year of his age, and the 22nd year of his presidency. (Jan. 23, 1817)

DWYER, Michael, and Miss Margaretta Burns, of Balto., were married in Annap., on Tues. morning last, by the Rev. Dr. Rafferty. (May 6, 1824)

EARLE, Thomas, died in Annap., Sat. morning last, aged about 40 years. (April 14, 1825)

EATON, Mr., from Ireland, drowned Sun., 5th inst., while crossing the Bay. (Sept. 9, 1790)

EATON, Gen. William, the Hero of Darne, died at Brinsfield, Mass. (June 26, 1811)

EDELEN, John, Esq., one of the Delegates from Chas. Co., to the General Assembly, died Friday evening at six o'clock. He had been elected Speaker pro tem on Thurs., and on the same day was attacked with pleurisy. (Feb. 23, 1832)

EDEN, the Hon. Mrs., wife of His Excellency [Gov. Robert Eden], last night between 11 and 12 o'clock, was safely delivered of a daughter. (June 7, 1770)

EDEN, John, Esq., died Sat., 1st inst., of St. M. Co.; formerly a Representative of this Province. (July 27, 1775)

EDGE, Mr. James, died lately in Tal. Co.; one of their worthy Representatives. (Jan. 20, 1757)

EDMISTON, Rev. Mr., rector of St. Anne's Parish, and Maria, only daughter of Mr. William Woodward, of Annap., were married Thurs. evening last [July 14]. (July 21, 1768)

EDMONDSON, Mr. Horatio, of Tal. Co., and Elizabeth Ann Lowndes, were married on Thurs. evening last, 13th inst., by Rev. Mr. Claxton. (Nov. 27, 1828)

ELDER, Mr. Alexander, who lived in A. A. Co., near Patuxent, was most barbarously murdered by his negro man Pompey, on the 30th of last month. (April 8, 1762)

ELLICOTT, George, died at Ellicott's Mills, on 9th inst., in his 72nd year. (April 19, 1832)

ELLICOTT, Henry, aged 26 years, a member of the Legislature, died
   Sun. night last, at Patuxent Forge. (Aug. 22, 1833)

ELLIOTT, Ambrose, a servant of Mr. Raitt's, was drowned in the
   Severn. (July 18, 1754)

ELLIOTT, Benjamin B., and Margaret Watson, all of A. A. Co., were
   married Thurs. evening last, at the Head of South River,
   by Rev. Mr. Waters. (Feb. 16, 1837)

ELLIOTT, Mrs. Catherine, died on Thurs., 4th inst., at her residence
   in A. A. Co., in her 90th year. (May 18, 1815)

ELLIOTT, Thomas, and Mrs. Susanna Nicholson, both of A. A. Co., were
   married in Annap., on Tues. last, by the Rev. Mr. Watkins.
   (Sept. 22, 1825)

ELLIS, Capt. John, late Commander of the ship Montague, died during
   his passage from Gibraltar to James River, Va. (Sept. 1,
   1747)

ELSON, Mr. William, overseer of Stephen West, P. G. Co., was murdered
   14th inst., by Negroes. (June 28, 1770)

ELTON, John H., Master Commandant of the U. S. Navy, died at Norfolk,
   Va., on Sat., aged 37. He was a native of New Jersey. (Oct.
   3, 1822)

EMMERSON, Patrick Henry, of Annap., son of the Hon. Peter Emmerson,
   a Seantor of Md., died on the 20th inst., in his 21st year.
   (March 29, 1821)

EMORY, Bishop, died. [John Emory, 1789 - 1835, Bishop of the Methodist Episcopal Church] (Dec. 24, 1835)

ENSOR, Mr. Joseph, merchant, of Balto. Town, and Miss Mary Bouchelle,
   were married Thurs. last [April 7], in Cecil Co. (April 14,
   1757)

ESTEP, Mr. Rezin, died at his residence in A. A. Co., on the night
   of 26th May, in his 67th year. (June 3, 1830)

ETHERINGTON, Capt., and his boy, were drowned Mon. last [April 13],
   by the capsizing of a boat while crossing over from Cambridge. Capt. Etherington was on his way to see his wife
   in P. G. Co., to take his leave. (April 16, 1772)

EVANS, Seth, a caulker, on Christmas Eve crossed the Patuxent to
   fetch a midwife to his wife. Both he and the midwife froze
   to death on the way over. (Jan. 10, 1754)

EVANS, William, proprietor of the Indian Queen Hotel, died in Balto.

on Sun., 28th ult., at the age of 56 years. (July 9, 1807)

EVE, Mr. Adam, died at his farm in Upper Merion Township, Montgomery Co., Penna., on Sat., 27th ult., aged about 104 years. [A long obit gives other biographical data.] (Nov. 22, 1821)

EVERETT, Rev. Joseph, died at Cambridge, on the Eastern Shore of this state, on Mon., 16th inst., in the 79th year of his age, and the 30th year of his ministry in the Methodist Church. (Oct. 25, 1809)

FAHEE, Thomas, died last Thurs. [July 12], in Va., from the effects of a rattlesnake bite. He was a post rider between this [place] and Alexandria. (July 19, 1764)

FAIRBAIRN, Benjamin, died in Annap., on Sat. last. (March 14, 1805)

FAIRFAX, Mrs. Jane, departed this life at Alexandria, on Mon. at 12 o'clock, relict of the late Bryan (Lord) Fairfax. (July 11, 1805)

FAIRFAX, the Hon. Col. William, died 2nd inst., at his seat on Potomac, in Fairfax Co., Va.; President of His Majesty's Council of that colony. (Sept. 15, 1757)

FARIS, Mr. William, died yesterday morning, an old inhabitant of this city. (Aug. 16, 1804)

FELL, Mr., master of a family, accidentally drowned Sunday last [July 7], by the capsizing of a canoe, in the Falls of Patapsco, with a daughter of Emanuel Teal. (July 11, 1754)

FENDALL, Mrs. Anne, wife of Dr. Benjamin Fendall, died at Cedar Hill, her husband's seat, aged 26 years and 9 days. (Feb. 24, 1785)

FENDALL, Benjamin, Esq., died lately at his seat on Patowmack, in Chas. Co.; formerly Clerk of that county. (April 26, 1764)

FENDALL, Mrs. Eleanor, wife of Benjamin Fendall, Esq., of Chas. Co., died Sun., 22nd inst., in the 49th year of her age. (April 26, 1759)

FENDALL, Mr. Philip Richard, Clerk of Chas. Co., and Sarah Lettice Lee, eldest daughter of the Hon. Richard Lee, Esq., the Naval Officer of North Patowmack, were married Sun. last [Sept. 30]. (Oct. 4, 1759)

FENDALL, Mrs. Priscilla, wife of Benjamin Fendall, Esq., of Chas. Co., died last August 25th, aged 49 years. (Sept. 15, 1763)

FENDALL, Mrs. Sarah Lettice, wife of Philip Richard Fendall, Clerk

of Chas. Co., died Thurs. last, 8th inst., after a short illness. (Jan. 22, 1761)

FENWICK, Martin Joseph, aged four years and seven months, second son
of Dr. Martin Fenwick, of South River, died 9th inst. (Dec.
29, 1831)

FERGUS, Capt. John, of the Regiment of Artillerists, died 21st ult.,
at Fort St. Philip (Plaquemine). (July 21, 1808)

FERGUSON, Rev. Colin, died 10th ult., in his 53rd year, at his farm
in Kent Co., the place of his birth. Rev. Colin Ferguson,
D. D., late principal of Washington College, received the
rudiments of his education at the University of Edinburgh.
He leaves a widow and two children. [Long obit.] (June 11,
1807)

FERGUSON, John F., was executed yesterday, for piracy. (From the
Balto. Patriot, March 14) (April 27, 1820)

FERGUSON, Robert, Sr., died Tues., Sept. 1, at Mulberry Grove,
Chas. Co., an old inhabitant of that county, and a native
of Scotland. He risked his rising fortunes in the same
bottom with (America's) liberties, at the time of the Revolution. He was Chief Judge of the Orphans Court. [Long
obit.] (Sept. 17, 1812)

FIDLER, Christopher, was killed by Indians on Nov. 8, in "the Great
Cove," Fred. Co. (Dec. 1, 1763)

FISH, Benjamin Thomas, drowned when the Kent Island ferry capsized.
(June 5, 1748)

FISHER, E. Burke, editor of the Pittsburgh Saturday Evening Visitor,
and Narcissa M'Keehan, of West Alexandria, were married 17th
inst., at the latter place. (Nov. 7, 1839)

FISHER, William, and Miss Hester Ann Wills, were married on Thurs.
evening last, in Annap., by the Rev. Mr. Emory. (Nov. 22,
1821)

FITZHUGH, Daniel Dulany, of Balto., and Miss Margaret Murray Mayna-
dier, were married Thurs. evening last [Jan. 4], by the Rev.
Mr. Judd, at Belvoir, the residence of Col. Henry Maynadier.
(Jan. 10, 1810)

FITZHUGH, William, Esq., of Va., and Mrs. Rousby, the widow of Mr.
John Rousby, were married last week. (Jan. 16, 1752)

FITZHUGH, William H., Esq., of Va., and Anna Maria, daughter of the
Hon. Charles Goldsborough, were married at Shoal Creek, Dor.

Co., on Tues., 11th inst., by the Rev. Mr. Bain. (Jan. 26,
1814)

FLEMMING, Mrs. Margaret, daughter of John Gordon, a block-maker and
French refugee, drowned in a squall on the 8th inst., when
the boat in which she was travelling from Annap. to Tal. Co.
overset. (July 12, 1753)

FLINT, Mr. John, of P. G. Co., was found dead on Friday morning
last [May 26], supposed to have been thrown from his horse.
(June 1, 1758)

FLUSSER, Charles T., and Miss Julia Waters, all of Annap., were
married on Sat. last, by the Rev. Dr. Rafferty. (Nov. 29,
1827)

FOARD, Joseph, stay-maker, aged about 24 years, died here last
Thurs. evening, of the pleurisy. (March 12, 1767)

FOOTNEY, Henry, one of the sect of Dunkers, was killed by lightning
in front of his house, about four miles from Frederick, one
day last week. (Aug. 2, 1753)

FORD, ---, the only son of Thomas Ford, of Balto. Co., died 2nd inst.,
when he was crushed to death by a tree. (Jan. 18, 1753)

FORD, Mrs. Catherine, wife of Philip Ford, died at Society Hill,
St. M. Co., on Jan. 2nd. (Jan. 9, 1823)

FORD, John F., died at his residence, St. M. Co., on Thurs., 26th
inst. [Dec.], youngest son of the late Joseph Ford, of the
same county. He leaves a widow. (Jan. 2, 1823)

FORD, Lewis, Esq., died on 2nd inst., at Prospect Hill, his residence
near Leonard-Town, St. M. Co. (July 31, 1823)

FORD, Philip, died on the 12th inst., in his 59th year, in St. M.
Co. (June 25, 1807)

FORD, Mrs. Susannah, died 27th ult., in M'Intosh Co., [Ga.?], aged
113 years. (Nov. 22, 1821)

FOREMAN, Mr. Joseph, and Rebecca Johnson, both of A. A. Co., were
married in Annap., by the Rev. Mr. Watkins, on Tues., 11th
inst. (Sept. 13, 1827)

FOREMAN, Samuel, and Ruth Grey, all of A. A. Co., were married
Thurs. last, by the Rev. Mr. Watkins. (Oct. 1, 1835)

FORNEY, John W., editor of the Lancaster Intelligencer and Journal,
and Elizabeth Matilda, daughter of Philip Reitzel, both of

that city, were married 22nd inst. (Nov. 7, 1839)

FORREST, George Thomas, and Jane Philips, all of Annap., were married
in Balto., 9th inst., by the Rev. Mr. Tippett. (July 19, 1838)

FORREST, Mrs. Henrietta, died a few days since, in St. M. Co., in her
84th year. (May 5, 1791)

FORREST, Gen. James, Register of Wills for St. M. Co., died at his
residence in that county last Friday. (Sept. 28, 1826)

FORREST, Julius, Esq., of Marlboro', and Sophia, daughter of Benjamin Ogle, were married on Tues., 23rd inst., at Bel Air,
P. G. Co., by Rev. Mr. Tyng. (Dec. 9, 1824)

FORREST, Gen. Uriah, died Sat. [July 6], at his seat near Georgetown.
On the next day his remains were interred in the Protestant
Episcopal Burying Ground of that place. He embarked early in
life in the Revolutionary War, and served with distinction
until the battle of Germantown, in which he sacrificed a
limb to his country. Fated ever after to support himself on
crutches, and to be a prey to the evils of impaired health,
his active and intelligent mind rose superior to his misfor-
tune, and his life has been equally distinguished by useful
and honourable enterprises. (July 18, 1805)

FORWOOD, Thomas, of Harf. Co., was killed in a shooting accident
at the residence of Mr. Turner on Spesutia Island. (Oct.
10, 1839)

FOUL, John, a lad lately belonging to Mr. Middleton and latterly a
hand on the brig Free Major, was drowned in the Bay. (Aug.
23, 1764)

FOWKE, Capt. Gerard, of Chas. Co., died March 19, 1783, in his 59th
year. (April 3, 1783)

FOWLER, Mr. Baruch, died Mon. last, at his residence on the north
side of Severn. (May 21, 1829)

FOWLER, Daniel, formerly an inhabitant of Annap., died Sun. last
[Aug. 23], at his dwelling on the north side of Severn.
(Aug. 27, 1812)

FOWLER, Miss Frances, daughter of the late Jubb Fowler, of Annap.,
died Friday evening last. (Aug. 19, 1830)

FOWLER, Jubb, died Tues. last [Sept. 9], at an advanced age, an
old and respectable inhabitant of Annap. (Sept. 11, 1827)

FOWLER, Mrs. Margaret, died yesterday in Annap. (May 30, 1810)

FOWLER, Mrs. Rebecca, late consort of Mr. William Fowler, died in
Annap. on Friday night last [June 1]. (June 6, 1810)

FOWLER, William, formerly a resident of Annap., died last week in
Q. A. Co., at the dwelling of Capt. James Wright, at an advanced age. (Aug. 17, 1826)

FOX, Mr., of the Theatre, died on the 15th ult. [March], at Charleston, S. C. (April 4, 1810)

FOXCROFT, Mrs. Elizabeth, died in Annap., on Sat. night last, in
her 53rd year. (Oct. 17, 1822)

FOXCROFT, Mrs. Sophia, consort of Mr. William Foxcroft, of Annap.,
died Sun. night last. (Aug. 11, 1825)

FRAILEY, Mr. William, died on Tues. last, at his residence in this
county. (Sept. 28, 1826)

FRAMPTON, ---, a young lad, aged about 15 years, son of a widow of
Annap., drowned Tues. afternoon last. (June 13, 1833)

FRANKLIN, Capt. Benjamin, died at his residence in A. A. Co., much
regretted. (Jan. 2, 1823)

FRANKLIN, Mrs. Eliza, consort of Thomas Franklin, of Annap., died
Mon. last [Nov. 13]. (Nov. 16, 1815)

FRANKLIN, George E., of Annap., and Maria Caroline, daughter of
the late Edward Johnson, Esq., of Balto., were married in
the latter city on Thurs. evening last, by Rev. Dr. Henshaw.
(June 14, 1838)

FRANKLIN, Capt. Jacob, Jr., died at his residence near West River,
on Friday last [Dec. 20]. The complaint which terminated
the earthly career of this worthy gentleman is supposed to
have been brought on by the fatigue and exposure which he
he endured during the late war. (Dec. 26, 1816) He was
38 years old. (Jan. 2, 1817)

FRANKLIN, Robert, died at his residence on West River, early this
month, at an advanced age. (Feb. 19, 1835)

FRANKLIN, Samuel, only son of Dr. Samuel Franklin of P. G. Co., in
his 13th year, was found drowned Thurs. morning last, in a
creek near the [St. John's?] College. (July 28, 1831)

FRANKLIN, Thomas, and Miss Eliza Mackubin, daughter if John C.
Mackubin, of Fred. Co., were married in Annap. on Sun. evening
last [Nov. 27], by Rev. Mr. Judd. (Dec. 1, 1808)

FRANKLIN, Thomas, and Miss Elizabeth Shaw, were married in Annap.,

on Thurs. evening last [Nov. 12], by the Rev. Mr. Davis.
(Nov. 19, 1818)

FRANKS, Mrs. Barbary, died at her residence in German Township, on
the Sabbath morning, 12th ult., in her 98th year. She was
born in Germany in 1741, and came to America in 1775 with
her father Conrad Brandenburg. She married Jacob Franks,
and they went to western Penna. She was the mother of 4
sons, 3 daughters, 64 grandchildren, 303 great-grandchildren,
and had 93 of her fourth generation. [Long obit is given.]
(June 6, 1839)

FRASER, Mr. George, died lately at his seat in P. G. Co., on the
Potowmack, nearly opposite to Alexandria. He was heretofore
for a number of years one of the Representatives of that
county. (Dec. 20, 1769)

FRAZER, Capt. Solomon, died at North Point, Balto. Co., on the 3rd
inst., an officer in the Revolution, in his 72nd year.
(March 16, 1826)

FREDERICK, G. H., died in Annap., on Thurs. last. (Nov. 24, 1808)

FRIEND, Robert, accidentally drowned Tues. last [June 10], a carpenter of the ship Severn. (June 12, 1755)

FULLER, Samuel, a servant to a saddler in this town, yesterday
morning, being disordered in his senses by a fever, and
alone, bled himself near the Jugular vein, and bled to death
in a short time. (Aug. 19, 1762)

FULTON, Lieut. John B., of the U. S. Revenue Service, and Julianna
Jacob, of A. A. Co., were married 7th inst., by the Rev. Mr.
Goldsborough. (Nov. 15, 1838)

FULTON, Robert, inventor, died yesterday morning [Feb. 24], between
nine and ten o'clock, aged about 42 years. He leaves a widow
and four children. [Long obit gives details of his career
as an inventor.] (March 2, 1815)

FULTON, Col. Samuel, and Miss Helen de Grand Pre, eldest daughter
of Gov. de Grand Pre, were married on the evening of 6th
Jan., at the house of His Excellency, the Governor, at
Baton Rouge. (Feb. 15, 1809)

GAITHER, Mrs. Anne, died on Mon. [Dec. 12], at an advanced age.
(Dec. 15, 1808)

GAITHER, Benjamin, and Miss Catherine Ridgely, were married in
Annap., on Tues. evening, by the Rev. Mr. Ryland. (Oct.
17, 1822)

GAITHER, Mrs. Catherine, consort of Benjamin Gaither, and daughter
of the late Absalom Ridgely, died Tues. morning, after a short
illness. (June 3, 1825)

GAITHER, Col. Edward, died Mon., 24th inst., at the Woodyard, the
seat of Stephen West, Esq. (Sept. 27, 1787)

GAITHER, Ephraim, of Mont. Co., and Miss Sarah E. Goldsborough, of
Annap., were married Tues. evening [May 16], by the Rev. Mr.
Davis. (May 18, 1820)

GAITHER, Col. Henry, died in George-Town (Columbia), in the 61st
year of his age, a Revolutionary officer. He was in every
battle Monmouth excepted, which was fought by the American
army. (July 3, 1811)

GAITHER, John, son of Rezin, died Sun. morning last, at the Head
of Severn. His wife died the preceding evening. Both were
buried in the same grave. They leave five children. (Jan.
26, 1832)

GAITHER, Mrs. Sarah, died Tues., 14th inst., in A. A. Co., relict
of Benjamin Gaither, formerly of the same county; in her
79th year. (Nov. 30, 1769)

GAITHER, Washington, and Henrietta Linthicum, both of A. A. Co.,
were married Tues., 16th inst., by the Rev. Mr. Linthicum.
(Dec. 25, 1828)

GALE, George, of Cecil Co., and Miss Anna Fitzhugh, daughter of
the late Judge Done, of Annap., were married in Balto., 17th
inst., by the Rev. John G. Blanchard, of Balto. (Dec. 20,
1832)

GALE, John, died on the 28th inst., in his 47th year. He was a
Delegate from Kent Co., and was in the discharge of the
important duties of legislation. (Dec. 31, 1807)

GALE, Levin, died at his residence near Elkton, on Thurs. morning
last, in his 51st year. (Dec. 25, 1834)

GALE, Capt. Mathias, died 6th inst., in Som. Co., brother of the
late Hon. Levin Gale. (Nov. 30, 1748)

GALLOWAY, Mrs. Ann, consort of Mr. Samuel Galloway, merchant, died
last week in childbed. (Dec. 23, 1756)

GALLOWAY, Benjamin, died in Hagerstown, on Thurs., 18th Aug., in
his 79th year. A native of A. A. Co., he was educated in
Eng. Soon after the adoption of the first state constitution, he was appointed the first Attorney-General of the

state. He leaves a wife with whom he lived more than 50 years.
[Long obit.] (Sept. 1, 1831)

GALLOWAY, Mr. John, died yesterday morning at his house at West
River; a merchant. (Oct. 14, 1747)

GALLOWAY, John, died on Wed. last [May 16], at Tulip Hill, on West
River. (May 23, 1810)

GALLOWAY, Joseph, died Mon. morning last [Sept. 11], at his house
near West River. (Sept. 14, 1752)

GALLOWAY, Joseph, died Wed., 13th ult., at Cumberland, All. Co.,
after a short illness. A resident of A. A. Co., he was aged
70 years. (March 14, 1805)

GALLOWAY, Mrs. Sarah, relict of the late John Galloway, of Tulip
Hill, and daughter of the late Benjamin Chew, formerly Chief
Justice, of Penna., died Sun., 28th ult., aged 73. [Long
obit.] (June 1, 1826)

GAMBRILL, Mrs. Anne, formerly of Annap., died Wed. last, in A. A.
Co. (July 19, 1832)

GAMBRILL, Mr. Horatio, and Miss Mary Davis, were married Thurs.
evening last by the Rev. Dr. Davis. (May 22, 1823)

GAMBRILL, Horatio, of Annap., aged 33, died Friday morning last.
He leaves a wife and family. (March 27, 1834)

GAMBRILL, Launcelot, formerly of Md., and Ann America, daughter of
Rev. Dr. Pierce, of Columbus, Ga., were married in the latter
place, on 9th inst., by Rev. Mr. Sanford. (July 26, 1838)

GAMBRILL, Richard, and Mary D. L. Iglehart, daughter of Richard
Iglehart, Esq., were married in A. A. Co., on the evening
of 17th inst., by the Rev. Mr. Shane. (May 26, 1825)

GAMBRILL, Mr. Richard, aged 19 years and six months, died at the
residence of his father, Augustine Gambrill, Esq., on the
Head of Severn, on Friday, 21st inst. [Long obit.] (Sept.
27, 1827)

GAMBRILL, Dr. Stevens, and Miss Elizabeth Gambrill, all of A. A. Co.,
were married on the 11th inst., by the Rev. Mr. Welch. (May
18, 1820)

GAMBRILL, Stevens, only son of Dr. Stevens Gambrill, died Thurs.,
20th inst., in his third year. Dr. Gambrill is a resident
of Brotherton. (June 26, 1834)

GANTT, Fielder, died at his residence in P. G. Co., on the 11th inst., in his 63rd year. (Oct. 14, 1824)

GANTT, Dr. Robert, died 13th ult., in the state of Alabama; formerly
    of Cal. Co., Md. (March 27, 1823)

GANTT, Dr. William T., and Kitty Worthington, daughter of Brice J.
    Worthington, all of A. A. Co., were married Tues., 2nd inst.
    (Dec. 11, 1828)

GARDINER, John M., of the U. S. Navy, and Miss Sophia Gassaway, of
    Annap., were married Friday evening last [Nov. 1], by the
    Rev. Mr. Higinbothom. (Nov. 7, 1805)

GARDINER, Lieut.-Commandant John M., U. S. N., died Wed., 30th ult.,
    at Doden, on the south side of South River. (Sept. 7, 1815)

GARDINER, Richard, of George, died Mon. last, at his residence near
    Annap. leaving a widow and three children. (April 28, 1836)

GARDNER, Mr. Richard, and Elizabeth Ann, youngest daughter of Mr.
    Howard Duvall, were married Tues. evening last, in South
    River Neck, by Rev. T. Riley. (Dec. 24, 1829)

GARLINER, Thomas, and Miss Susan Brewer, all of Annap., were married
    on Tues. evening last [March 14], by the Rev. Mr. Watkins.
    (March 16, 1820)

GARSTON, Thomas, one of the owners of the Annapolis packet, was
    drowned off the mouth of the Magothy on Friday last en route
    from Annap., to Balto. (Feb. 28, 1793)

GASKINS, James R., of Balto., and Eleanora Sewell, of A. A. Co.,
    were married Tues., 15th inst., by the Rev. Dr. Hammond.
    (Dec. 24, 1835)

GASSAWAY, Mrs., of Elk-Ridge, departed this life. (Oct. 31, 1805)

GASSAWAY, Amelia Pinckney, youngest daughter of Louis and Rebecca
    Gassaway, died Sun. morning last, in her fifth year. (March
    27, 1834)

GASSAWAY, Capt. Henry, a meritorious officer in the Revolutionary
    army, died in Annap. on Mon. night last. (Feb. 11, 1818)
    He died on Feb. 10, 1818. (Feb. 26, 1818)

GASSAWAY, Capt. John, died last Thurs. [June 10], at his plantation
    near South River, in his 55th year; for a number of years in
    the Commission of the Peace, for three years Sheriff, and
    for eight years one of the Representatives of A. A. Co.
    (June 17, 1762)

GASSAWAY, Gen. John, died in Annap., on Sun. evening last. He was

an officer of merit in the Revolutionary army, and for many
years past held the office of Register of Wills of this county.
(June 29, 1820)

GASSAWAY, Dr. John, died Tues. night last [Dec. 10], in Annap.; he
lived at Rhode River. (Dec. 12, 1811)

GASSAWAY, Louis, and Miss Rebecca Henry, both of Annap., were married
last evening [June 20], by the Rev. Mr. Smith. (June 21,
1809)

GASSAWAY, Louis G., and Ellen, daughter of the late John Brewer, Esq.,
were married in Annap., yesterday morning, by the Rev. Mr.
McElhiney. Mr. Gassaway is a resident of Wash., D. C. (May
18, 1837)

GASSAWAY, Mr. Thomas, died lately at his house near South River.
(Jan. 27, 1774)

GASSAWAY, Dr. Thomas J., of Q. A. Co., and Rebecca Hardcastle of
Caroline Co. were married Thurs., 22nd ult., by the Rev. James
Smith. (Dec. 6, 1827)

GASSAWAY, Dr. Thomas Jefferson, died 15th inst., in his 28th year,
at his residence in Q. A. Co. He was a native of Annap.
(Oct. 29, 1829)

GASTON, the Hon. William, of N. C., and Miss Eliza Ann Worthington,
eldest daughter of Dr. Charles Worthington, of George-Town,
D. C., were married Tues., 3rd inst. (Sept. 12, 1816)

GEDDES, Capt. David, died on Friday [March 6], at Balto., an old inhabitant of Fell's Point. (March 12, 1807)

GEDDES, David R., died on Tues. [July 23], in Annap. (July 25, 1816)

GEORGE, Mr. Joshua, died on Sat. last, in Caecil [sic] County, for
many years a Representative of that county [in the Maryland
Assembly], and a prosecutor in that and in two other counties.
(Nov. 9, 1748)

GEORGE II, King of Great Britain, died on October 25, 1760, in the
77th year of his age, and in the 34th year of his reign.
(Jan. 1, 1761)

GETTY, Robert, of George-Town, and Miss Margaret Wilmot, of Annap.,
were married Tues. evening last [Dec. 27], by the Rev. Mr.
Judd. (Dec. 29, 1808)

GHISELIN, Reverdy, Clerk of the Provincial Court, died Sun., 2nd
inst. (April 6, 1775)

GHISELIN, Dr. Reverdy, one of the Honourable Council of this state, and Miss Margaret Bowie, daughter of His Excellency, the Governor, were married on Tues. evening [Dec. 25], by the Rev. Mr. Duke. (Dec. 27, 1804)

GIBSON, Mrs. Anne O., relict of the late John Gibson, Esq., of Magothy, died Mon., 6th inst. (Aug. 16, 1821)

GIBSON, George H., died at Prince Frederick, Cal. Co.; a member of the Bar of that county. (Nov. 1, 1832)

GIBSON, Mr. Horatio, died in Jan., on the north side of Severn. (Feb. 11, 1830)

GIBSON, Mr. Horatio S., and Miss Eliza Burnett, both of A. A. Co., were married Tues. evening last, by Rev. Mr. Riley. (May 28, 1829)

GIBSON, John, died at his seat near Magothy River, on Mon. morning last [Dec. 6]. (Dec. 9, 1819)

GIBSON, William, late Clerk of the Balto. Co. Court, died Sun. evening, 29th inst. (May 3, 1832)

GILES, Edward, died last Mon. night, in Annap., one of the Delegates to Congress from this state. (March 13, 1783)

GILL, Elizabeth, a young woman, was killed by lightning which struck the house of Mrs. Buchanan, widow of Dr. Buchanan, about three miles from Balto. Town, on Mon. last. (July 30, 1752)

GILL, Richard, son of Richard W., and Anne E. Gill, died in Annap., 3rd inst., aged two years and six months. (Oct. 11, 1838)

GILL, Richard W., of Balto. City, and Miss Ann E. Deale, of Annap., were married Thurs. evening last, by the Rev. Mr. Pinckney. (May 14, 1835)

GILLILAND, William, last Friday se'ennight was shot through the head and was scalped near Fort Frederick. (Dec. 23, 1756)

GILLIS, Capt. Ezekiel, died Mon. evening last [Jan. 9], at his plantation near Annap., after a tedious indisposition for above seven months; in the 51st year of his age; one of the gentlemen for the commission of the peace of this county. (Jan. 11, 1749)

GLASGOW, Rev. Mr. Patrick, died Thurs. last [March 15], in Wor. Co., the rector of Allhallows Parish in that county. (March 22, 1753)

GLOVER, Edmund, died in Annap. on Thurs. last, in his 26th year. (March 16, 1826)

GLOVER, Mrs. Eleanor. died in Annap., on Wed., the 26th inst., after a lingering illness. (Aug. 3, 1820)

GLOVER, John, died Mon. evening, aged about 45 years. (May 8, 1823)

GLOVER, William, died Wed., 25th inst. (Jan. 31, 1810)

GLOVER, William, and Miss Mary Ann Beard, all of Annap., were married on Sun. evening last [Feb. 25], by the Rev. Mr. Emory. (March 1, 1821)

GODDARD, William, died at Providence, R. I., on Tues. morning last [Dec. 30]. He was first editor of the Providence Gazette, which paper he established in 1762. He had just completed his 77th year. (Jan. 8, 1818)

GOLDER, ---, son of Mr. Golder, of Annap., died as a result of eating some mushrooms gathered by Francis Keys. (Aug. 15, 1765)

GOLDER, Mr., died last night as a result of eating some mushrooms, which he had eaten the previous week. For some time before his death he had lost the use of his limbs, and his skin had turned a very blackish hue. (Aug. 22, 1765)

GOLDER, Archibald, of Balto., and Miss Elizabeth Howard, also of Balto., were married Sun. evening last, by Rev. Ralph Higinbothom. (April 2, 1812)

GOLDER, John, Esq., of Annap., and Miss Margaret Matilda McMechen were married Thurs. evening last [July 16], near Philadelphia. (July 23, 1812)

GOLDSBOROUGH, Mrs. Achsah, died in Mont. Co., Md., at the residence of her son-in-law, Mr. Thomas Owen, on Mon., 7th inst., in her 68th year, consort of the late Dr. Richard Y. Goldsborough, of Cambridge, Md. She was a resident of Annap. for 12 or 14 years. (Sept. 10, 1835)

GOLDSBOROUGH, Mrs. Catherine, relict of Thomas Goldsborough, died in Tal. Co., on the 22nd ult., at the seat of Robert Banning after a short illness. (Dec. 1, 1825)

GOLDSBOROUGH, the Hon. Charles, Esq., died at his house in Cambridge, on Tues. morning last, one of His Lordship's Council of State, and Commissary General of the Province. He was a gentleman eminent for many years in the knowledge and practice of the law, and was formerly one of the Representatives for Dor. Co. (July 16, 1767)

GOLDSBOROUGH, the Hon. Charles, died about half-past three, at his

residence on Shoal Creek, near Cambridge, Dor. Co., Md.
(Dec. 18, 1834)

GOLDSBOROUGH, Mrs. Henrietta Maria, died lately at her seat at "Peach
Blossom," Tal. Co. (Nov. 21, 1771)

GOLDSBOROUGH, Mr. Howes, died last week in Dor. Co.; Clerk of that
county. He is succeeded in office by Mr. John Caile.
(April 8, 1746)

GOLDSBOROUGH, Mr. Nicholas, died last week in Tal. Co., in a very
advanced age, formerly and for many years a magistrate and
representative of that county. (Oct. 2, 1766)

GOLDSBOROUGH, Robert, Jr., of Cambridge, drowned while crossing
the Bay, on Sun., 5th inst. He was in his 24th year. (Sept.
9, 1790)

GOLDSBOROUGH, Robert Henry, died on Thurs. morning, 9th inst., in
his fifth year, son of the Governor of Maryland. (Sept. 16,
1819)

GOLDSBOROUGH, the Hon. William, Esq., died Sun. last [Sept. 21],
at his seat near Talbot Court House; one of His Lordship's
Council, and Judge of the Court of Vice-Admiralty in this
Province. (Sept. 25, 1760)

GOLDSBOROUGH, William J., and Catherine Slicer, all of Annap., were
married in Annap., on Tues., by Rev. N. J. Watkins. (April
7, 1831)

GOLDSBOROUGH, William T., Esq., of Dor. Co., and Mary Ellen, youngest
daughter of the late Edward Lloyd, of Wye House, Tal. Co.,
were married in Annap., on Thurs. last, by Rev. Mr. McElhiney.
(Nov. 2, 1837)

GOOCH, Sir William, Bart., late Governor of Virginia: news of his
death is received by letter from London. (March 12, 1752)

GOODMAN, Joseph, blacksmith, drowned last week attempting to ride
over the Falls of Patapsco. He leaves four children, and a
wife big with her fifth. (March 12, 1767)

GOODMAN, Mrs. Sarah, died yesterday in Annap. (Nov. 11, 1813)

GOODMAN, William, and Mrs. Sarah Goodwin, were married on Sun.
evening, 8th inst., by Rev. Mr. Fechtig. (March 12, 1818)

GOODWIN, Richard, and Matilda Phelps, all of Annap., were married
Thurs. last, by Rev. Dr. Davis. (April 27, 1826)

GOOTIE, Miss Priscilla, died Friday last, in her 40th year. (Sept.
12, 1833)

GORDON, Mrs. Christian, of the Woodyard, P. G. Co., died Thurs.,
18th inst., after a long and painful illness. (Oct. 25, 1770)

GORDON, John, blockmaker, drowned in a squall, on the 8th inst.
(July 12, 1753)

GORDON, Robert, Esq., died Sun. evening last [Sept. 9], of gout in
his lungs, in his 77th year. He was one of the Aldermen of
Annap., and one of the representatives for Annap. in the Lower
House of Assembly, as also, one of the Judges of the Provincial Court and one of the Commissioners of the Loan Office.
On Tues. last his remains were honourably interred, the
funeral sermon being delivered by the Rev. Mr. Bacon. (Sept.
13, 1753)

GORDON, Rev. Dr. William, died at Ipswich, Eng., in the month of
Oct. last; author of The History of the American Revolution.
(March 3, 1808)

GOTT, Edwin, died on Thurs. 15th inst., in his 29th year. He leaves
a wife of four months, and eight days, and a mother. (Aug.
22, 1822)

GOTT, Rispah, daughter of the late Joseph Gott of A. A. Co., died
Sun. morning last, in Annap., in her 58th year. She was a
member of the Methodist Church for over 20 years. (Feb. 1,
1827)

GOUGH, Miss Cecilia, died Sat., 14th inst., at the seat of her brother,
Capt. Joseph Gough, near Leonard-Town. (May 26, 1825)

GOUGH, Mr. Peter, Jr., died in St. M. Co., on Sat., 27th ult., in
his 21st year, youngest son of Capt. Joseph Gough, near
Leonard-Town. (April 8, 1824)

GOVER, ---, a young child of Mr. Ephraim Gover, of P. G. Co., aged
about three years old, was killed by lightning on Friday
last. (June 13, 1771)

GOVER, Mary C., wife of Capt. Samuel Gover, died 19th inst., near
Friendship, A. A. Co., in her 47th year. (July 27, 1837)

GOWAN, George D'Oleir, of London, and Sarah Clementine, daughter of
the late Thomas Hamilton Bowie, were married Thurs. evening
by Rev. Mr. McElhiney. (June 28, 1838)

GRAMMER, Anna Janetta Henrietta, youngest daughter of Gottleb I.
Grammer, died yesterday. (April 7, 1836)

GRAMMER, Mr. C., died at Balto. on Sun. morning last, in his 23rd
year, eldest son of Mr. F. Grammer, of Annap. (Oct. 6, 1803)

GRAMMER, Mrs. Elizabeth, died at her residence on the north side of Severn, on April 20th, aged 66, consort of Mr. Frederick Grammer. Her son died recently. (May 1, 1817)

GRAMMER, Frederick, Jr., died yesterday morning, in Annap. (Feb. 6, 1806)

GRAMMER, Mr. Frederick, died Thurs., 15th inst., at his late residence, Pleasant Plains, on the north side of Severn, in his 67th year. (Oct. 29, 1818)

GRAMMER, Dr. Frederick L., and Margaret Schwrar, both of Annap., were married Thurs. evening last, by the Rev. Mr. Guest. (March 7, 1833)

GRAMMER, Mr. Henry, died Sat. morning, at the residence of his father, Mr. Frederick Grammer, in his 35th year. (March 6, 1817)

GRAMMER, John A., youngest son of the late Frederick Grammer, died Sun. morning last, in his 41st year. (Sept. 13, 1832)

GRANT, Hector, died Friday last. He was executed at Chester, Kent Co., with James Horney and Esther Anderson, for the murder of their master. The men were hanged and the woman burned. (May 20, 1746)

GRAVES, Ann Maria, aged 19 years, a native of Ireland, whose parents and family for some years have resided at Montreal (U. C.), died yesterday. (Nov. 1, 1832)

GRAVES, Edward U., and Miss C. Grawbager, were married in Troy, N. Y. (May 10, 1832)

GRAY, Capt. Benjamin, of Cal. Co., and Miss Esther Lowes, daughter of the late Tubman K. Lowes, of Som. Co., were married Thurs., 14th inst., by the Rev. Mr. Stone. (Nov. 21, 1816)

GRAY, Col. Benjamin, of Cal. Co., died Friday, 21st inst., at Judge Wilkinson's, aged 33 years, 9 months, and 21 days. He leaves a wife, children, and a sister. (June 3, 1824)

GRAY, George L., formerly editor of the Baltimore Anti-Democrat, died at St. Helena, on March 24th last. (June 2, 1808)

GRAY, Capt. Joseph Cox, died lately in Dor. Co., for many years and at the time of his death one of the representatives of that county. (May 24, 1764)

GRAY, Mr. Richard, died in Annap., on 6th inst. He leaves a wife and several children. (Aug. 10, 1826)

GREEN, Mrs. Anna Catherine, died last Thurs. morning [March 23],

relict of the late Jonas Green, Printer of this Province. She
was buried Friday in St. Anne's Churchyard. (March 30, 1775)

GREEN, Mrs. Anne, relict of the late Frederick Green, died Wed., 23rd
ult., in her 80th year. (Oct. 1, 1835)

GREEN, Mr. Jonas, died Sat. evening last [April 11], at his late
dwelling house, for 28 years Printer to this Province, and
for 21 years publisher of the Maryland Gazette; he was one of
the aldermen of this city. (April 16, 1767)

GREEN, Col. Joseph, died at his residence in Chas. Co., on the 4th
inst., in his 66th year. (Jan. 12, 1826)

GREEN, Mr. Lewis, and Miss Eliza Carey were married Tues., 14th
inst., in Frederick-Town, by Rev. Mr. Shaeffer. (March 23,
1815)

GREEN, Mr. Lewis, died in Frederick-Town, son of the late Frederick
Green, and brother of the editor of the Maryland Gazette.
He leaves a wife and three infant children. (Feb. 9, 1826)

GREEN, Mrs. Mary, consort of William S. Green of Annap., died Thurs.
morning. She leaves several children. (April 8, 1830)

GREEN, Robert, was killed by John Wilmot, in Balto. Co., with a
compass staff. He leaves a wife and six children, all under
seven years. Wilmot was found guilty of manslaughter at the
Balto. Co. Assizes last week. (April 15, 1756)

GREEN, Timothy, printer, died Mon. morning last [Oct. 3], after a
short illness, with a violent fever, in his 60th year. He
formerly conducted his business in Boston with Mr. Samuel
Kneeland, but upon the decease of his father in 1757, he
removed to this town, where he followed the business until
his decease; "New London, October 7." (Oct. 27, 1763)

GREEN, William S., clerk of the A. A. Co. Court, and Matilda E.
Bowie, were married Sat. evening last by the Rev. Mr. Blanchard. (Sept. 27, 1832)

GREENWELL, Joseph W., and Lydia Ann Coulter, daughter of Henry
Coulter, of Annap., were married in George-Town, D. C.,
on the 8th inst., by Rev. Mr. Dougherty. (Nov. 24, 1825)

GREGORY, Benjamin P., of Albany, N.Y., and Miss Ann Maria Shaffer
of Annap., were married Thurs. morning, Sept. 4, by the Rev.
Mr. James. (Oct. 2, 1834)

GRESHAM, Mr. John, member [of the House of Delegates] for Kent Co.,
died there lately. (Jan. 23, 1752)

GRIFFITH, Capt. David, of Balto., and Emily Brewer Thompson, of
    Annap., were married Sun. morning last, by the Rev. Mr.
    Decker. (May 17, 1838)

GROSVENOR, Mrs. Mary, died and was buried in Annap., where she was
    born. [Long obit is given.] (Dec. 7, 1815)

GROVE, Mr. Solomon, Esq., died in A. A. Co., on Thurs., in his 54th
    year. (Sept. 28, 1826)

GROVER, John, of Cal. Co., had his house blown down by a tornado
    on March 17th. His eldest daughter and a child in her arms
    were killed. (April 9, 1752)

GROVES, Mrs. Elizabeth, died Wed., 15th inst., in her 34th year;
    consort of Solomon Groves. She leaves an aged mother, a
    husband, and a numerous train of relatives. (March 23, 1826)

GRYMES, the Hon. Philip, Esq., one of the Council for the Colony of
    Virginia, died there the latter end of December. (Jan. 28,
    1762)

GUEST, Elizabeth E., only daughter of the Rev. Job Guest, of Annap.,
    died Sun., 2nd Oct. [Long obit is given.] (Oct. 6, 1831)

GWINN, Henrietta, daughter of the late John Gwinn of Chas. Co., died
    Mon., aged about eight years. (Sept. 22, 1831)

GWINN, John, Jr., died at Fells Point, Balto., on Feb. 11, a resident
    of Annap., in his 51st year, leaving a wife and six children.
    (Feb. 19, 1807)

GWINN, John, Esq., of Annap., Clerk to the late General Court, de-
    parted this life on Friday night last [Feb. 23], in his 54th
    year. (March 1, 1809)

GWINN, Dr. John, and Miss Louisa Hobbs, were married Thurs. evening
    by the Rev. Mr. Davis. (Nov. 13, 1817)

GWINN, Mrs. Louisa, consort of Dr. John Gwinn, formerly of Balto.,
    died last week in St. M. Co. (Sept. 8, 1825)

HADDAWAY, Capt. Wrathburn B., of Tal. Co., and Mary C. Philips, of
    Annap., were married Wed. evening, 8th inst., by Rev. Mr.
    Waters. (May 16, 1833)

HAGERTY, Rev. John, died in Balto., on the evening of the 4th inst.,
    in his 77th year. He was a minister of the Methodist Episco-
    pal Church for nearly half a century. (Sept. 11, 1823)

HAGNER, Peter, of Washington, and Miss Frances Randall, of Annap.,

were married on Tues. [April 22], by the Rev. Mr. Higinbotham.
(April 24, 1806)

HALL, Capt., of the army, died at Winchester, Eng., aged 91. He was
Surgeon's Mate on the Centurion, and went round the world
with Lord Anson in 1740. [Long obit is given.] (July 10,
1806)

HALL, Mr. Aquila, of Balto. Co., was reportedly shot to death on
Christmas Day, as he was walking in his orchard, by one of
his negroes. (Dec. 31 - Jan. 7, 1728/9)

HALL, Betty Ann, daughter of the late William I. Hall, aged about
12 years, died Sun. last. (April 3, 1834)

HALL, Dr. Blake, and Miss Rachel Sprigg Watkins were married in A.
A. Co. on Tues. evening last by Rev. Dr. Rafferty. (Nov.
30, 1826)

HALL, Edward, Esq., departed this life on Sat., 10th inst., at his
residence near West River. (July 15, 1813)

HALL, Edward, Esq., died in A. A. Co. on Sat. night last; formerly
Commissioner of Loans for the United States, for the State
of Maryland. (Oct. 13, 1825)

HALL, Mrs. Eleanor, died on 10th inst., at Collington Meadows, P.
G. Co., in her 25th year, wife of Francis Hall, and daughter
of Richard B. Hall, Esq. (March 1, 1792)

HALL, Mrs. Eleanor, died in Annap. on Sat. last, in her 66th year;
relict of the late John Hall, Esq. (Dec. 12, 1805)

HALL, Major Henry, died Tues. last at his plantation near the Head
of South River, aged 50 years; a magistrate and a representative. (May 20, 1756)

HALL, Henry, one of the magistrates and late representative of A. A.
Co., died Thurs., 11th inst. (Jan. 18, 1770)

HALL, Henry, Sr., died Sun., Dec. 23, 1798, in his 49th year. (Jan.
3, 1799)

HALL, Mr. Henry, and Miss Ann Garsten, both of Annap., were married
Thurs. evening last by Rev. Mr. Higinbothom. (Oct. 6, 1803)

HALL, Henry S., died Sun. morning last. (Sept. 13, 1825)

HALL, Jasper, on Thurs. evening last, accidentally drowned in the
Dock. (July 2, 1767)

HALL, John, Esq., one of the representatives for this city, and

Miss Eleanor Dorsey were married Sun. last [Aug. 23]. (Aug. 27, 1767)

HALL, John, Esq., of Annap., died Wed., 8th inst., in his 68th year. (March 16, 1797)

HALL, John, late a resident of Q. A. Co., died 4th April, in his 19th year. (April 30, 1801)

HALL, Dr. Joseph, died in A. A. Co., Wed., 24th inst., in his 45th year. (Nov. 28, 1822)

HALL, Joseph B., printer, died in Balto., Thurs. last, in his 25th year. (Oct. 6, 1831)

HALL, Joshua, of Annap., and Mary Ann Harmon of A. A. Co., were married 3rd inst., by the Rev. Dr. Hammond. (Jan. 12, 1826)

HALL, Mrs. Mary, relict of Thomas Hall, late Register of Wills for A. A. Co., died Friday morning. (Oct. 29, 1829)

HALL, Thomas, Esq., of Hagerstown, and Miss Anne Pottenger, of Balto., were married in the latter city on Thurs. evening, 27th ult., by the Rev. Mr. Bend. (Nov. 3, 1808)

HALL, Thomas, son of Henry S. Hall, of Annap., died Friday morning, 24th inst. (March 2, 1815)

HALL, Thomas H., Register of Wills, and Miss Mary Watkins, were married Tues. last at South River, by Rev. Dr. Davis. (July 25, 1822)

HALL, Thomas H., Register of Wills for A. A. Co., died Mon., 11th inst. (Aug. 14, 1828)

HALL, Thomas W., Esq., died on Sat. last, at his residence near the Head of South River. (April 10, 1828)

HALL, William, of Annap., and Miss Caroline Weedon, were married Thurs. evening last at Sandy Point Farm on north side of Severn by Rev. Mr. Watkins. (Sept. 21, 1820)

HALL, William I., and Miss Margaret Harwood, all of A. A. Co., were married Thurs. evening last [Nov. 18], by the Rev. Mr. Gibson. (Nov. 25, 1819)

HALL, Col. William I., of South River, died Thurs., 6th inst., in his 41st year. He leaves a widow and four children. (Sept. 13, 1832)

HALL, William T., died in Annap. on Thurs. evening last. [Long obit is given. (Feb. 9, 1826)

HALLAM, Lewis, the father of the American Theatre, died at Philadelphia on the 1st inst., in his 75th year. (Nov. 17, 1808)

HALLAM, Mr. William L., died in New York on 24th ult., in his 30th
year. (Sept. 1, 1825)

HAMILTON, Dr. Alexander, of Annap., and Miss Margaret Dulany, daughter
of the Hon. Daniel Dulany, Esq., were married Friday last
[May 29]. (June 2, 1747)

HAMILTON, Alexander, M. D., died Tues. last, at his house in Annap.,
aged 44 years. (May 13, 1756) William Murdock will settle
the estate. (Sept. 1, 1757)

HAMILTON, Alexander, was buried Sat. last. (July 19, 1804) [Alex-
ander Hamilton, 1757 - 1804, first Secretary of the Treasury,
was killed in a duel by Aaron Burr.]

HAMILTON, Dr. John, died Mon. morning [March 28], about three o'clock,
in his 72nd year. (March 31, 1768)

HAMILTON, Mrs. Mary, consort of Samuel H. Hamilton and daughter of
of William C. Peach, died 10th Feb., at her late residence
at West River, A. A. Co. (March 1, 1832)

HAMILTON, Samuel H., of A. A. Co., and Elizabeth Duvall, of P. G.
Co., were married Thurs. evening last by Rev. Mr. Watkins.
(May 16, 1833)

HAMILTON, Mr. William, merchant of P. G. Co., was killed on Thurs.,
5th inst., near Patuxent Bridge, by the accidental discharge
of a gun. He leaves a young widow, "now near her time."
(July 12, 1759) Martha Hamilton is administratrix. (Oct.
18, 1759)

HAMMOND, Mrs. Ann Kitty, eldest daughter of Ellis Thomas, Esq., of
A. A. Co., died 5th Aug., aged 35. (Sept. 13, 1827)

HAMMOND, the Hon. Charles, Esq., died Sun. night, Sept. 13, aged 80,
at his seat on the north side of Severn; President of the
Council and Treasurer of the Western Shore. (Sept. 17, 1772)

HAMMOND, Mr. Denton, died Sat. last [March 2], at his seat at the
Head of Severn. (March 7, 1782)

HAMMOND, Denton A., and Elizabeth Reiner, both of A. A. Co., were
married Tues., 12th inst., at the residence of Dr. Mewburn.
(March 21, 1833)

HAMMOND, Mrs. Elizabeth, wife of Denton A. Hammond, died July 10th
in her 26th year, at the residence of Dr. Mewburn, in A. A.
Co. (July 17, 1834)

HAMMOND, Mr. George W., and Miss Elizabeth Harmon, both of A. A. Co.,
    were married Thurs. evening, Oct. 28th, by the Rev. Mr.
    Shane. (Nov. 11, 1830)

HAMMOND, Henry, son of the late Major Philip Hammond, died at the
    Head of Severn, in his 18th year. (Feb. 9, 1826)

HAMMOND, Henry, aged 53 years, a local preacher belonging to the
    Methodist Society, died in Annap. on Friday night last. (Feb.
    26, 1829)

HAMMOND, Henry, and Miss Ruth H. Maccubbin, all of Annap., were
    married Thurs. evening last, by the Rev. Mr. Blanchard. (Dec.
    19, 1833)

HAMMOND, Henry, of Annap., died Friday evening last. (April 20, 1837)

HAMMOND, John, drowned off the mouth of the Magothy on Friday last
    en route from Annap. to Balto. (Feb. 28, 1793)

HAMMOND, John, son of Charles, died Wed., 13th inst., at 58 minutes
    past 10 o'clock, in his 28th year. (April 21, 1796)

HAMMOND, John L., and Miss Charlotte Maccubbin, were married Tues.,
    18th inst., at the Head of Severn. (Feb. 27, 1812)

HAMMOND, Dr. John W., and Miss Sarah Pinckney, daughter of Jonathan
    Pinckney, Esq., were married on Thurs. evening, 26th inst.,
    by the Rev. Dr. Rafferty. (June 16, 1825)

HAMMOND, Lucretia, daughter of Denton A. Hammond, aged six weeks,
    died July 9th, at the residence of Dr. Mewburn in A. A. Co.
    (July 17, 1834)

HAMMOND, Mrs. Margaret S., died Thurs. night last, at the residence
    of Mr. William Brown, in Annap. (Dec. 20, 1827)

HAMMOND, Matthias, died Sat. last [Nov. 11]. (Nov. 16, 1786)
    Philip Hammond is executor. (May 17, 1787)

HAMMOND, Mr. Matthias, and Miss Eliza Brown, were married Thurs.,
    17th inst., at the Head of Severn, by Rev. Mr. Welch. (May
    21, 1812)

HAMMOND, Dr. Matthias, died at his residence in A. A. Co. on Sept.
    7th, in the zenith of manhood. (Sept. 9, 1819)

HAMMOND, Mr. Mordecai, died this day in Annap., in confinement, a
    gentleman formerly in the commission of the peace for A. A.
    Co. (Jan. 27, 1747) William Cockey and Joshua Owings
    advertise they will sell a choice parcel of Negroes belonging

to the late Hammond on April 24th next. (Feb. 10, 1747)
George Steuart is administrator. (June 9, 1747)

HAMMOND, Major Nathan, died lately at his plantation on Elk Ridge
in the 54th year of his age; formerly High Sheriff of A. A.
Co. (May 6, 1762) Anne Hammond is executrix. (June 17,
1762)

HAMMOND, Nathan, of Annap., and Sarah Jane Tate of Washington, D.C.,
were married Thurs. last. by O. B. Brown. (Dec. 25, 1834)

HAMMOND, Nicholas, Esq., late President of the Farmers Branch Bank
at Easton, died Thurs. evening last, 11th inst., in his 73rd
year at his residence in Tal. Co. (Nov. 18, 1830)

HAMMOND, Mr. Philip, Esq., died Sat. last [May 3], at the Head of
Severn, one of the Representatives for A. A. Co., and for
many years past successively chosen to serve in that station.
He was appointed Speaker in 11 sessions. [Long obit is
given.] (May 8, 1760) Charles Hammond, Jr., is executor.
(July 31, 1760). At an election to choose a Representative
for A. A. Co., in the room of Philip Hammond, Esq., dec.,
the latter's son John Hammond was unanimously chosen to
succeed his father. (Oct. 16, 1760)

HAMMOND, Mr. Philip, died Mon. last, a gentleman of a most respectable
character. (May 8, 1783)

HAMMOND, Major Philip, Sr., died Sat. night last. (Nov. 28, 1822)

HAMMOND, Madam Rachel, died Sat. last [Feb. 25], worthy consort of
the Hon. Col. Charles Hammond, at his plantation on the
Severn. (March 1, 1749)

HAMMOND, Mrs. Rachel, relict of Philip Hammond, died Tues. morning
last [April 11], in her 75th year. (April 13, 1786)

HAMMOND, Rachel Ann, third daughter of Dr. William Hammond, died
Thurs., 20th inst., on the north side of Severn, aged 4
years, 11 months, and 18 days. (Nov. 27, 1834)

HAMMOND, Rezin, of Annap., son of Major Nathan Hammond, and Rebecca
Hawkins of the north side of Severn, were married Thurs.
evening last [Sept. 2]. (Sept. 4, 1760)

HAMMOND, Col. Rezin, departed this life at his farm in A. A. Co., on
Friday, 1st inst., in his 64th year. [Long obit gives details
of his service in the American Revolution, the State Convention,
and the State Legislature.] At an advanced age he retired
from the turmoil of the world to the peaceful quiet of his
farm. (Sept. 6, 1809)

HAMMOND, Thomas, and Miss Margaret Boone, all of A. A. Co., were
married Thurs. last, 24th ult., by the Rev. Mr. Watkins, on
the north side of Severn. (July 1, 1824)

HAMMOND, Col. William, of Balto. Town, died of small pox. (Jan. 16,
1752) Sarah Hammond is executrix. (July 9, 1752)

HAMMOND, William, died on Tues. morning [April 30], in his 47th
year; a resident of Annap. (April 2, 1807)

HAMPTON, Wade, died on his way to New Orleans, proceeding to take
command of the army. (Nov. 29, 1809)

HANBURY, Mr. Capel, merchant, died in London. His business is
carried on by Osgood Hanbury, the surviving partner. (Aug.
17, 1769)

HANCOCK, Orlando, and Elizabeth Johnson, both of A. A. Co., were
married 14th inst., by the Rev. Mr. Watkins. (Sept. 28,
1826)

HANDS, Bedingfield, Esq., died lately in Kent Co., Treasurer of the
Eastern Shore, and one of His Lordship's Justices of the
Provincial Court. (Sept. 28, 1769)

HANDY, Mrs. Ann G., consort of Wm. Handy, Esq., died suddenly, 11th
inst., in Som. Co., in her 30th year. (Feb. 23, 1832)

HANDY, Gordon M., of Snow Hill, Wor. Co., and Ann, eldest daughter
of Dr. D. Claude, of Annap., were married Thurs. evening
last by the Rev. Mr. McElhiney. (June 7, 1838)

HANDY, Capt. John, died Nov. 6th in Som. Co., of a nervous fever; a
Representative and a Magistrate. (Dec. 2, 1756)

HANLON, David, of Annap., and Miss Harriet Moss, daughter of James
Moss of Hackett's Point, were married at the latter place
on Sun. evening last [Feb. 27], by the Rev. Mr. Higinbothom.
(March 3, 1808)

HANLON, Mr. David, a native of Ireland, died in Annap. on Thurs.
morning, leaving a widow and children. (Oct. 13, 1825)

HANLON, Henrietta Maria Clare, died at her residence in A. A. Co.,
on 10th inst., in her 14th year. (Nov. 13, 1828)

HANLON, Robert Moss, son of the late David Hanlon, died in A. A.
Co., on Wed. last, in his 10th year. (Feb. 16, 1832)

HANSON, Mr., was found dead in Chas. Co., on the road. He is
supposed to have died by a fall from his horse. (Dec. 21,
1748)

HANSON, Alexander C., Jr., and Miss Priscilla Dorsey, were married
Mon. evening last [June 25], by the Rev. Mr. Higinbothom.
(June 27, 1805)

HANSON, Alexander Contee, died in Annap. on Jan. 16th, in his 56th
year; Chancellor of the State of Md. (Jan. 23, 1806)

HANSON, Charles W., and Miss Rebecca Ridgely, daughter of Gen. Charles
Ridgely, were married Thurs. evening last, by the Rev. George
Dashiell. (Oct. 8, 1807)

HANSON, Mrs. Elizabeth, died Sun., 9th inst., in her 52nd year;
wife of Walter Hanson, Esq., of Chas. Co. She leaves a husband, children, and other relatives. (May 20, 1773)

HANSON, Mrs. Rebecca, died on Tues. [June 21], in her 47th year, the
relict of A. C. Hanson, late Chancellor of the State. (June
26, 1806)

HANSON, Col. Robert, died last Friday at a good old age, at his seat
near Port Tobacco, for many years a Representative and Chief
Magistrate of Chas. Co. (Aug. 3, 1748)

HARDESTY, Mr. George, and Miss Priscilla Boswell, all of Cal. Co.,
were married in that county on Tues. morning last, by Rev.
Mr. Coffin. (Nov. 15, 1838)

HARDESTY, Richard C., and Matilda Holland, both of Annap., were
married Tues. evening last, by the Rev. Mr. Blanchard. (May
3, 1832)

HARDING, Robert, belonging to the Miles River Packet, drowned yesterday. (June 5, 1766)

HARMAN, Master Ephraim Augustine, only surviving son of Col. Ephraim
Augustine Harman, died Friday last [March 1], in Caecil Co.,
aged 17. He was heir to Bohemia Manor, a very fine estate
in Cecil Co., which by his death, falls to his sister. (March
6, 1751)

HARPER, Gen. Robert Goodloe, died Friday morning last, aged 60 years.
(Jan. 20, 1825)

HARRIS, David, died at Balto., Thurs. last; Cashier of the Office of
Discount and Deposit in that city. He was one of the early
soldiers of our Revolutionary War. In the year 1775 he
joined the American army, under Gen. Washington, before Boston. (Nov. 22, 1809)

HARRIS, Edward, blockmaker of Annap., last Sat. morning [March 14],
was seized with an apoplexy and died within a few minutes.
(March 19, 1761)

HARRIS, Frances Hatton, died Thurs., 29th June, in her 70th year
(July 6, 1815)

HARRIS, Gwynn, President of the Executive Council of Md., died
Sun. last, at Bath, Berkeley Springs, Va. (From the Balto.
Chronicle) (Aug. 17, 1837)

HARRIS, Isaac, died in Annap. on Mon. last [April 4], in the 78th
year of his age. (April 7, 1808)

HARRIS, Jane, aged 17 years, died 21st inst., at the residence of
her father, Col. Joseph Harris, in St. M. Co. (Nov. 3, 1831)

HARRIS, John, late of Annap., died at "Mount Tirzah," the Chas.
Co. residence of his uncle Gwinn Harris, on the 11th inst.,
in his 35th year. (March 31, 1831)

HARRIS, Samuel, died Thurs., 20th inst., after a short illness, the
only son of William Harris, of the Clifts, Cal. Co. (Jan.
27, 1774)

HARRIS, Mr. Thomas, one of the representatives for Q. A. Co., died
there last Tues., of the small pox. (March 20, 1760)

HARRIS, Thomas, Esq., Clerk of the Court of Appeals for the Western
Shore, died in Annap. on Wed. night, June 24th, in his 60th
year. (July 2, 1829)

HARRIS, William, died the 22nd of last month, at his plantation on
Fairly Creek, in Kent Co.; formerly a representative and
twice Sheriff of that county. (July 13, 1748)

HARRISON, Col. Benjamin, of "Berkly," Va., was killed last Friday
[July 12], in Chas. City Co., when lightning struck his
house, killing him and his two youngest daughters; "Williamsburg, July 18." (Aug. 16, 1745)

HARRISON, Mrs. Dorothy, died the 5th of last month, wife of Col.
Richard Harrison, of Chas. Co. She was the daughter of Col.
Robert Hanson, late of said county, dec. She was in the 31st
year of her age. (April 9, 1752)

HARRISON, James, and Frances Clayton, both of Annap., were married
Tues. evening last, by the Rev. Mr. Guest. (March 7, 1833)

HARRISON, Mrs. Mary, consort of Samuel Harrison, died in London-
Town, A. A. Co., on the 1st inst. (Dec. 8, 1825)

HARRISON, Rev. Mr. Richard, died on Sat. evening last [Jan. 15],
at his house in St. Luke's Parish, Q. A. Co.; rector of that
parish for 20 years past. (Jan. 20, 1763)

HARRISON, Robert Hanson, died 2nd inst., at his seat on the Potomac
     River, Chas. Co., in his 45th year. He was Chief Judge of
     the General Court of Maryland. He served the U. S. in the
     late war. (April 8, 1790) Walter H. Harrison is admini-
     strator. (June 17, 1790)

HARRISON, Mr. Samuel, of John, and Miss Harriet Smith, both of South
     River, were married on the evening of the 26th ult., by Rev.
     Mr. Watkins. (July 5, 1827)

HARRISON, Dr. Walter, died at his residence near Herring Bay, A. A.
     Co., on Sat., 6th inst., in his 75th year. (March 11, 1830)

HARRISON, Washington, of Balto. City, and Margaret Dorsey, daughter
     of Major Thomas Dorsey of A. A. Co., were married Tues.
     evening, 19th inst., by Rev. Mr. McElhiney. (Jan. 28, 1836)

HARRISON, the Hon. William, Esq., member of the Senate of Maryland,
     died Tues., 21st ult., at his residence in Chas. Co. (Aug.
     13, 1789)

HARSNIP, Robert, cabinet maker, on last Tues. afternoon [May 4],
     was standing under the gallows, and fixing directions for
     fixing the cross-piece, when it fell and struck him upon the
     head. He died next morning. (May 6, 1762)

HART, Mr. Daniel, and Miss Harriet Smith, were married on Thurs.
     evening last [Nov. 18], by the Rev. Mr. Joseph Wyatt. (Nov.
     25, 1813)

HART, Elizabeth, eldest daughter of Daniel Hart, died in Annap.
     on Mon. last, in her 15th year. (Aug. 30, 1832)

HARWOOD, Mrs. Anne, died on Sun. morning last, at 12 o'clock, at
     South River, in her 85th year. (Sept. 27, 1804)

HARWOOD, Mr. Benjamin, of Richard, and Miss Henrietta Maria Battee,
     were married on Thurs. evening last [Oct. 10], at the seat
     of Col. Richard Harwood, by the Rev. Mr. Compton. (Oct.
     17, 1811)

HARWOOD, Benjamin, late Trustee of Maryland, and Treasurer of the
     Western Shore, died Friday, Jan. 27th, in his 75th year.
     [Long obit is given.] (Feb. 2, 1826)

HARWOOD, Benjamin, son of Richard, died Tues. last at his seat in
     South River Neck. (Jan. 29, 1835)

HARWOOD, Edward, died on Friday evening, 3rd ult., in Upper Marl-
     borough. (Nov. 9, 1820)

HARWOOD, Mr. Edwin, eldest son of the late Judge Harwood, died Sat.
     morning last, in his 22nd year. (Oct. 21, 1824)

HARWOOD, Henry H., died in Annap. on Tues. morning. (July 18, 1839)
    He died Tues., 16th inst.; President of the Farmers Bank of
    Maryland, [Long obit is given.] (July 25, 1839)

HARWOOD, Henry Hall, of Annap., and the amiable Miss Elizabeth
    Lloyd, also of Annap., were married on Thurs. evening last
    [Feb. 14], by the Rev. Mr. Higinbothom. (Feb. 21, 1805)

HARWOOD, Henry S., son of the late Nicholas Harwood, Esq., of Annap.,
    died Mon. morning last, at the residence of Col. Duvall.
    (Jan. 5, 1826)

HARWOOD, James, died Friday evening last [Oct. 11], in the 24th
    year of his age; a resident of Annap. (Oct. 17, 1811)

HARWOOD, John Edmund, died at German-Town, near Philadelphia, on
    Thurs. last [Sept. 21], formerly of the New Theatre. (Sept.
    27, 1809)

HARWOOD, Mr. Joseph, died at his residence in A. A. Co., on Mon.
    last. (May 15, 1828)

HARWOOD, Mrs. Lucy, of West River, A. A. Co., died in Philadelphia,
    3rd inst., in her 68th year. (Sept. 10, 1835)

HARWOOD, Mrs. Margaret, relict of the late Thomas Harwood, died in
    Annap., on Friday, 24th inst., in her 76th year. (Aug. 30,
    1821)

HARWOOD, Mrs. Matilda, consort of Joseph Harwood, Esq., died in A.
    A. Co., on Mon. last. (Sept. 8, 1825)

HARWOOD, Nicholas, died Thurs. last, 4th inst., an old inhabitant of
    Annap., in his 65th year. This gentleman began the career of
    life about the commencement of the Revolution. Through the
    whole of our struggle for independence, he was the open and
    avowed friend of those rights we then contended for. He was
    early appointed to the office of Clerk of A. A. Co. Court,
    which he continued to hold until the day of his death. (Oct.
    10, 1810)

HARWOOD, Peter, died yesterday, in his 94th year. He lived all his
    time in A. A. Co. (Oct. 7, 1756)

HARWOOD, Capt. Richard, died Mon. last [Sept. 2], at his house near
    West River; for many years he was one of our magistrates.
    (Sept. 5, 1754)

HARWOOD, Richard, son of Thomas, and Miss Sally Callahan, daughter
    of John Callahan, Esq., of Annap., were married Tues. evening
    last by Rev. Mr. Higinbothom. (March 31, 1803)

HARWOOD, Col. Richard, and Mrs. Lucinda Battee, all of A. A. Co., were married on Sun. [June 1], by the Rev. Mr. Compton. (June 5, 1806)

HARWOOD, Col. Richard, died on Tues. last in his 89th year, at his seat in A. A. Co. (Feb. 23, 1826)

HARWOOD, Richard, son of Thomas, Adjutant-General of Maryland, died Sat. last in his 61st year. (April 9, 1835)

HARWOOD, Richard H., died Friday night, 21st inst., in Annap. (May 27, 1819)

HARWOOD, Mrs. Sally, wife of Richard Harwood, of Thos., Adjutant-General of Maryland, and eldest daughter of the late John Callahan, died 22nd inst., in her 50th year. [Long obit is given.] (April 25, 1833)

HARWOOD, Sprigg, Esq., of A. A. Co., and Elizabeth Ann Mills, second daughter of William P. Mills, Esq., of Balto. Co., were married Thurs. evening last at Mt. Dilton, by the Rev. Wm. Pinckney, of P. G. Co. (June 8, 1837)

HARWOOD, Thomas, Esq., son of Mrs. Anne Harwood, died Sun. evening last, the same day that his mother died, in his 62nd year; Treasurer of the Western Shore of Maryland. (Sept. 27, 1804)

HARWOOD, Thomas, late Clerk of the City Court of Balto., died Sat. last, in his 50th year. [Long obit, from the Balto. Chronicle.] (Feb. 1, 1827)

HARWOOD, William, Esq., died yesterday afternoon, late Clerk of the House of Delegates of Maryland. He was in his 56th year. (July 5, 1804) [Long obit is given in the July 12, 1804, issue.]

HARWOOD, William, of Richard, of Thomas, and Hester C. Loockerman, all of this city, were married Thurs. evening last, by the Rev. Mr. McElhiney. (Nov. 27, 1834)

HASSELBACH, Miss Anne, died Sat. morning last, at the residence of her brother-in-law, Mr. John A. Grammer, of A. A. Co.; she was a daughter of John Hasselbach, of Fred. Co. (July 16, 1829)

HASSELBACH, John, Jr., died in Fred. Co., on 7th inst., in his 23rd year. (Aug. 17, 1826)

HATHERLY, John, of Elk Ridge, lost two of his children last Thurs., when his convict servant murdered two boys, aged 9 an 11, and a girl, aged 14. The servant's name was Jeremiah Swift. (March 20, 1751) John, aged 12, and Elizabeth, aged 14, died. Benjamin, aged 10, recovered. (April 10, 1751)

HATHERLY, John, late Examiner-General of the Western Shore of this
   state, died on Friday, April 28th. (May 4, 1815)

HATTON, Mrs. Lucy, died about a fortnight ago, when her dwelling
   house near Piscataway burned. She escaped, but attempting to
   return and rescue her two sons she perished with them. (Aug.
   29, 1750)

HAWKINS, Mr. John, Jr., died Sun. morning last, in P. G. Co., after
   a few hours' illness; aged 44 years; one of the Representatives of the county. (Feb. 24, 1757)

HAWKINS, Col. Josias, died 30th ult., at his seat in Chas. Co.,
   in his 54th year. (Nov. 12, 1789)

HAYDEN, George, of Annap., and Mrs. Mary Selby, of A. A. Co., were
   married Sun. evening last, by the Rev. Mr. Guest. (June 14,
   1832)

HAYWARD, George, Esq., Attorney-at-Law, died lately in Wor. Co.
   (March 4, 1773)

HEAGER, Capt. John, died after two days illness, in Antigua, late
   master of the schooner Chester River, which arrived yesterday from Antigua. (June 5, 1760)

HEARN, Mrs., of Wor. Co., was killed by lightning one day last week.
   (July 16, 1761)

HEATH, James, of Cecil Co., and Susanna, daughter of John Hall of
   Swan Town, Cecil Co., were married Thurs. last. [Oct. 25].
   (Nov. 1, 1759)

HEATH, James, died Thurs. last [Nov. 27], at his plantation in Balto.
   Co., in the prime of life, one of the representatives of
   that county. (Dec. 4, 1766)

HEATH, Mr. Robert, and Adeline Johnson, both of A. A. Co., were
   married Thurs. evening last, by the Rev. Mr. Watkins. (Nov.
   21, 1833)

HEBB, William, and Miss Sarah Baily, both of St. M. Co., were married
   on Tues., 21st inst., by the Rev. Dr. Barclay, (March 29,
   1809)

HEERMANCE, Mr., of N. Y. State, and Miss Maria Wootten, were married
   Thurs., 12th inst., at Mrs. Crabb's, in A. A. Co. (May 26,
   1791)

HEISTER, Gen. Daniel, died Wed. last, at the seat of government, a
   representative in Congress from the State of Maryland. The

friends of liberty have lost in him an early asserter of his
country's rights. The House of Representatives as a tribute
of respect to his memory have resolved to wear crape for 30
days. His body is to be conveyed to Hagerstown, where he
lately resided, and there interred. (March 15, 1804)

HEMSLEY, Philemon, of Q. A. Co., a member of the Society of the
Middle Temple, died in London, May 12, 1752, aged 24 years,
of the small pox. [The obit. contains the long epitaph on
his tombstone.] (Aug. 27, 1752)

HENDERSON, Mr. Jacob, died Wed. last [Aug. 21], in P. G. Co., for
many years the rector of St. Barnaby's Parish in that county.
(Aug. 28, 1751) Mary Henderson and Robert Tyler, Jr., are
executors. (Oct. 23, 1751)

HENDERSON, Richard, merchant of Bladensburg, and Sarah Brice, second
daughter of John Brice, Esq., of Annap., were married Thurs.
last [Nov. 19]. (Nov. 26, 1761)

HENDRY, Mrs. Anne, died Tues. last, at an advanced age, in Annap.
(April 29, 1830)

HENDRY, Thomas, and Miss Margaret Slicer, all of Annap., were married
on Sun. evening last [Nov. 4], by the Rev. Mr. Guest. (Nov.
18, 1819)

HENDRY, Thomas, an old inhabitant of Annap., died Friday night.
(Feb. 1, 1827)

HENRY, James, Esq., died 9th Dec. last, at his seat Fleetby, Northum-
berland Co., Va., aged 73 years. He was a member of the old
Congress. (Feb. 7, 1805)

HENRY, Mrs. Margaret, wife of the Hon. John Henry, Esq., died Wed.,
11th inst., in her 23rd year. (March 26, 1789)

HENRY, Robert Jenkins, Esq., of Som. Co., and Gertrude Rousby, daughter of the late Hon. John Rousby, Esq., dec.; were married
last week in Tal. Co. (June 3, 1746)

HENRY, Col. Robert Jenkins, died some few days ago, at his brother's
in Dor. Co.; of Som. Co., one of His Lordship's Council of
State, a provincial magistrate, and one of the judges of the
Assize for the Eastern Shore. (Oct. 23, 1766)

HENWOOD, Mr. Robert, died 25th ult., of Annap., one of the senior
members of the Well-Meaning Society. He leaves a wife and
five small children. (Dec. 2, 1773)

HEPBURN, John, died Mon., 14th inst., at his house in Upper Marl-

borough, in his 65th year, for many years one of the Judges
of the Provincial Court. (Aug. 24, 1775)

HEPBURN, Mrs. Mary, died Friday evening last [Aug. 10], at Upper
Marlborough in her 56th year. (Aug. 16, 1770)

HEPBURN, Dr. Samuel, died suddenly at Upper Marlborough, on the 11th
inst., in his 26th year of his age. (May 19, 1808)

HERON, Mr. Robert, died Friday, 3rd inst., in Dor. Co.; Collector
of His Majesty's Customs for the Port of Pocomoke. (June
16, 1774)

HERSCHELL, Sir William, died lately in England, the celebrated astronomer, 86 years of age. (Oct. 17, 1822)

HERSMAN, Matthias, died 18th ult., at Pattersons Creek, in Hampshire
Co., Va. The deceased was a native of Germany, aged by the
most accurate accounts, 125 years old. He had three wives
in Germany, and one in this country; "Baltimore, May 13."
(May 21, 1801)

HERVEY, Edmund [Edward?], and Miss Elenor Saunders, both of A. A.
Co., were married 10th inst., near Q. A. Co., by the Rev.
Mr. Watkins. (Jan. 19, 1826)

HEWES, Mr. John, proprietor of the Federal Gazette, and Miss Rachel
T. Ellicott, daughter of Mr. Elias Ellicott, were married
on Wed., 15th inst., at Friends' Meeting, in Balto. (Jan.
23, 1812)

HEWITT, Thomas William, died in Annap. on Sat. morning last [March
10], in his 42nd year. (March 14, 1810)

HIGGINS, Mrs. Grace, died in Annap. on Sat. morning last, in her
90th year. (April 11, 1810)

HIGGINS, Joshua Clarke, died Sat. last, 25th ult., at his home
near the Head of South River. (March 2, 1815)

HIGGINS, Richard, died Tues. morning last [Nov. 17], in his 63rd
year. (Nov. 19, 1807) He was in his 66th year. (Nov. 26,
1807)

HIGINBOTHOM, James S., died at Balto., on Sat. night last, after a
long and painful illness. He was a Lieut. in the American
Navy, in his 25th year. (Oct. 22, 1807)

HIGINBOTHOM, Rev. Ralph, Vice President of St. John's College, departed this life yesterday morning. (April 22, 1813)

HILL, Mrs. Althea, a native of A. A. Co., Md., and consort of Morgan

Hill of Big Prairie, New Madrid Co., Mo., died Wed., 9th inst.,
in her 38th year. (April 21, 1836)

HILL, Henry, of A. A. Co., and Mary, eldest daughter of the Hon.
Philip Thomas, Esq., one of His Lordship's Council, were
married last Thurs. at West River. (May 18, 1748)

HILL, Mr. Henry, only son of Mr. Joseph Hill, on Wed. last [Aug. 21],
was killed by a fall in his tobacco house. He was about 25
years of age, and left a widow and a young child. He was
buried on Sat., 24th inst. [Long account of the accident is
given.] (Aug. 28, 1751)

HILL, Mr. James, died Thurs., 2nd inst., near Staunton, Va., in his
87th year. He was a soldier in the old Indian Wars, in Byrd's
Campaign, Braddock's defeat, and throughout the whole of the
Revolutionary contest. (June 30, 1808)

HILL, Mr. Joseph, died Sun. last [Oct. 25] at his plantation near town;
an eminent planter and one of the people called Quakers, who
by honest industry accumulated a very good estate. (Oct.
29, 1761) Robert Pleasants and Thomas Sprigg are executors.
(Nov. 19, 1761)

HILL, Margaret, died Tues. last [Sept. 24], at her father's house
near Annap.; only daughter of Joseph Hill. (Sept. 27, 1745)
[The issue of Jan. 28, 1746, contains an ode on the death
of Peggy Hill.]

HILL, Richard, Jr., died March 18 past, in Madeira, eldest son of
Dr. Hill, formerly of this province. (May 15, 1755)

HILL, Dr. Richard, formerly of this Province, and lately of Madeira,
died on the 29th of last month. (From the Pennsylvania
Gazette) (Feb. 11, 1762)

HILL, Mrs. Sarah, widow, died last week at her plantation near South
River, aged 83, one of the people called Quakers. Her twin
sister is still living. (March 13, 1755)

HILL, Mrs. Sarah, died last Sun. evening [Jan. 11], after a week's
illness, of a pleurisy; one of the people called Quakers;
wife of Mr. Joseph Hill, near Annap. (Jan. 15, 1761)

HILL, William, late of Antigua, merchant, died here Sun. last [Jan.
8]. (Jan. 12, 1769)

HINCKLE, Rev. Moses M., of the Methodist Episcopal Church, and
Amelia Fleming, of Frederick-Town, were married in the latter
town on the morning of the 16th inst., by the Rev. Mr. Senthen.
(Aug. 25, 1825)

HINDMAN, Mr. Jacob, died Tues. last [Sept. 9], at his plantation in
   Tal. Co.; formerly a representative of his county, and in
   other public stations. (Sept. 11, 1766)

HODGES, Benjamin, of P. G. Co., and Miss Elizabeth Jenings, of Annap.,
   were married Thurs. evening last [Oct. 13], by the Rev. Mr.
   Judd. (Oct. 20, 1808)

HODGES, Charles, and Lucille Ann Grey, were married on the evening
   of the 7th inst., by Rev. Gibbons. (Aug. 23, 1827)

HODGES, Charles, and Ann Matilda Harwood, all of A. A. Co., were
   married Tues. evening, 20th inst., by Rev. Mr. Wright. (Jan.
   29, 1835)

HODGES, John T., and Elizabeth, second daughter of Brice J. Worthington, Esq., were married Tues. morning, 20th inst., by the
   Rev. Mr. McElhiney. (Jan. 29, 1835)

HODGES, Mr. William, and Miss Sarah Jacob, both of A. A. Co., were
   married in All Hallows Parish on Tues. evening last by the
   Rev. Dr. Davis. (Oct. 28, 1824)

HODGKIN, Thomas B., died at Balto., Wed., 27th ult., in his 69th
   year; formerly Clerk of the General Court of the United
   States. (March 7, 1805)

HODGSON, Michael, at the beginning of this month, was suffocated
   to death at a fire in Kent Co. (April 24, 1760)

HOGAN, Anne, a married woman big with child, accidentally drowned
   at the mouth of South River on Wed. last week [Oct. 23].
   (Oct. 30, 1754)

HOHNE, Mrs. Anne S., died Friday evening last, consort of Wesley
   M. Hohne. (Dec. 29, 1836)

HOHNE, Christopher, died Friday last of apoplexy, aged 75 years,
   a soldier of the Revolution. (April 4, 1833)

HOHNE, Elizabeth, daughter of Christopher Hohne, of Annap., died
   Friday, 6th inst., in her 25th year. (Aug. 12, 1830)

HOHNE, Mr. Westall M., and Mrs. Mary Duvall, all of Annap., were
   married Sun. evening last, by Rev. R. S. Vinton. (Dec. 7,
   1837)

HOHNE, Westoll, and Miss Sophie Cross, all of Annap., were married
   on Thurs. evening last [Oct. 19], by the Rev. Mr. Watkins.
   (Oct. 26, 1820)

HOLDEN, John, a sailor, drowned last Sat., when he fell in between
   a ship and brig in the dock. (Feb. 21, 1765)

HOLLAND, Edward, died in Annap. on Sat. night last [March 3].
(March 7, 1810)

HOLLAND, Edward, and Elizabeth Popham, all of A. A. Co., were married
Thurs. last, by Rev. Lipscomb. (June 14, 1832)

HOLLAND, George, aged about six years, son of James Holland of this
city, died Mon. morning last. (March 5, 1829)

HOLLAND, Mr. Henry S., and Miss Susan Darnall, both of Annap., were
married Tues. evening last [June 21], by the Rev. Mr. Wyatt.
(June 23, 1814)

HOLLAND, Isaac, and Miss Mary Sherbert, all of Annap., were married
on Thurs. evening last [April 27], by the Rev. Mr. Watkins.
(May 4, 1820)

HOLLAND, Mr. Isaac, died on Tues. morning, at the Half-Way House
between Balto. and Annap., in his 61st year. He was formerly a resident of Annap. (Sept. 21, 1826)

HOLLAND, Isaac, and Mrs. Elizabeth Disney, were married Tues. evening,
2nd inst., by Rev. Mr. Hamilton. (Jan. 11, 1838)

HOLLAND, James, and Miss Anne Sands, both of Annap., were married
Sun. evening last, by the Rev. Mr. Higinbothom. (Feb. 20,
1806)

HOLLAND, Mr. James, died yesterday evening, in Annap., after a short
but severe illness, in his 53rd year. (Dec. 6, 1832)

HOLLAND, James S., formerly of Annap., and Miss Elizabeth Jane,
youngest daughter of the late George W. Grant of Washington
City, were married in the latter city on Thurs., 5th inst.,
by Rev. Josiah Vanden. (Dec. 12, 1839)

HOLLAND, Joseph, a native of Annap., died at Mobile, Alabama, 14th
ult., of yellow fever, in his 46th year. (Oct. 10, 1839)

HOLLAND, Mrs. Mary, consort of Isaac Holland, formerly of Annap.,
died in Washington, Tues., 8th inst., aged 36 years. She
leaves a husband and six children. (March 16, 1837)

HOLLAND, Nehemiah, and Miss Anne Glover, all of Annap., were married
on Tues. evening last [Aug. 25], by the Rev. Mr. Wyatt. (Aug.
27, 1812)

HOLLIDAY, Jesse, of Balto., and Mrs. Margaret L. Hunt, of A. A. Co.,
were married in Annap., Sun. evening, 18th inst., by the
Rev. Mr. Vinton. (Nov. 22, 1838)

HOLLINGSWORTH, Mr. Francis, died in Balto., on the 14th inst., in
his 53rd year. (Feb. 23, 1826)

HOLLYDAY, Henry, High Sheriff of Q. A. Co., and Anne Robins were
    married on Sat. last [Dec. 9], in Tal. Co. (Dec. 13, 1749)

HOLLYDAY, Col. James, died Thurs. morning last [Oct. 8], in Q. A.
    Co.; Naval Officer of the Port of Oxford, Treasurer of the
    Eastern Shore, and one of His Lordship's Honourable Council.
    (Oct. 14, 1747)

HOLLYDAY, Madam Sarah, of Md., died in London, where she had gone
    on a visit to her only daughter. (June 26, 1755)

HOLTON, Mr. William, died at his residence in St. M. Co., on the
    Patuxent, eldest son of the late Capt. William Holton, of
    the same county. He was an amiable young gentleman, and
    leaves a widow and two children. (Jan. 22, 1824)

HOOD, Charles W., of A. A. Co., and Hannah H., youngest daughter of
    Walter Worthington, Esq., of Balto. Co., were married Tues.,
    1st inst., by Rev. Benj. Hood. (Dec. 17, 1835)

HOOD, Miss Hester, died Sept. 24th, at the head of South River, in
    her 98th year. Her sister Elizabeth died about two weeks
    since, aged 88 years. (Oct. 2, 1828)

HOOD, James, was murdered by his convict servant man from Elk Ridge,
    one Hubbard, who last Sat. was committed to gaol. (April
    18, 1765)

HOOD, Mr. William, ship-carpenter, was killed yesterday at West
    River, by a fall from a scaffolding. (April 7, 1747)

HOOD, William, Jr., committed suicide on Friday, 11th inst., aged
    about 40 years. He leaves a wife and 11 small children.
    (July 17, 1823)

HOOE, Robert Townshend, departed this life at Alexandria, on Thurs.
    evening, 16th inst., in his 66th year. At an early period
    of his life, he was selected as a member of the Maryland
    Convention. In 1776 he received from the Convention the
    appointment of Lieutenant Colonel in the 12th Battalion.
    (March 29, 1809)

HOOK, Richard, and Mary Cadle, both of A. A. Co., were married
    27th inst., by the Rev. Job Guest. (Dec. 29, 1831)

HOOPER, the Hon. Henry, died on Mon. evening [April 20], aged over
    80 years of age; Chief Justice of the Provincial Court and
    one of His Lordship's Council of State. He was formerly a
    Representative for Dor. Co., and for many years Speaker of
    the Lower House of the Assembly. (April 23, 1767) While
    his body lay in the house of his daughter, Mrs. Hicks, near

Cambridge, the house, a brick dwelling, was destroyed by fire, and his corpse was rescued from the flames with much difficulty. (May 14, 1767)

HOPEWELL, James R., Esq., of St. M. Co., and Antoinetta, daughter of Thomas Culbreath, were married Wed. morning, 1st inst., by the Rev. Mr. McElhiney. (Nov. 9, 1837)

HOPKINS, Benjamin, and Elizabeth Ann Gaither, both of Annap., were married Thurs. evening last, by Rev. Mr. Guest. (Feb. 28, 1833)

HOPKINS, Mr. Edward, and Miss Mary Davis, all of Annap., were married Thurs. evening last, by Rev. Mr. Riley. (Dec. 24, 1829)

HOPKINS, Ezekiel, and Miss Maria Hopkins, both of A. A. Co., were married Thurs. evening last, by Rev. Mr. Wright. (Dec. 18, 1834)

HOPKINS, Mr. Isaiah, of A. A. Co., and Hannah, daughter of Capt. George Barber, of Annap., were married in the county on Tues. evening last. (Nov. 10, 1825)

HOPKINS, James L., and Matilda Ann Hopkins, all of A. A. Co., were married Thurs. evening last, by Rev. Mr. Waters. (Dec. 24, 1835)

HOPKINS, Joseph, who lived in the counting house of Messrs. Pollard and Cornthwait, Bowly's Wharf, Balto., died July 7th. (July 29, 1802)

HOPKINS, Mr. Philip, and Ann Maria Willigman, all of Annap., were married Sun. evening last, by the Rev. Mr. Vinton. (Nov. 23, 1837)

HOPKINSON, Rev. Thomas, died May 26th, aged between 30 and 40 years, at Cedar Hill, the seat of Dr. B. Fendall. (June 19, 1788)

HOPPER, John, was murdered last fall by his brother-in-law Richard Nicholson, of A. A. Co., who was tried for murder Sat., found guilty of manslaughter, and burnt in the hand. (April 20, 1758)

HOPPER, Miss Sally, eldest daughter of Col. William Hopper, died last week in Q. A. Co. (May 7, 1761)

HOPPER, Col. William, formerly a representative of Q. A. Co., died recently. (April 16, 1772)

HORNBROOK, Thomas, was horned Friday last in Balto. Co., for horse stealing. (May 21, 1752)

HORNER, James, was executed in Dor. Co. last week, pursuant to his
    sentence at the Provincial Court for rape. (May 8, 1760)

HORNEY, James, was executed at Chester, Kent Co., with Hector Grant,
    and Esther Anderson for the murder of their master. The men
    were hanged, and the woman burned. (May 20, 1746)

HOSKINS, Mr. John, expired on Friday night, 18th inst., in the midst
    of inexpressible tortures, in St. M. Co.; aged 40 or 50 years,
    who about 10 weeks ago was bit in the leg by a mad dog. (May
    31, 1764)

HOVELL, Capt. James, master of the snow Beaumont, perished when his
    ship foundered soon after leaving the Capes last month. (Oct.
    31, 1754)

HOWARD, Mr., living near Annap., died of "jail fever." (July 9,
    1767)

HOWARD, Miss Ann, youngest daughter of the late Samuel H. Howard,
    of Annap., died Mon. last [Sept. 23], in her 14th year.
    (Sept. 26, 1811)

HOWARD, Mr. Beale, drowned Friday last [May 24], going up Patapsco
    in a sloop in a sudden squall of wind; he was jerked over-
    board by the foresheet, and drowned. He was a young man.
    (May 30, 1754)

HOWARD, Benjamin, Esq., Sheriff of A. A. Co., died at the seat of
    Mrs. Martha Howard, in A. A. Co., on 11th inst., in his
    29th year. (April 21, 1791)

HOWARD, Benjamin Marion, son of J. Howard, Esq., died at Howard
    Grove in A. A. Co., on Tues. morning, 7th inst. (Feb. 16,
    1832)

HOWARD, Charles, was killed 14th inst., by the fall of a tree, near
    the Fork of Patuxent. (Feb. 21, 1750)

HOWARD, Charles, of Balto., and Elizabeth Key, daughter of Francis
    S. Key, of George-Town, D. C., were married on the 8th inst.,
    by the Rev. Mr. Addison, in the latter city. (Nov. 17, 1825)

HOWARD, Mrs. Elizabeth S., consort of Joseph Howard, Esq., died at
    her late residence at South River, A. A. Co., on the 31st
    March; in her 39th year. (April 15, 1824)

HOWARD, George, son of Brice, formerly a Delegate to the Maryland
    Legislature, died last week at his residence in this county.
    (Jan. 17, 1827)

HOWARD, Mrs. Jane, died in Annap., on Sat. night last, at an ad-
    vanced age. (Sept. 18, 1823)

HOWARD, John E., Jr., eldest son of our Revolutionary veteran of
that name, died a few days since at Mercersburg, Penna.
(From the Balto. Chronicle). (Oct. 24, 1822)

HOWARD, Col. John Eager, died Friday evening, 12th inst., so greatly
distinguished as a hero of the Revolution, aged 75. (From
the Baltimore Gazette). (Oct. 18, 1827)

HOWARD, Joseph, of A. A. Co., and Miss Elizabeth Susanna Bowie, of
P. G. Co., were married on Tues. evening, 4th inst., near
Queen Anne, by the Rev. Mr. Scott. (April 12, 1809)

HOWARD, Mrs. Martha, died June 11th, in her 66th year, at her late
dwelling in A. A. Co. (June 22, 1815)

HOWARD, Martha, second daughter of Joseph Howard, Esq., died Sun.,
5th Feb., at Howard Grove, A. A. Co., in her 15th year.
(Feb. 16, 1832)

HOWARD, Mrs. Mary, relict of the late Samuel Harvey Howard, of Annap.,
died 17th inst. (Jan. 1, 1829)

HOWARD, Samuel Harvey, died on Friday morning last [April 24], in
his 57th year; Register of the Court of Chancery of the State
of Maryland. (April 30, 1807)

HOWARD, William, and Margaret Davis, both of South River, A. A. Co.,
were married 18th inst., by the Rev. Mr. Watkins. (Sept.
25, 1828)

HUBBERT, John, was executed here Friday last for the murder of his
master. (Oct. 10, 1765)

HUGHES, George W., U. S. Civil Engineer, and Ann Sarah, daughter of
Virgil Maxcy, were married in Washington on Tues., 16th inst.,
by the Rev. J. L. Woart. (Dec. 25, 1834)

HUGHES, Jeremiah, and Miss Priscilla Jacob, were married Thurs.
last [July 9], at South River, by the Rev. Mr. Barclay.
(July 16, 1807)

HUGHES, Mrs. Priscilla, consort of Jeremiah Hughes, Esq., editor
of the Maryland Republican, died yesterday in Annap. (Nov.
9, 1826)

HULL, the Hon. William, died at Newtown, Mass., on the 29th ult.,
in his 73rd year, a field officer in the Army of the Revolution, and late a Brigadier-General of the U. S. Army.
(Dec. 8, 1825)

HUMES, Joseph, jeweller of Annap., was executed today for breaking and entering the store of Lyde Goodwin, merchant of Annap. (Sept. 21, 1748)

HUMPHREY, the Rev. John, and Mrs. Lawrence, were married last Tues. evening. (Feb. 2 - Feb. 9, 1733)

HUNTER, James, and Miss Elizabeth Glover, all of Annap., were married Thurs. last [May 17], by the Rev. Dr. Judd. (May 23, 1810)

HUNTER, James, and Miss Mary Miller, were married Thurs. evening last [May 20], by the Rev. Mr. Guest. (May 27, 1819)

HUNTER, Mr. James, died in A. A. Co. on Sat. last, son of Mr. John Hunter. (Jan. 12, 1826)

HUNTER, James, died Sun. evening, in his 55th year, long known as the Host of the Union Hotel in Annap. He leaves a widow and children. (Nov. 19, 1835)

HUNTER, James W., printer, and Frederica Grammer, all of Annap., were married Sun. evening last by Rev. Mr. Vinton. (Oct. 11, 1838)

HUNTER, John, a collier, died Tues. last, in Balto. Co., at Bush River Furnace. (Dec. 9, 1756)

HUNTER, Mr. John, and Miss Rowena Watkins, both of A. A. Co., were married on Sun. evening last, by the Rev. Dr. Wells. (Aug. 31, 1826)

HUNTER, Mrs. Margaret, consort of Mr. John Hunter, died in A. A. Co., on Thurs. evening last. (Oct. 21, 1824)

HUNTER, Rev. Mr. Samuel, rector of All Saints Parish in Fred. Co., died last week. (Oct. 12, 1758)

HUNTER, William, Esq., died on Wed. se'ennight [Aug. 12], at his house in Williamsburg; one of His Majesty's Deputy Post Masters General of the Continent of North America, and Printer the General Assembly of this colony [Virginia]. ("Williamsburg, Aug. 21.") (Sept. 3, 1761)

HURST, Abraham, and Mary, daughter of the late Philemon Green, were married in Annap. on Thurs. evening last, by Rev. Dr. Davis. (March 15, 1827)

HURST, Mr. Bennett, died Sun. morning last, in Annap. (Nov. 1, 1827)

HURST, Mrs. Elizabeth, wife of John Hurst of Annap., died Sun. last, 27th inst. For several years she had been a member of the Methodist Church. (Jan. 31, 1833)

HURST, Jacob, and Miss Ann Bromwell, were married Sun. evening in
    Annap., by the Rev. Mr. Griffith. (Jan. 15, 1824)

HURST, Mrs. Margaret, died Friday last in this city, in her 85th year.
    (April 21, 1808)

HURST, Mrs. Mary, consort of Bennett Hurst of this city, died on
    Sat. night last, after a lingering illness. (May 10, 1821)

HUSFORD, George, a servant man, dropped suddenly dead last Tues.
    [July 3], near town, from drinking cold water while over-
    heated. (July 5, 1764)

HUTCHINGS, Mrs. Mary, died last Mon. [Feb. 13], in Kent Island, aged
    52 years, wife of Mr. James Hutchings. She was a good wife,
    mother, mistress, and neighbor. (Feb. 16, 1764)

HUTTON, Jonathan, and Miss Eliza Plain, were married in Annap. on
    Tues. evening, by Rev. Mr. Nind. (July 28, 1814)

HUTTON, Mrs. Margaret, relict of the late Samuel Hutton, died Mon.
    last. (Sept. 20, 1838)

HUTTON, Mr. Samuel, died in Annap. on Friday morning last [May 18],
    in his 53rd year. (May 23, 1810)

HYDE, Daniel T., and Miss Anne Merriken, both of Annap., were married
    on Sun. evening last [Sept. 7], by the Rev. Mr. Welch. (Sept.
    10, 1818)

HYDE, Mr. Frederick, and Miss Jane Phelps, all of Annap., were married
    Thurs. evening last, by the Rev. Mr. Watkins. (May 22, 1823)

HYDE, George W., and Mary Whitright, of A. A. Co., were married on
    Thurs. evening last at West River, by the Rev. Mr. Watkins.
    (Nov. 29, 1827)

HYDE, John, died Mon. morning [Sept. 13], in Annap. (Sept. 23, 1819)

HYDE, Mary Ann, youngest daughter of Mr. Frederick C. Hyde, died
    Sun. last. (April 3, 1834)

HYDE, Mrs. Sarah, relict of the late Mr. John Hyde, of Annap., died
    Thurs. morning last. (Feb. 23, 1826)

HYDE, William J., of Balto., and Lucretia Tilly of Annap. were
    married Tues., 23rd inst., by the Rev. Mr. Gere. (Aug. 1,
    1833)

HYNSON, Col. Charles, died a few days ago in Chester-Town, for many
    years Chief Justice of Kent Co.; Deputy-Commissary, and
    formerly one of their representatives. (March 9, 1748)

HYNSON, John, died owning 150 acres on Eastern Neck Island, Kent
Co. Frances Hynson is the executrix. (Sept. 17, 1761)

IGLEHART, Mr. James, Sr., died at his residence in A. A. Co., on
Sun. last, after a severe illness, at an advanced age.
(Dec. 8, 1825)

IGLEHART, John, of A. A. Co., and Miss Eleanor Smoot, were married
on Tues., 23rd ult., in Chas. Co., by the Rev. Mr. Weems.
(May 1, 1811)

IGLEHART, Thomas, Esq., aged 32 years, died Friday last. (Sept. 28,
1826)

IJAMS, Mrs. Rachel, consort of Capt. John Ijams, died at her residence
in A. A. Co., 5th inst., in her 56th year. (March 10, 1831)

INCH, Mr. John, died here Mon. morning last [March 14], aged 42
years, a goldsmith of Annap. Yesterday his funeral was
solemnized in a very decent manner, being attended by a
procession of the Brethren of the Lodge. (March 17, 1763)
Jane Inch, widow, and Baruch Maybury, son-in-law of John
Inch, are administrators. (March 24, 1763)

IRELAND, Joseph, Jr., and Amelia Brice, all of Kent Co., were
married on Wed. morning, 31st of Aug., by the Rev. P. F.
Smith. (Sept. 8, 1825)

IRELAND, Thomas, of Annap., and Elizabeth Ann Nicols, of A. A. Co.,
were married Thurs. evening last, by Rev. Poisal. (Nov. 5,
1835)

IRWIN, John: By a letter from Scotland to a gentleman here, we have
an account that John Irwin, well known in this province for
his dispatch and integrity in taking up runaways, and sometimes for goodnaturedly helping them off, was hanged Nov. last
at Edinburgh for a robbery and murder committed by him on
the highway. (June 28, 1745)

ISAACS, Benjamin, and Elizabeth Woodfield, both of A. A. Co., were
married Sunday evening last, by the Rev. Mr. Watkins. (Sept.
20, 1827)

ISRAEL, Arid, Clerk of the Baltimore County Court, died Tues., the
9th, after a lingering illness. (April 18, 1833)

JACK, negro, died Sun., 20th inst., at the plantation of George
Calvert, Esq., in P. G. Co., in his 120th year. (May 23,
1810)

JACKSON, Mrs. Ann, aged 83 years, and a relict of a Revolutionary

soldier of Annap., died Friday morning of an injury received
on the foot, which terminated in lockjaw. (Sept. 6, 1832)

JACKSON, Johnson, a ship carpenter, drowned last Sat. afternoon
[Sept. 1], in Kent Narrows. (Sept. 4, 1751)

JACKSON, Mrs. Rachel, wife of Andrew Jackson, President-elect of the
United States, died Dec. 22nd, at "The Hermitage," in her
62nd year. [Long obit is given.] (Jan. 15, 1829)

JACOB, Mr. David L., died in Annap., yesterday. (Aug. 6, 1829)

JACOB, Mr. Ezekiel, died Sun. last in his 50th year. He leaves a
widow and five children. (Jan. 10, 1805)

JACOB, Mrs. Nancy, relict of the late Ezekiel Jacob, died Sun. last
in her 84th year. She was one of the earliest members of the
Methodist Episcopal Church in this state. (Feb. 9, 1837)

JACOB, Samuel, of South River, died Mon. morning last. (July 5,
1806)

JACOB, Zachariah, of Balto. Co., died in Balto. on the 17th, in his
99th year. (June 26, 1811)

JAMES, Samuel, died Mon. [July 7]; of South River. (July 10, 1806)

JAQUES, John L., died near Vienna, Dor. Co., on 1st inst. (Oct. 13,
1825)

JARVIS, Mrs. Mary, widow of the late John Jarvis of Annap., died
Wed., 29th ult., at an advanced age. (June 6, 1833)

JARVIS, Nathan, departed this life on Sun. morning last [April 15],
in his 39th year; printer, of Annap. (April 18, 1810)

JAVIS [sic], John, an old inhabitant of Annap., died on Tues. morning
last [Sept. 15], at an advanced age. (Sept. 17, 1818)

JEFFERSON, Thomas, former President of the United States: obituary
notices of. (July 13, 1826)

JEMMY, negro, was executed Friday last at Port Tobacco, for poisoning
Mr. Chase. (July 10, 1755)

JENIFER, Daniel, of St. Thomas, Esq., died 16th inst., in Annap.,
in his 67th year. He held many important offices. (Nov. 18,
1790)

JENIFER, Daniel, of St. Thomas, died 14th inst., in Chas. Co. (May
23, 1790)

JENIFER, Mrs. Elizabeth, died Sun., Nov. 27, of a pleuritic fever,
wife of Mr. Daniel Jenifer, and eldest daughter of Walter
Hanson; aged 25 years. (Dec. 25, 1757)

JENIFER, Joseph, died in A. A. Co. on Friday last [Aug. 11]. (Aug.
15, 1810)

JENIFER, Mrs. Sarah, died Wed., 19th ult., wife of Dr. Daniel Jenifer
of Port Tobacco, in Chas. Co. (April 3, 1800)

JENINGS, the Hon. Edmund, died at Bath, Eng., formerly of Annap.;
lawyer, formerly a member of His Lordship's Council of
State, and Secretary of the Province. (June 24, 1756)

JENKINS, Mr. Augustine, and Miss Araminta Wootton, all of South
River, were married Thurs., 11th inst., by the Rev. Mr.
Watkins. (May 25, 1826)

JENKINS, Thomas, and Elizabeth Day, all of A. A. Co., were married
Thurs. evening last, by the Rev. Mr. Watkins. (Feb. 21,
1833)

JENNINGS, James, of Annap., drowned off the mouth of the Magothy
on Friday last, en route from Annap. to Balto. (Feb. 28,
1793)

JENNINGS, Mr. Thomas, died Sun. last [Aug. 26] here; Chief Clerk
of the Land Office, and for a great many years, in the
commission of the Peace for A. A. Co. (Aug. 30, 1759)
Rebecca Jennings is administratrix. (Nov. 8, 1759)

JENTLE, Jonathan, died Sun., 29th ult., at the head of South River.
(Feb. 16, 1832)

JEWELL, Mr. Joseph, of Annap., died suddenly, Sat. last, leaving a
widow and two children. (Nov. 28, 1833)

JOBSON, Mr. Thomas, died last Friday [May 19], at his plantation on
Patuxent River, in A. A. Co., in his 56th year; formerly an
inhabitant of, and one of the Common Council men of, Annap.
For nearly 30 years successively he was chosen Sergeant at
Arms to the Hon. Lower House of the Assembly. (May 24, 1749)

JOE, mulatto, was executed 1st inst., in Cecil Co., for the murder
of his master. (Feb. 13, 1751)

JOHNS, Capt. Isaac, died on his passage from London, 12 days after
sailing from England. He leaves here a sorrowful young widow
and one child. His ship, of which he was late Commander,
arrived in Patowmack with convicts. (Oct. 3, 1754)

JOHNS, John, died 18th inst., at West River, in his 64th year; a
veteran of the Revolutionary War. (Aug. 29, 1822)

JOHNS, Kensey, Esq., died Thurs. last [May 26], at his house at West
    River; High Sheriff of that county [A. A.]; aged no more than
    42 years. (June 2, 1763)

JOHNSON, Capt. Archibald, formerly of Annap., on 3rd inst. was
    unfortunately drowned in the Nanticoke River. (July 12, 1764)

JOHNSON, Col. Baker, died at Frederick-Town, on 18th inst. (July
    3, 1811)

JOHNSON, Elisha, and Miss Anne Mills, all of Herring Creek, were
    married Sun. [May 25], by the Rev. Mr. Compton. (May 29,
    1806)

JOHNSON, Mrs. Elizabeth, consort of Dr. Thomas W. Johnson, died on
    Sun., 29th March, in her 32nd year, leaving seven children.
    (April 9, 1829)

JOHNSON, James, merchant of Annap., died last Thurs. [Sept. 6], at
    the house of Mr. Maxwell, in Patuxent; aged 30 years. (Sept.
    13, 1759) George Maxwell and Robert Swan, administrators.
    (Sept. 20, 1759)

JOHNSON, Mr. John, inspector of St. Leonard's Creek warehouse, in
    Cal. Co., having crossed the creek in a canoe, in order to
    breakfast at his own dwelling, on the 4th inst., was seized
    with an apoplectic fit, as is supposed, just as he was going
    into the canoe. He was found dead, with his head at the
    edge of the water. He was a bachelor, 34 years old. (Oct.
    27, 1763)

JOHNSON, the Hon. John, Chancellor of this State, died Friday last.
    Having lately been appointed by the Executive of the State
    to be a Commissioner on the part of this state, to unite
    with the Virginia Commissioners in establishing a boundary
    line between Virginia and Maryland, he left home on the 27th
    and had proceeded as far as Hancock-Town, Wash. Co., where
    his death occurred. He leaves a widow and several small
    children. (Aug. 5, 1824)

JOHNSON, Mrs. Mary, aged 71, died in Annap., Thurs. last. (June 14,
    1832)

JOHNSON, Mrs. Ruth, died Mon. last, at the residence of Mrs. Carroll
    of Annap., in her [75th?] year. (June 19, 1828)

JOHNSON, Thomas, died owning a lot adjoining the Town Fence. Anyone
    wishing to rent the lot should apply to Mrs. Susanna Johnson.
    (Aug. 7, 1751)

JOHNSON, Thomas, Esq., one of the representatives of A. A. Co., and

Anne Jennings, daughter of the late Mr. Justice Jennings, were married Sun. evening last [Feb. 16], by the Rev. Mr. Read. (Feb. 20, 1766)

JOHNSON, Thomas, died on Tues. morning, 26th ult., at Rose Hill, the seat of John Grahame, near the close of his 87th year, a venerable patriot, and a native of Cal. Co. For the last 40 years he was a resident of Fred. Co. He was the first Governor of the State after the Declaration of Independence. His body was interred in the family burial vault, in the Episcopal burial ground of Frederick. (Nov. 18, 1819)

JOHNSON, Thomas, printer, died in Annap., on Sun. morning last. (Oct. 30, 1828)

JOHNSON, Mr. Zachariah, and Miss Priscilla Mace, all of Annap., were married Sun. evening last, by the Rev. George Wells. (Jan. 16, 1817)

JOHNSTON, Gabriel, Governor of North Carolina, died July 17th, at Eden House (From the Virginia Gazette of July 24). (Aug. 6, 1752)

JOHNSTON, George, Esq., died Friday last [Aug. 31], at Alexandria. an eminent practitioner of the law in Virginia and in this province. (Sept. 4, 1766)

JOICE, Abel, of A. A. Co., and Mary Jane Marriott, of Balto., were married in the latter city on Sun. morning, 1st inst., by Rev. Crosby. (Dec. 5, 1839)

JONES, Dr. Alfred, of Q. A. Co., and Eliza Gassaway of this city, were married in Annap., Tues. morning, by the Rev. John G. Blanchard. (May 20, 1830)

JONES, Benjamin, was killed Friday evening [Sept. 12], in a drunken frolic at Queen Anne Town, P. G. Co., leaving a wife and two small children. (Sept. 18, 1755)

JONES, Edward, and Elizabeth Ann Ball, all of A. A. Co., were married Thurs. evening, by the Rev. Mr. Waters. (June 7, 1832)

JONES, Mrs. Elizabeth, died Thurs., 31 July, wife of Charles Jones, of Mont. Co. (Sept. 11, 1788)

JONES, Mrs. Elizabeth, consort of Edward Jones of South River, died Wed., 27th ult. She leaves three daughters. (Dec. 5, 1839)

JONES, Rev. Mr. Hugh, died 8th inst., in Cecil Co., for a great number of years rector of St. Stephen's Parish there, which last July resigned to his nephew, the Rev. William Barroll. (Sept. 18, 1760)

JONES, Capt. John, of the sloop Unity, of Balto. Town, died of ill
treatment received after his ship was taken on the voyage to
Jamaica, and carried to Cape Tiberoom. (May 4, 1758)

JONES, Mrs. Margaret, consort of Major Richard Jones, died 28th ult.,
leaving five young children. (Dec. 1, 1825)

JONES, Nathan A., of Wash. City, and Ann Eliza, daughter of George
Stewart, Esq., of A. A. Co., were married on Tues., by the
Rev. Mr. Maud. (April 18, 1833)

JONES, Philip, Jr., son of Capt. Philip Jones, Sr., on Thurs. last
[Oct. 5], being the first day of the Balto. Fair, as some
people were riding a race towards evening, Jones, a very
hopeful youth, who was one of those who fell off his horse
when in full speed, and died in a few minutes, without
speaking a word. (Oct. 11, 1749)

JONES, Capt. Philip, died Sat. last [March 10], at his plantation
on the north side of Severn, in his 80th year. (March 15,
1753)

JONES, R. I. C., and Mary G., daughter of Louis C. Pascault, Esq.,
all of Kent Island, Q. A. Co., were married at Bellevue, on
4th inst., by the Rev. Mr. Carey. (Sept. 13, 1838)

JONES, Major-General Samuel, died 15th ult. in Port Tobacco, in his
49th year; a member of the General Assembly of Maryland, from
Chas. Co. At an early period in life he entered into the
army at the commencement of the American struggle for liberty,
and served as an officer until very near the end of the war,
when circumstances forced him to retire. He has for some
time past held the commission of Major-General in the Militia
of the State, and for the last four years has been a member
of the House of Delegates. (Feb. 2, 1804)

JONES, Walter M., Esq., of Mulberry Fields, died Friday last, in his
24th year, leaving a widow and three young children. (Aug.
28, 1823)

JORDAN, John Morton, died July 23rd, in Bermudas, where he sailed
June 13, for a change of air; some time Agent for the Lord
Proprietary of this province. He leaves a wife and son.
(Sept. 26, 1771) Reuben Meriwether, administrator. (March
4, 1773)

JOURNEY, Sabret, of South River, died 28th ult., leaving a large
family. (May 4, 1837)

JOYCE, John, died on Tues. morning last [Dec. 19], at his residence
in A. A. Co., in his 25th year. (Dec. 21, 1815)

JUBB, James, and Ann E. Rockhold, all of A. A. Co., were married on
Thurs. evening last, by the Rev. Dr. Hammond. (May 12, 1836)

JURNEY, Richard H., and Elizabeth Carr, all of A. A. Co., were married
Thurs., 23rd inst., by Rev. Thomas G. Waters. (May 30, 1839)

KANE, Capt. John, and Miss Dorothy Seward, of Dor. Co., were married
Sun. evening last, by the Rev. Mr. Watkins. (Oct. 11, 1832)

KARNEY, Major Thomas, died in Annap., Friday last, 18th inst., in
his 57th year. He was born in Armagh, Ireland, on Dec. 25,
1777, and emigrated to the United States in June, 1801.
During the war with Great Britain he was commissioned by
President Madison as a First Lieut. in the 14th Regt. of
U. S. infantry. He was Auditor-General of Maryland. He
leaves a widow and a large family of children. (July 24,
1834)

KEATINGE, George, of Westminster, Fred. Co., and Miss Mary Ann Caton,
of Annap., were married in this city on Mon. last [July 14],
by the Rev. Mr. Watkins. (July 17, 1817)

KEENE, Mr. Lawrence, of the U. S. Navy, and Miss Maria Martin, eldest
daughter of Luther Martin, Esq., of Balto., were married in
that city on Friday evening, by the Rev. Mr. Inglis. (April
21, 1808)

KEITH, Mrs. Anne, died on Mon. morning last [Feb. 16], in an advanced
age. (Feb. 21, 1805)

KELLY, John, of Thames St., Fells Point, Balto., died 7th July, of
a fever. (July 29, 1802)

KEMP, Mrs. Elizabeth, consort of the Right Rev. James Kemp, died in
Balto., on 14th inst. (Aug. 17, 1826)

KEMP, Right Rev. James, Bishop of the Protestant Episcopal Diocese
of Maryland, died Sun., 28th ult., at his residence in
Balto. (Nov. 1, 1827)

KEMP, Joseph, and Miss Frances Richards, were married Sun., [Feb.
15], by the Rev. Mr. Wyatt. (Feb. 19, 1807)

KENNALL, William Alexander, and Eleanor Walter Wilson, all of Som.
Co., were married Aug. 2nd, in Spring Hill Church, Som. Co.,
by Rev. Richard J. Waters. (Aug. 10, 1837)

KENNEDY, Thomas, died; for many years he had been in the House of
Delegates or Senate of Maryland, and at the time of his
death was in the House of Delegates. (Oct. 25, 1832)

KENT, DeWitt, Esq., of P. G. Co., and Miss Juliana Sudler, were

married Tues. morning, at Bellefield, north side of Severn,
by Rev. Dr. Henshaw. (Oct. 9, 1834)

KENT, Mrs. Eleanor Lee, consort of His Excellency, Joseph Kent, the
Governor of this State, died in P. G. Co., on Mon., 14th
inst., in her 45th year. (Aug. 17, 1826)

KENT, the Hon. Joseph, Governor of the State of Maryland, and Miss
Alice Lee Contee, only daughter of the late H. B. Contee,
were married at Bromont, Chas. Co., by the Rev. Mr. Marr.
(July 24, 1828)

KENT, Dr. Joseph, the beloved and respected Senator of the United
States from Maryland, and formerly Governor of Maryland, died
yesterday, killed by a fall from his horse. (From the Washington, D.C., National Intelligencer) (Nov. 30, 1837)

KENT, Mrs. Mary Anne, consort of Col. Robert W. Kent, died on Friday
last at her residence on South River. (Feb. 28, 1828)

KENT, Capt. Robert, of P. G. Co., and Miss Mary Ann Maccubbin, of
Annap., were married on Tues. evening last [June 7], by the
Rev. Mr. Nind. (June 9, 1814)

KENT, Robert, son of the Hon. Joseph Kent, late Governor of Maryland,
died Sun. evening last, 15th inst., in Lancaster, in his 19th
year. He had been but a few weeks resident in our city, and
had just commenced the study of law under Mr. Buchanan. (From
the Lancaster Journal) (May 26, 1831)

KENT, Thomas R., Esq., and Sarah O., eldest daughter of the late
Gov. Martin, were married 1st inst., at the Wilderness, in
Tal. Co. (Nov. 9, 1837)

KENT, Wallace, third son of the Hon. Joseph Kent, Governor of Maryland, died 9th inst., at the residence of his father in P.
G. Co., in his 16th year. (Nov. 16, 1826)

KERBY, Mr. George, of A. A. Co., and Miss Rebecca Fowler, of Annap.,
were married on Sun. evening last [Oct. 20], by the Rev. Mr.
Ryland. (Oct. 24, 1811)

KERR, Capt. Archibald, and Mrs. Henrietta Maria Sterrett, both of
Balto., were married in Annap., on the 30th ult., by the Rev.
Mr. Wells. (Dec. 8, 1825)

KEY, Mrs., relict of the late Philip Key, died a few days ago in
St. M. Co. (April 16, 1772)

KEY, Mrs. Ann, died Thurs., 18th inst., widow of the late Philip
Barton Key, of George-Town. (Dec. 25, 1834)

KEY, Mrs. Ann Arnold, relict of the late Francis Key, of Cecil Co.,
   died on the 5th inst., at the seat of Henry Maynadier, in her
   84th year. (Jan. 30, 1811)

KEY, Mrs. Ann Pheobe, relict of the late John Ross Key, died on Thurs.,
   8th inst., in her 74th year, at the house of R. B. Taney, Esq.,
   in Balto. Her husband was a resident of Fred. Co. (July 15,
   1830)

KEY, Edmund, died on Sun. last [May 4], at Upper Marlborough, P. G.
   Co., Attorney General of this Province, and one of the representatives for St. M. Co. (May 8, 1766) Thomas Key of St.
   M. Co., was elected a representative for that county in
   the room of his brother Edmund. (June 26, 1766)

KEY, Francis, of St. M. Co., and Anne Arnold Ross, eldest daughter
   of John Ross, Esq., of Annap., were married. (Dec. 14, 1752)

KEY, Francis, Clerk of Cecil Co., died a few days ago at Charles-Town,
   of an inflammatory fever. (Nov. 22, 1770)

KEY, Francis S., of the U. S. N., and Miss Elizabeth Lloyd, daughter
   of Henry H. Harwood, of Annap., were married in Balto., on
   5th inst., by the Rev. Mr. Shane. (April 13, 1826)

KEY, the Hon. Philip, died at his seat in St. M. Co., in his 68th
   year, on Mon., 20th inst. (Aug. 30, 1764)

KEY, Philip Barton, died a few days since of pleurisy, at Chester-
   Town, on his journey home from Northward; late Sheriff of
   St. M. Co. (Dec. 2, 1756)

KEY, Philip Barton, died on the 28th ult., at his seat near George-
   Town. He sat as a representative in the 10th, 11th, and
   12th Congresses from the adjoining district of Maryland.
   As a lawyer he stood in the first rank of his profession;
   as a gentleman he was greatly respected, even by those who
   admired him least as a politician. (Aug. 17, 1815)

KEY, Capt. Richard Ward, died Wed. last [April 10], in St. M. Co.,
   after a long illness, clerk of that county. (April 18, 1765)

KEY, Thomas, died in St. M. Co., only surviving son of the late
   Philip Key, and one of the representatives of that county.
   (April 2, 1772)

KEYS, Francis, constable, died last Thurs., as a result of eating
   mushrooms he had gathered. (Aug. 15, 1765)

KILGOUR, the Hon. Charles J., died Tues. morning last, Associate
   Judge of the Judicial District comprising Mont., A. A.,
   Cal., and Carroll Counties. (Aug. 31, 1837)

KILMAN, Nicholas, and Miss Sarah Whitney, both of Annap., were married
Sun. evening last by the Rev. Mr. Bartow. (April 29, 1830)

KILTY, Mrs. Elizabeth, consort of William Kilty, Esq., Chancellor
of Maryland, departed this life on Wed., 21st inst. (Oct.
29, 1807)

KILTY, Mr. George A., died at La Guayra, in his 20th year. He was
a native of Annap., and a son of the late Capt. John Kilty.
(Aug. 4, 1825)

KILTY, John, died Mon. evening last [May 27], late Register of the
Land Office for the Western Shore of Maryland. (May 29, 1811)

KILTY, the Hon. William, Chancellor of this State, departed this life
yesterday morning, in the 64th year of his age. (Oct. 11,
1821)

KILTY, William, printer, died Sat. last, in the 27th year of his
age. The order of I. O. F. attended his funeral. (May 19,
1836)

KILTY, William, Esq., died Friday night last, at the residence of
James Miller near this city. (Aug. 16, 1838)

KIMBER, John, mate of Capt. Martin, lately drowned in Chester
River. (Dec. 9, 1746)

KING, Mrs. Elizabeth, wife of Mr. William King, died Tues., 12th
inst., at George-Town in Mont. Co. She was an affectionate
wife and a dutiful daughter. (Feb. 28, 1793)

KING, Levin R., Esq., died in Som. Co., aged 49. (Dec. 8, 1825)

KING, Robert, Jr., died in Wor. Co., Clerk of that county. (April
9, 1752)

KING, Robert, accidentally drowned at George-Town, Fred. Co., on
Tues. last week [June 19], a man who had a wife and six
children. (June 28, 1764)

KING, Mr. Thomas, and Miss Mary Hardesty, both of Annap., were
married in Balto., on Sun. evening last, by the Rev. Dr.
Jennings. (April 21, 1825)

KING, Thomas, a Revolutionary Soldier, died yesterday morning, in
his 76th year. (March 29, 1832)

KIRBY, Mrs. Mary, wife of William Kirby, died in Annap. She leaves
two children. (Jan. 5, 1832)

KIRBY, Mr. Samuel, and Eleanor Ann Hunter, were married Sun. last,
by Rev. Mr. Riley. (May 28, 1829)

KIRBY, William, and Mary Taylor, all of Annap., were married Thurs., 29th ult., by the Rev. Mr. Smith. (Oct. 6, 1825)

KIRBY, Mr. William, of Annap., and Miss Ann Malonee, of A. A. Co., were married in Annap., on Thurs. evening last, by the Rev. Mr. Gere. (Oct. 24, 1833)

KNAPP, John, died in the city of Washington on the 31st ult., for many years a clerk in the office of the Comptroller of the Treasury. (Aug. 10, 1820)

KNIGHT, Alexander, overseer of Mr. Bordley, last Monday se'ennight was driving his cart home from town, when it accidentally ran over him, and bruised him so much that he died soon after. (Jan. 24, 1750)

KNIGHT, Mr. William, died on Thurs. last [April 17], in Cecil Co., after a short illness; Clerk and Deputy Commissary for that county. (April 23, 1746)

KNIGHT, William, and Mrs. Elizabeth Young, were married Thurs. evening last, by the Rev. Mr. Wyatt. (March 5, 1807)

KNIGHTON, John, died Sat., 29th Sept., after a short illness, aged 23 years. (Oct. 4, 1838)

KNOX, General, died October 25, 1806; "Boston, November 4." (Nov. 20, 1806)

LAFAYETTE, [Marquis de], the last surviving General of the Army of the Revolution, died. (June 26, 1834)

LAFAYETTE, Madame, died at Paris on Dec. 24, 1807. (March 3, 1808)

LAKE, Rev. Mr. Charles, died at Wye River, on the last day of July, at an advanced age; Rector of St. James Parish, and formerly rector of this parish. (Aug. 16, 1764)

de L'ALLIE, M. Nyol, died Sun. last, Aug. 1st, long a teacher of the French language at St. John's College. He never exceeded the bounds of that small pittance allowed him as a tutor. (Aug. 5, 1802)

LAMARDE, John, committed suicide while a prisoner in the Baltimore County jail. (Dec. 18, 1817)

LAMB, John, and Ann Norman, all of Annap., were married on Sun. evening last, by the Rev. Mr. Wells. (July 27, 1826)

LAMB, John, blacksmith, formerly of Annap., died Mon., 19th inst., at an advanced age. Lately he had resided in A.A. Co. (June 19, 1834)

LAMB, Mrs. Margaret, of Annap., died Friday evening last. (Aug. 24, 1837)

LAMB, Thomas, on Thurs. last had a sentence of death passed on him by the Provincial Court, for murder of a mulatto. (May 5, 1747). We hear he was executed 13th inst., in P. G. Co.

LAMBDIN, Mr. Thomas, died Thurs. morning last. (Dec. 29, 1831)

LANDMAN, Mr. Thomas, and Mrs. Susan Shephard, all of Annap., were married Sunday evening last, by the Rev. Mr. Griffith. (Feb. 10, 1825)

LANE, Mrs. Mary, a native of Cal. Co., but for the last 10 years a resident of Annap., died Wed., 16th inst. She leaves a son and two daughters. (March 24, 1831)

LANE, Nathan, of A. A. Co., and Miss Mary Williamson, of Cal. Co., were married on Thurs. evening (April 13), by the Rev. Mr. Compton. (April 19, 1809)

LANG, Rev. Mr. John, died last Mon., in the evening, rector of St. James Parish, A.A. Co. (Sept. 28, 1748)

LANSDALE, Thomas, of A. A. Co., and Harriet, second daughter of the late Dr. Samuel Franklin of P. G. Co., were married Thurs. evening last in P. G. Co., by the Rev. Mr. Mackenheimer. (Dec. 18, 1834)

LAPEAR, Matthew, was executed this day for breaking open and robbing the store of Dr. James Walker, near Patapsco Ferry. (Sept. 21, 1748)

LARK, James, and Miss Mary Ann Heath, all of A. A. Co., were married the 4th of July, by Rev. N. J. Watkins. (July 16, 1835)

LASHLY, George, last week, a somewhat weak-minded, was drowned as the result of a practical joke, in Cecil Co. He leaves a wife and seven children, the eldest not eleven years old. (Sept. 18, 1760)

LATIMER, Randolph B., died at his plantation in Chas. Co., on Mon. evening [July 8]. (July 18, 1805)

LAURENSON, William, ran away from his master some time ago. A body presumed to be his was found (recently) in South River. (June 6, 1754)

LAWRENCE, Benjamin, planter of Elk Ridge, died last Saturday [Jan. 4], when walking across a field with a pipe in his mouth; he fell forward, ran the pipe stem into the roof of his mouth. (Jan. 9, 1755)

LAWSON, Mr. Alexander, died last week at his house in Balto. Town, after a long and tedious indisposition of the Gout. (Oct. 23, 1760)

LAWSON, Mr. Alexander, a young gentleman of Balto., and Elizabeth Brown, only daughter of Mr. Charles Brown, of Q. A. Co., were married a few days ago. (Jan. 20, 1763)

LAWSON, the Misses Dorothy, Elizabeth, and Margaret, daughters of Alexander Lawson, drowned four days ago, when the ice broke on their father's furnace pond, at his iron works in Balto. Co. (Dec. 28, 1752)

LE COMPTE, Benjamin W., for many years an able and faithful repre- sentative of Dor. Co., in the State Legislature, died at Cambridge, on the 22nd inst., in his 35th year. (Nov. 29, 1821)

LE COMPTE, Mr. Thomas D., aged 39, a native of the Eastern Shore of Md., died at the residence of Col. H. Runnels, in this town on Friday, 6th inst. (Monticello, Miss., paper). (Sept. 9, 1830)

LEE, Capt. Arthur, died last Sun. evening [July 13], in Chas. Co.; one of the Representatives for that county. (July 17, 1760)

LEE, Edward, and Miss Juliana, daughter of William Collison, were married Thurs. evening last in A. A. Co., by the Rev. Mr. Watkins. (Sept. 13, 1827)

LEE, Francis, died last week in Cecil Co.; Clerk of that county. (Oct. 4, 1749)

LEE, Mrs. Grace, relict of the late Hon. Richard Lee, died at Blen- heim, on the 16th inst., aged about 76. (Oct. 29, 1789)

LEE, Mr. Hancock, merchant of Nottingham, died Sun., 4th inst., at Upper Marlborough, after a tedious illness. (Nov. 15, 1759)

LEE, Major-General Henry, died March 25th, in his 61st year, at the house of a friend on Cumberland Island, Ga., on his return from the West Indies to his native state, Virginia. He was a conspicuous officer in the Revolutionary army...[A long obit gives details of his military career, and the public offices he held since the Revolution.]. He leaves behind him a valuable historical work entitled "Memoirs of the War in the Southern Department of the United States." (April 23, 1818)

LEE, Rev. Jesse, departed this life, on the 12th inst., at Hills- borough, on the Eastern Shore of Md., in his 59th year, late chaplain to Congress, and for 33 years a respectable itinerant preacher among the Methodists. He was interred at the Methodist graveyard in Balto., at his own request. (Sept. 26, 1816)

LEE, Mrs. Mary, died at George-Town, 21st ult.; the lady of Thomas Sim Lee, Esq. (Feb. 7, 1805)

LEE, Hon. Richard, Esq., died at Blenheim, Chas. Co., on Jan. 26, in his 81st year. (Feb. 15, 1787)

LEE, Russell, died at Blenheim, in Chas. Co., 4th ult., only surviving son of the late Philip Thomas Lee, in his 18th year. His death was occasioned by a fall from his horse the day before. He was buried in the family burial ground of his ancestors. (Oct. 3, 1793)

LEE, Mr. Stephen, Sr., of South River, A. A. Co., died Thurs. night last, 26th inst. (Jan. 31, 1833)

LEE, Stephen Lewis, and Miss Caroline Elizabeth Stockett Duncan, all of South River, were married Friday night last, by Rev. Nicholas I. Watkins. (July 25, 1833)

LEE, Hon. Thomas, President of the Colony of Virginia, died there 13th inst. (Nov. 21, 1750)

LEE, Thomas Sim, died on Tues., the 9th, at Needwood, Fred. Co., in his 75th year of age. He bore a conspicuous part in the arduous struggle for independence. He was the second Governor of Maryland, and was immediate successor of the late Governor Johnson. (Nov. 18, 1819)

LEGG, Mrs. Hester, consort of William Legg, of South River, A. A. Co., died Friday last, in her 37th year. She leaves a husband and five children. [Long obit.] (April 16, 1829)

LEGG, Mrs. Prudence, died in Annap., Tues., 27th ult., in her 58th year. (Sept. 5, 1833)

LEIDLER, John, was thrown from his horse and killed in Chas. Co., on the 7th inst. (Dec. 16, 1773)

LENDRUM, Lieut. Thomas W., of the U. S. Army, and Maria, daughter of the late John Callahan, Esq., were married in Annap. on Friday, by the Rev. Mr. Blanchard. (July 19, 1827)

LESTER, Capt., master of the ship Friends' Adventure, which arrived in Patuxent a few days ago, died on his passage. (May 20-May 27, 1729)

LE VACHER, Mrs. Anne, died in Balto., 9th inst., in her 86th year. (March 16, 1837)

LEVELY, Mr. John S., formerly of Balto., died yesterday morning in this city. (Oct. 25, 1821)

LEVY, Mrs. Anne, wife of Jacob Levy, and daughter of Mrs. Jane Maggs of Balto., died in that city on Thurs. last [Dec. 8], in her 23rd year. (Dec. 15, 1808)

LEWIS, Mrs. Eliz., died Thurs. evening last [March 15], at Hackett's Point, in her 27th year. (March 21, 1810)

LEWIS, John, on Sat. last [Oct. 3], was thrown from his horse, and killed, in Dor. Co. (Oct. 7, 1747)

LEWIS, the Hon. John, on Thurs., 17th inst., died of the gout in his stomach, at his house in Gloster Co. [Va.]...for many years one of His Majesty's Council for the Province of Va.; "Williamsburg, Jan. 25." (Feb. 7, 1754)

LEWIS, Capt. John, late Commander of the ship Eagle of London (which arrived in Choptank after a passage of 13 weeks), died on his passage. (Aug. 9, 1764)

LIGHTFOOT, Michael, Esq., died Thurs. last [Nov. 26] here,...our Provincial Treasurer. Yesterday, Dr. Samuel Preston Moore was appointed by the General Assembly in his stead. (Dec. 12, 1754)

LINCOLN, Maj.-Gen. Benjamin, late collector of the port of Boston, died at his seat at Higham, Mass., on the 9th inst. (May 23, 1810)

LINGAN, General, was murdered in Balto. His remains were conveyed to the vicinity of George-Town, where they were interred. The murder was a "monument to Jacobin intolerance and perfidy." (Dec. 2, 1813)

LINGAN, Mr. Nicholas, merchant of George-Town, and Miss Ann Hanson of Chas. Co. were married Thurs. last. (Oct. 22, 1789)

LINSTEAD, William, a respectable citizen of A. A. Co., was found dead Tues. morning in the Basin near the City Dock (From the Balto. American). (April 19, 1832)

LINTHICUM, Miss, daughter of Hezekiah Linthicum, drowned Sun., on the South River. (July 2, 1767)

LINTHICUM, Abner, Sr., and Mrs. Elizabeth Pitcher, were married 2nd inst., by the Rev. Mr. French. (Dec. 18, 1828)

LINTHICUM, Mr. Stephen, died Tues. last, on the north side of Severn. (Sept. 17, 1829)

LISLE, Tobias, Esq., Governor of Gambia, went from this Province last
Summer for London in the Princess of Gambia. He had the mis-
fortune to fall overboard, and although he was presently got
on board again, he expired soon after. (Dec. 11, 1760)

LITTLE, Col. Peter, died Friday last, at his residence in Balto. Co.
(Feb. 11, 1830)

LITTLETON, Rev. Thomas, died at his residence, Sweet Spring, in this
county on 19th inst., in his 73rd year. He was born in London, and served in the Revolutionary War. He joined the
Methodist Episcopal Church a short time before the Revolution.
(Sept. 9, 1830)

LIVINGSTON, Edward, and Marie-Louise-Magdeline-Valentine-Davezac-
Castra Moreau, widow of the late Louis Moreau de Lassy, were
married at New Orleans, 4th June, by the Rev. Father Walsh.
(July 11, 1805)

LIVINGSTON, Rev. William, died in Balto., Rector and Founder of the
First African Protestant Episcopal Church in Balto. (May 18,
1837)

LLEWELLIN, Mr. Richard, died of the small pox on Tues. last [June
22], in Q. A. Co., on his return home from Philadelphia,
where he had been on a party of pleasure; the eldest son of
Mr. John Llewellin of St. M. Co. (June 24, 1762)

LLOYD, Mrs. Alicia, wife of Edward Lloyd, Esq., died at Wye House,
Sun., 8th inst., in her 32nd year. (From the Easton Advo-
cate). (July 12, 1838)

LLOYD, Mrs. Anna Maria, died on Tues., 30th of last month; the consort of Robert Lloyd, Esq., and one of the daughters of the
late Hon. Richard Tilghman. (Sept. 8, 1763)

LLOYD, Daniel, Esq., youngest son of Col. Edward Lloyd, of Tal. Co.,
and Miss Virginia Upshur, were married Thurs. last by Rev.
Mr. Blanchard. (Nov. 29, 1832)

LLOYD, Edward, who rented a small house and tract of land in Q. A.
Co., was killed by lightning, on Wed. morning last week
[May 15]. (May 23, 1754)

LLOYD, Edward, of this Province, and Elizabeth Tayloe, eldest daughter of the Hon. John Tayloe, Esq., of Va., were married 12th
ult. (Dec. 10, 1767)

LLOYD, Col. Edward, Esq., died at his seat on Wye River, in Tal. Co.;
formerly one of His Lordship's Council of State, and Agent
and Receiver General for this Province. (Feb. 8, 1770)

LLOYD, Edward, Jr., Esq., of Tal. Co., and Alicia, eldest daughter
of Mr. M'Blair, were married in Balto., on Tues., 30th ult.,
by the Rev. Dr. Glendy. (Dec. 9, 1824)

LLOYD, Mrs. Elizabeth, died in Annap. on Thurs., in her 75th year.
She was buried on Wye Farm. [Long obit.] (Feb. 24, 1825)

LLOYD, Robert, Esq., of Q. A. Co., Speaker of the Lower House of the
Assembly, died Mon., 16th inst. (July 19, 1770)

LOMAS, John, died in Liverpool last winter; for many years an
inhabitant of Annap. (June 30, 1757)

LOOCKERMAN, Mr. Richard, of Tal. Co., and Miss Fanny Chase, daughter
of J. T. Chase, Esq., of Annap., were married Sat. evening.
(Oct. 6, 1803)

LOOCKERMAN, Richard, of Annap., died 11th inst., at his farm in
Caroline Co. (Nov. 13, 1834)

LOOCKERMAN, William, one of the owners of the Annapolis packet, was
drowned Friday last off the mouth of the Magothy on Friday
last en route from Annap. to Balto. (Feb. 28, 1793)

LOTHIAN, Alexander, died Sat. last, Jan. 28, in St. M. Co., in his
43rd year. (Feb. 16, 1769)

LOWE, Hon. Nicholas: elegy on his death. (Dec. 24, 1728)

LOWE, Mr. Stead, and Miss Laetitia Young, daughter of the late
Benjamin Young, Esq., were married Tuesday last week [Aug.
9]. (Aug. 18, 1757)

LOWNDES, Lieut. Charles of the U. S. Navy, and Sarah S., second
daughter of Edward Lloyd, Esq., were married on the evening
of 4th inst., at Wye House, Tal. Co., by Rev. Hodgkiss.
(May 18, 1826)

LOWNDES, Charistopher, merchant of Bladensburg, and Elizabeth, third
daughter of the Hon. Benjamin Tasker, were married last Thurs.
(May 19, 1747)

LUCAR, John, and his half-aunt Catherine Clinton, were married at
Middleton (Monmouth) a few weeks ago. The bride was a widow,
daughter of Thomas Tilton, who married John's sister Mary
Lucar. (From the Trenton Federalist). (March 13, 1800)

LUCAS, Miss Elizabeth, of Annap., died Friday last, at the residence of Col. Boyle. (Jan. 11, 1838)

LUCAS, Capt. James, of the ship Friendship, died a few days ago,
at Balto., lately from Rotterdam, with Palatines. (Nov.
23, 1752)

LUCAS, Robert, a founder, was drowned on Tues. last [Oct. 7], on Bodkin Point. (Oct. 14, 1746)

LUCKETT, Mr., died in a powder magazine explosion at Fort Cumberland.
(Oct. 19, 1758)

LUSBY, Mrs., of Kent Co., was drowned Wed. last, 28 July, at the
mouth of the Chester River, below Poole's Island. (Aug. 5,
1773)

LUSBY, Miss Anne, died in Annapolis, on Friday last. (Aug. 11, 1825)

LUSBY, Eli, and Elizabeth Sanders, both of A. A. Co., were married
Tues. evening last, by the Rev. N. I. Watkins. (Jan. 14,
1830)

LUSBY, Eli, and Sophia D. Journey, of A. A. Co., were married on
Thurs. last, by Rev. N. J. Watkins. (April 4, 1839)

LUSBY, James, died Wed., 7th ult., in his 35th year; a resident of
Annap. (Sept. 8, 1808)

LUSBY, Robert, died at his residence in A. A. Co., on Tues., at an
advanced age. (Sept. 8, 1831)

LUX, Capt. Darby, died Sun. night last [Oct. 14], of pleurisy, in
his 53rd year; a resident of Baltimore Town. He was a Magistrate and Representative. (Oct. 17, 1750)

LUX, Mr. Darby, merchant of Barbadoes, and Rachel Ridgely, who has
a fortune of £ 2000 sterling, were married last week in
Balto. Co. (Nov. 15, 1764)

LYLES, David C., died in the village of Friendship, Md., on Sat.,
5th inst., in his 46th year. (Dec. 10, 1835)

LYNCH, Samuel, and Angelica Williams, all of A. A. Co., were married
on Thurs. last, by Rev. Mr. Watkins. (Feb. 1, 1838)

LYNN, ---, son of Mr. Lynn, of Fred. Co., was found dead and scalped,
as were two boys living near Lawrence Wilson's in that county.
(March 4, 1756)

LYNN, Capt. David, died at his residence in Cumberland, 11th inst.,
in his 78th year; a soldier of the Revolution. [Long obit
is given.] (April 23, 1835)

LYONS, the Hon. Peter, President of the Court of Appeals of the
Commonwealth of Virginia, died at his seat in Hanover Co.,
in the 75th year of his age. (Aug. 16, 1809)

M'ALWAIN, Mrs., a young married lady from Fred. Co., died in a fire

at the house of Mrs. Key, near Carpenter's Point. Mrs. M'Alwain had lived with Mrs. Key as a child, and had intended to
lie in with her first child. (Nov. 2, 1775)

McBLAIR, Lyde Goodwin, of Balto., and Matilda Chase Loockerman, of
Annap., were married Thurs. evening last, by Rev. Dr. Humphreys.
(Jan. 30, 1834)

M'CAULEY, Mrs. Ann, departed this life on Tues., 22nd inst., in her
83rd year, in A. A. Co. (July 1, 1813)

MACAULEY, Miss Ann, died in A. A. Co., on 22nd Sept. (Oct. 9, 1828)

MACAULEY, Miss Mary, died Friday last, in A. A. Co. (Nov. 29, 1832)

M'CENEY, Joseph, died Thurs., 2nd inst., at his residence in A. A.
Co., in his 50th year. He was Sheriff of the County for
five years. In one year he lost his two oldest sons. He
leaves a widow and five children. (Oct. 9, 1823)

McCOY, Morris, was executed on the gallows near this city yesterday.
(Jan. 24, 1771)

MACCUBBIN, Charles L., died in Annap. on Tues. morning last; he
was Assistant Clerk of the Senate of this state. His body
was yesterday committed to the grave with military and masonic
honors. (Jan. 22, 1824)

MACCUBBIN, Mrs. Eleanor, relict of the late John Maccubbin, of A. A.
Co., died Wed., 8th inst., at her residence in Annap., in
her 70th year. (Oct. 16, 1828)

MACCUBBIN, John C., formerly of this city, died Thurs. last, in
Balto. (Oct. 1, 1829)

MACCUBBIN, Mrs. Mary Ann, died Sat., 5th inst.; the late consort of
Samuel Maccubbin, Esq., of West River, in her 65th year.
She was one of the earliest and oldest members of the Metho-
dist Episcopal Church. (Dec. 10, 1835)

MACCUBBIN, Moses, died Friday evening last, in his 57th year. (Oct.
25, 1832)

MACCUBBIN, Nicholas, merchant of Annap., and Mary, only daughter of
Dr. Charles Carroll, of Annap., were married Tues. last
[July 21]. (July 28, 1747)

MACCUBBIN, Samuel, died 27th inst., in his 75th year. (Nov. 29,
1838)

MACCUBBIN, William; on Thurs. last, his body was found dead near

the Calverton Mills. The deceased was about 19 years old,
the son of Mr. Moses Maccubbin of Balto. A coroner's jury
brought in a verdict of willful murder. "Balto., Oct. 25."
(Nov. 6, 1817)

McCULLOCH, Mr. David, merchant, and Mary, eldest daughter of Mr.
James Dick, merchant, were married yesterday at London-Town,
by Rev. Mr. Deans. (July 5, 1759)

McCULLOCH, Mr. James, died 13th inst., in his 66th year, at Roe-
Down, the residence of his sister, Mrs. Brogden. [Long obit
is given.] (Nov. 16, 1826)

McCULLOH, Anthony, merchant, died Sun. last, Feb. 18, at Queens
Town, in Q. A. Co. (Feb. 22, 1770)

M'DONALD, Mrs. Elizabeth, died in Annap., on the night of 9th inst.
(July 24, 1823)

M'DONALD, James, of Fred. Co., froze to death, while riding home from
a drinking party on Christmas Eve. (Jan. 10, 1760)

MacDONOUGH, Mrs. Lucy Ann, consort of Capt. Thomas MacDonough, of
the U. S. Navy, died at Middletown (Conn.) aged 35 years.
(Aug. 25, 1825)

M'ELDERRY, Thomas, died on the 27th inst. [May], in the City of
Baltimore; one of the Senators in the State Legislature.
(June 13, 1810)

McFARLANE, Mr. Alexander, of St. M. Co., was found drowned in the
Potomac River on Friday last [July 25]. (July 31, 1766)

McGILL, James, accidentally drowned last Mon. evening [Oct. 2].
(Oct. 25, 1753)

MacGILL, James, died Wed., Oct. 20, at Joppa, in Balto. Co.; of a
fever, in his 25th year, eldest son of Rev. James MacGill;
he was educated in the profession of physic. (Nov. 11, 1756)

M'GILL, Robert, of P. G. Co., and Miss Helen Stockett, of South River,
were married on Thurs. evening [May 21], by the Rev. Mr. Lane.
(June 28, 1804)

McGRATH, Christopher Charles, comedian, died Feb. 24, 1799, at Reading
Berks. Co., Penna.; lines on his death are published. (April
4, 1799)

M'GRATH, Rev. Owen, died on Thurs., the 8th, at Alexandria, Va.
(Feb. 26, 1810)

McGRATH, Mr. Patrick, Professor of Humanity at St. John's Coll.,
died last Sunday morning, 6th inst. (Sept. 10, 1795)

MACKALL, Benjamin, Jr., a Representative for Cal. Co., and Rebecca
Covington, of P. G. Co., were married Sat. last. (April 29,
1756)

MACKALL, Mr. James John, died Friday last [Jan. 3], formerly a Representative of Cal. Co. (Jan. 9, 1772)

M'KEAN, Thomas, LL. D., former Governor of the State of Pennsylvania,
died 24th ult. (July 3, 1817)

M'KENNIE, Donald, overseer of William Digges, was found murdered in
Balto. Co., on March 29. (April 3, April 10, 1751)

M'KENNY, Francis, was killed on Tues. last, at a horse race in Tal.
Co. Court House. One of the horses fell, and killed him.
(May 26, 1763)

M'KENZIE, James, died a Sun. last; a merchant, and a young gentleman of Glasgow. (Sept. 21, 1748)

McKIM, Isaac, a representative in Congress, died Mon. last, in
Baltimore. (April 5, 1838)

MACKLIN, William, fireman, was killed in a fire in Balto. ("Balto.
Chronicle, Feb. 26.") (March 5, 1835)

MACKUBBIN, John, was buried here last Sat., aged 88. He was born
in this county, and died of old age. (May 7, 1752)

MACKUBIN, Frederick, and Miss De Auchbrune, were married on Sun.
last [Dec. 12], by the Rev. Mr. Judd. (Dec. 15, 1808)

MACKUBIN, Mr. Frederick, on Tues. last, was killed on his farm, on
the North side of Severn, by the fall of a tree. He leaves
a young widow, two children, and his parents. (Feb. 1, 1816)

M'KUBIN, George, Esq., and Miss Eleanor Maccubbin, were married on
Tues. evening [Oct. 27], by the Rev. Mr. Nind. (Oct. 29, 1812)

MACKUBIN, James, Jr., and Miss Mary Ann Merriken, were married on
Thurs. 1st inst., by the Rev. Mr. Welch.(Dec. 15, 1808)

MACKUBIN, James, died 31st inst., at Bellefield, near Annap., in
his 75th year. He was Chief Judge of the Orphans Court.
He leaves an afflicted daughter and family. (Sept. 4, 1834)

MACKUBIN, Richard, died on the morning of the 8th inst., at his
residence in A. A. Co., in his 59th year; formerly a merchant
of Annap. (Nov. 15, 1821)

McLACHLAN, James, Esq., late of Kent Co., in this Province, died

lately at Newport, in Rhode Island. He was an upright and
active magistrate. [Long obit is given.] (Oct. 6, 1768)

McLEOD, Mrs. Elizabeth, widow, died Tues. evening last [Jan. 2], who
for many years kept a respectable and well frequented tavern
in this city. (Jan. 4, 1759) William Roberts and Robert
Couden are execs. (Jan. 11, 1759)

M'NEIR, George, and Miss Elizabeth Thompson, all of Annap., were
married (in Annap.) on Sun., 1st inst., by the Rev. Mr.
Wells. (Sept. 12, 1816)

McNEIR, George, died Sat., in his 79th year. He was born in Annap.,
but for the last 50 years had been a resident of the city.
(Jan. 25, 1838)

McNEIR, Thomas, died in Annap., on Sun. morning last, in his 39th
year. He leaves a widow and three small children. (June
26, 1828)

M'NEIR, William, of Annap., and Miss Mary Ann Maccubbin, were married
on Tues. evening last [April 17], in Balto., by the Rev. Mr.
Henshaw. (April 19, 1821)

MACNEMARA, Michael, Esq., died yesterday, after a lingering indisposition; for many years Clerk of the Lower House of Assembly,
and one of the Aldermen of the city. (Nov. 5, 1767)

McNULTY, William, was killed in a fire in Baltimore. ("Balto.
Chronicle, Feb. 26.") (March 5, 1835)

McPARLEN, Mr. George, died suddenly on Tues. (Jan. 8, 1829)

M'PARLIN, William M., and Miss Cassandra Woodward, of P. G. Co., were
married Sun. evening last, by the Rev. George Wells. The
groom was a resident of Annap. (Dec. 19, 1816)

M'PHERSON, Miss Catherine, died on the 23rd (March), at her residence in Chas. Co., in her 68th year. (April 4, 1816)

McPHERSON, John, died Sat., March 19, aged between 50 and 60. While
on his way to his residence near Benedict, his horse ran
against a tree. (April 21, 1785)

McPHERSON, Col. John, died in Frederick-Town last week. (Dec. 10,
1829)

McPHERSON, Dr. William S., of Frederick City, and Mrs. Harriett
Neth of this city, were married on Tues. evening, by Rev.
McElhiney. (July 23, 1835)

MACE, John, and Elizabeth Thomas, all of Annap., were married Sun.
evening last, by Rev. Davis. (May 18, 1826)

MADISON, Mrs. Eleanor, mother of Ex-President Madison, died at Mont-
pelier, Va., on Wed., Feb. 11, aged 98 years. (Feb. 19, 1829)

MAGRUDER, Alexander C., of Annap., and Miss Rebecca Thomas, daughter
of Dr. Philip Thomas of Frederick Town, were married in the
latter place on Tues., Nov. 14, by the Rev. George C. Bower.
(Nov. 28, 1805)

MAGRUDER, Master Francis, died last week at George-Town on Patowmack, in his 21st year. It is imagined that his death was
occasioned by too violent exercise at fives [a kind of
handball played in Eng,--Webster's New World Dictionary.].
This ought to be a caution to others. (Dec. 22, 1763)

MAGRUDER, George L., of Upper Marlborough, P. G. Co., and Henrietta
Randall, daughter of the late John Randall, Esq., were
married Tues. evening last, by Rev. Blanchard. (Jan. 1,
1829)

MAGRUDER, Mr. John, died a few days ago, in P. G. Co., for many
years in the Commission of the Peace, and one of the Representatives in that county. (Aug. 29, 1750)

MAGRUDER, John, died Friday last [Sept. 3], in his 18th year, son
of Mr. Zadock Magruder. (Sept. 9, 1773)

MAGRUDER, John Reed, died Mon. evening last, at his residence near
Upper Marlborough, P. G. Co. (Dec. 16, 1830)

MAGRUDER, Mrs. Nancy H., died on Tues., 31st ult., wife of John
Read Magruder, Jr., of P. G. Co. (June 9, 1808)

MAGRUDER, Mrs. Rebecca B., consort of Alexander C. Magruder of
Annap., died Thurs. last, 27th ult., at the residence of her
father, in Frederick-Town. (Nov. 3, 1814)

MAGUIRE, Patrick, of Balto., and Julia Ann Kilghman, of the same
place, were married in Annap., Mon., 13th inst., by the
Rev. Mr. Watkins. (Aug. 23, 1832)

MAHAFFY, Hugh, Jr., was murdered. His widow Margaret is in Cecil
Co. gaol, charged with murdering her husband. (March 28,
1750)

MALCOLM, Rev. Alexander, died a few days ago, at an advanced age,
in Q. A. Co.; Rector of St. Paul's Parish in that county, a
gentleman who has obliged the world with several learned
performances in the Mathematics, Music, and Grammer. (June
30, 1763)

MALONE, Denton, and Miss Anne Kirby, all of Annap., were married
Thurs. evening last by the Rev. Mr. Watkins. (Nov. 15, 1821)

MANN, George, died 10th inst., in Annap., aged 43 years. (April 16,
    1795)

MANN, Mrs. Mary, died Sat. morning last [July 6], relict of the late
    George Mann, of Annap. (July 10, 1811)

MANN, Miss Sally, died 19th ult., in Chas. Co., at the residence of
    her brother. She was formerly a resident of Annap. (Oct. 3,
    1822)

MANN, William H., died in Annap., on Thurs. evening last [May 9],
    in his 30th year. (May 16, 1816)

MANSFIELD, John, of London, and Miss Mary B. Smith, of Balto., daugh-
    ter of General Smith, were married in the latter place by the
    Rev. Dr. Bond. (Dec. 6, 1809)

MANSHIP, Mr. Samuel, and Miss Eliza Gray, all of Annap., were married
    Tues. evening last, by the Rev. Mr. Griffith. (Dec. 25, 1823)

MARLE, Edmund, of Fred. Co., was killed or carried off by a party
    of Indians. (Oct. 9, 1755)

MARLOW, ---, of Piscattaway, in P. G. Co., died. He was suffering
    from small pox, and was so disordered in his senses that he
    got away from his nurse and was later found dead in Mattawoman
    [Creek], frozen in the ice. (Jan. 24, 1765)

MARLOW, Samuel, of P. G. Co., was accidentally drowned in South
    River on Tues., Oct. 24. (Oct. 26, 1769)

MARLOW, William, an ingenious and skillful smith, accidentally
    drowned on Sun. last [June 14]. (June 18, 1752)

MARRIOTT, Barzillai, and Elizabeth, youngest daughter of the late
    Amasa Linthicum, all of A. A. Co., were married 11th inst.,
    in Balto., on Thurs. evening, by Rev. William Collier. (Dec.
    18, 1834)

MARRIOTT, Bushrod W., of Annap., and Catherine Waters, of P. G. Co.,
    were married Thurs. last, in P. G. Co., by Rev. Mr. Macken-
    heimer. (Dec. 6, 1832)

MARRIOTT, Mrs. Elizabeth, widow, died Thurs. last. She kept the
    Ship Tavern, in South East Street. She is said to have died
    worth over 3000 pounds. (March 6, 1755)

MARRIOTT, Ephraim, and Miss Sarah Nicholls, all of A. A. Co., were
    married on Thurs. last [Oct. 1], by the Rev. Mr. Coleman.
    (Oct. 8, 1818)

MARRIOTT, Mr. Evan, died Wed. evening, 4th inst., at Snow Hill, the residence of Charles Hammond, in his 27th year. (Feb. 12, 1835)

MARRIOTT, Mr. John, of A. A. Co., died Sun. last, 7th inst. He was a member of the Methodist Church. He leaves three small children. (Feb. 11, 1830)

MARRIOTT, Rachel F., died Sun. last, 13th inst., at the residence of James H. Marriott, a daughter and only child of Bushrod W. Marriott, aged 10 months, 19 days. (July 24, 1834)

MARRIOTT, Rezin H., died in Annap., on Thurs. last [May 11], of the prevailing epidemic. (May 18, 1815)

MARRIOTT, Richard, of A. A. Co., died Mon. last [Oct. 28]. (Oct. 31, 1805)

MARRIOTT, Dr. Richard, and Miss Margaret Stewart, were married on Tues. evening, 9th inst., by the Rev. Dr. Rafferty. (Jan. 17, 1827)

MARRIOTT, Gen. William H., of Annap., and Jane, daughter of John McKim, Jr., were married in Balto., on Tues. evening, by the Rev. Duncan. (Nov. 7, 1822)

MARTIN, Mr., student of medicine in Balto., was killed Sat. morning last, in a duel with Mr. Carr, also a student of medicine. (Balto. Chronicle). (Feb. 7, 1828)

MARTIN, Daniel, of Tal. Co., and Miss Mary C. Maccubbin, of this place, were married in Annap., on Tues. evening [Feb. 6], by the Rev. Mr. Ryland. (Feb. 8, 1816)

MARTIN, the Hon. Daniel, Governor of Maryland, died Friday, 8th inst. (July 14, 1831)

MARTIN, Dr. Ennals, died at his residence in Easton, Md., on Tues. evening, 16th inst. (Dec. 25, 1834)

MARTIN, John W., of Cambridge, Md., and Evelina, second daughter of Gov. Martin, were married Tues. evening, 26th of Nov., by Rev. Dr. Henry M. Mason, at "The Wilderness," residence of the late Gov. Martin. (Dec. 5, 1839)

MARTIN, Luther, died at New York, on the evening of the 8th inst., a distinguished patriot and jurist, in his 82nd year. (July 20, 1826)

MARTIN, the Hon. William Bond, Chief Justice of the Fourth Judicial Circuit in Md., died Friday morning last, 3rd inst., at his residence in Cambridge. (April 9, 1835)

MARTIN, William Thomas, died last week on Wed. morning [Aug. 28], in
his 16th year; second son to the Hon. Josiah Martin, Esq.,
of N. Y., he read Philosophy in the Higher Class of our
Academy, "Philadelphia, Sept. 5." (Sept. 26, 1754)

MASON, Gen. A. T., of Va., was killed in a duel with J. M. McCarty,
the morning of Feb. 6. The duel was held in Bladensburg,
Md. The deceased was a democratic candidate for Congress from
Loudon Co., Va., and was late Senator. (Feb. 11, 1819)

MASON, Mrs. Anne, died Sat., Nov. 13th, at her house in Stafford
Co., Va., widow and relict of Col. George Mason, in her 63rd
year. (Dec. 23, 1762)

MASON, George, Esq., of Va., and Ann Eilbeck, daughter of William
Eilbeck, merchant of Chas. Co., were married the 3rd of last
month. (May 2, 1750)

MASON, Mrs. Mary, lady of Thomson Mason, of Loudon Co., Va., died
Oct. 21, at Westwood, the seat of Mr. Scott, in Prince William
Co., on her return home from a visit to her father. (Nov.
14, 1771)

MATLOCK, James, died Friday last at the Alms House, where he had
stopped for a few days; apparently 40 or 50 years old. He
was supposed to be from St. Mary's Co., and was looking for
a situation as a teacher. (Feb. 16, 1832)

MATTHEWS, Mr. James, brother of Dr. W. Matthews, of Cecil Co., was
killed Mon., 16th inst., in a duel with Mr. Richard Heath,
eldest son of Daniel C. Heath of Cecil Co. (Jan. 21, 1791)
The duel was fought in the border of Newcastle Co., near
Mr. Ellis' Tavern.

MATTINGLY, Capt. Edward, died on Wed., 5th inst., in his 69th year,
an officer in the Revolution. In early life he entered
the tented field in the defence of our rights and in the
eventful struggle aided to establish American liberty. He
has since lived in retirement in St. M. Co. (Sept. 20, 1821)

MATTINGLY, Capt. Joseph, died at St. Inigoes, St. M. Co., the 24th
inst. (Dec. 30, 1790)

MAULDIN, Mr. Francis, died lately in Caecil Co., one of the Representatives of that county. (Feb. 18, 1762)

MAULSBY, Gen. I. D., died 14th inst., at his residence near Bel Air,
late member of the Legislature, and R. W. G. S. Warden of
the Grand Lodge of Maryland. (June 20, 1839)

MAXCY, Cornelia Elizabeth, youngest daughter of Virgil Maxcy, Esq.,
died 26th ult., at West River. (Dec. 4, 1823)

MAXCY, Rev. Jonathan, President of Columbia College, died at his
residence at that place on the 4th inst. (June 22, 1820)

MAXCY, Juliana Howard, youngest daughter of the Hon. Virgil Maxcy,
died on the 1st inst., at Tulip Hill. (March 12, 1818)

MAXCY, Levi, Esq., died at Wrentham, Mass., on the 12th inst., aged
85, as distinguished by his genius as by his venerable and
benevolent character. He was the father of the late Dr.
Maxcy, of South Carolina. (Nov. 2, 1826)

MAXCY, Virgil, Esq., of Balto., and Mary Galloway, of West River,
A. A. Co., were married at Philadelphia, on 22nd inst., by
Rev. Bishop White. (March 6, 1811)

MAXWELL, George, merchant of Benedict Town, and Elizabeth Trippe,
were married Sun. last, in Dor. Co. (May 27, 1756)

MAXWELL, Capt. James, died lately at his plantation in Gunpowder Neck,
Harf. Co. He leaves six children. (Feb. 27, 1777)

MAYER, George C., died on Tues. [Oct. 15], late of the city of
Balto. (Oct. 17, 1811)

MAYER, Henry Ernst, of George-Town, and Miss Mary Grammer, daughter
of Frederick Grammer, of Annap., were married on Sun. evening
last [Aug. 14], by the Rev. Mr. Mackenheimer. (Aug. 18, 1808)

MAYER, Henry E., died in Balto., Sun. last, 28th ult., in his 52nd
year; a native of Germany but for several years a resident
of Annap. He leaves a wife and five children. [Long obit
is given.] (Sept. 1, 1831)

MAYER, Miss Louisa, died at Pleasant Plains, the seat of Andrew
Grammer, on Sun. morning. (Sept. 5, 1822)

MAYER, Mrs. Mary, died 3rd inst., in Balto., relict of the late
Henry E. Mayer, of Sandy point, in Annap. She was in her
42nd year, and was the youngest daughter of the late Frederick
Grammer. (Sept. 13, 1832)

MA[Y]NADIER, Rev. Daniel, died 30th ult., at his house near Cambridge,
rector of Great Choptank Parish, Dor. Co. (Jan. 21, 1773)

MAYNADIER, Mrs. Elizabeth, consort of Col. Henry Maynadier of Annap.,
died Friday last. (Feb. 16, 1832). Long obit is printed
later. (Feb. 23, 1832)

MAYNADIER, Miss Hannah, died at the residence of her brother, Col.
Maynadier, in Annap., on Sept. 2nd. Her sister Margaret died
recently. (Sept. 8, 1825)

MAYNADIER, Margaret, died in Annap. on Tues. morning. (Sept. 1, 1825)

MAYNARD, Mrs. Anna, consort of Samuel Maynard, Esq., and daughter of
the late John Callahan, Esq., died yesterday morning. (March
14, 1833)

MAYNARD, James Pelham, and Miss Julia Owen, both of Annap., were
married on Sun. last [Jan. 26], by the Rev. Mr. Higinbothom.
(Jan. 30, 1806)

MAYNARD, Mrs. Mary, of Annap., died Thurs. morning, 1st Jan., at an
advanced age. (Jan. 8, 1818)

MAYNARD, Samuel, and Miss Anne Callahan, both of Annap., were married
on Thurs. evening last, by the Rev. Mr. Judd. (May 19, 1808)

MAYO, Capt. Isaac, U. S. N., and Sarah, daughter of the Hon. Theo-
doric Bland, were married Tues. last, by Rev. J. G. Blanchard.
(Sept. 26, 1833)

MEAD, Mrs., consort of Samuel Mead of Annap., died Tues. morning last,
at an advanced age. (Jan. 19, 1826)

MEAD, Benjamin, of Annap., and Miss Louisa C. Rousell, of Balto.,
were married in the latter city on Tues. evening last, by
the Rev. Mr. Tydings. (Nov. 30, 1820)

MECONEKEN, William E., died in Q. A. Co., on the 13th inst., in his
53rd year. (July 20, 1826)

MEDCALFE, Mrs. Dorothea, relict of George Medcalfe, died Mon. night,
26th inst., of typhus pleurisy. She leaves two children.
(Dec. 29, 1831)

MEDKIFF, George, died in Annap., on Sat. evening, 12th inst. (Aug.
17, 1820)

MEEKS, Aquila, was found dead after the wreck of the sloop Betsy,
March 4. (March 5, 1812)

MEEKS, James, was found deat after the wreck of the sloop Betsy,
March 4. (March 5, 1812)

MELLINGER, George, aged about 25 years, was found murdered on Aug.
23, on the land of Harry D. Gough, near the Belle-Air Road,
about 12 miles from Balto. (Aug. 29, 1799)

MEETEET, William, died Friday last at half past twelve, in his 46th
year. [Long obit is given.] (April 18, 1833)

MERCER, John, of West River, and Mary, only daughter of Thomas

Swann, of Alexandria, Va., were married on the 25th of June,
by the Rev. Mr. Norris. (July 2, 1818)

MERCER, the Hon. John F., delegate to Congress for the state of Virginia, and Miss Sprigg, of Annap., were married 3rd inst.
(Feb. 17, 1785)

MERCER, Col. John F., died on the night of 30th inst., at Philadelphia, in his 64th year. The deceased resided at West River,
Md. At a very early age, Col. Mercer took up arms in the
defence of his country, and after the close of the war was
sent from Virginia, his native state, to the Old Congress as
a delegate. On his marriage he removed to Maryland, where
he commenced the practice of law; but he was soon appointed
by the Legislature of Maryland a Member of the Convention
which framed our present Constitution. Some years ago he was
chosen a Member of the House of Representatives for the
Congressional District of Maryland....(He was) Governor of
Maryland,...and (later) a member of the House of Delegates
in the General Assembly of Maryland. He was in Philadelphia
to consult a physician about his health. His remains were
deposited in the churchyard of St. Peter's, in Philadelphia.
(Sept. 13, 1821)

MERCER, Mrs. Sophia, wife of John Francis Mercer, departed this life
on Friday, 25th ult., at West River Farm, the seat of her
ancestors for several occasions. (Oct. 1, 1812)

MEREDITH, Hugh, overseer of Richard Cooper, was murdered by his
master. Cooper, an old man of over four score years, was
committed to prison in Dor. Co. (Sept. 5, 1754)

MERRIKEN, Mrs. Mary Ann, died Sat., 5th inst., in her 36th year, at
the residence of her father in A. A. Co.; consort of Rev.
Richard H. Merriken of Balto., and eldest daughter of the
Rev. Benjamin Hood. (Sept. 17, 1835)

MERRIKEN, Capt. John, died on the evening of the 8th inst., at his
residence on the North side of Severn, in his 65th year. He
served as an officer in the Revolutionary Army. (April 15,
1824)

MERRIKEN, Robert, and Miss Sarah Welsh, both of Severn, were married
on Tues. last [Feb. 18], by the Rev. Mr. Fleming. (Feb. 20,
1806)

MIDDLEMORE, Dr. Josias, died Thurs., Feb. 27, at his house in Balto.
Co.,...of gout in his head and stomach, in his 73rd year.
He came from England in 1720. His only son Francis died a few
years earlier in his 19th year. [Long obit is given.]
(April 3, 1755)

MIDDLETON, William, died April 12, at his residence on Poole's Island, in his 19th year. (April 25, 1805)

MIDDLETON, William, First Officer of the schooner Linnett, of Balto., died at St. Jago de Cuba, on Oct. 14. (Dec. 10, 1807)

MILBURNE, Stephen, of St. M. Co., was murdered on or about June 10. Warrants have been issued for the arrest of his nephews William and James Milburne. Proclamation of a reward is made. (July 8, 1819)

MILLARD, Col. Enoch J., Register of Wills for St. M. Co., died Friday, 20th inst., at his residence in Leonard-Town, in his 63rd year. (March 26, 1835)

MILLER, Mrs., wife of James Miller, merchant of Bladensburg, died Sat. last. [Nov. 27]. (Dec. 2, 1773)

MILLER, Mrs. Caroline, consort of Mr. James Miller, died Thurs. evening, 16th inst., in her 20th year, at the residence of her father, Mr. John Quynn, in Annap., after having been married for only seven months. (Aug. 23, 1827)

MILLER, Mr. Edward, died yesterday morning, on the North side of Severn, in his 25th year, eldest son of Mr. Peter Miller, near Annap. (March 6, 1823)

MILLER, James, of A. A. Co., and Caroline, eldest daughter of John Quynn, of Annap., were married Tues. evening last, by Rev. Dr. Davis. (Jan. 4, 1827)

MILLER, James, of A. A. Co., and Louisa, daughter of John Quynn, of Annap., were married Sun. evening last, by Rev. Vinton. (Jan. 22, 1829)

MILLER, James E., of Annap., and Miss Louisa Bray, of Balto., were married in Balto., on Thurs. evening last, by the Rev. Mr. Bartow. (Nov. 14, 1822)

MILLER, John, and Elizabeth Rebecca Webster, were married Tues., June 28, near Port Tobacco, by Rev. Walter McPherson. On this occasion, the eldest of 12 brothers and sisters was married by the youngest, both widowers; and by this event the said Miller became son to his son William Cox, who previous to this, by his last marriage became son, nephew, and brother to his wife's oldest sister. (Aug. 25, 1791)

MILLER, John, and Miss Margaret Schurar, all of Annap., were married Sun. evening last [June 28], by the Rev. Mr. Guest. (July 2, 1818)

MILLER, Mr. John, Sr., died in Annap., on Sat. morning last, in his

65th year of age. He was a member of the Methodist Church.
(April 22, 1824)

MILLER, Mrs. Margaret, relict of John Miller, died yesterday morning
in Annap., at a good old age. (Dec. 29, 1831)

MILLER, Peter, died at his residence near Annap., on the 23rd inst.,
in his 67th year. (May 28, 1835)

MILLER, Peter, and Miss Delilah Jane Clarke, all of A. A. Co., were
married Tues. morning last, at the residence of Leonard
Iglehart, by Rev. Dr. Waters. (March 28, 1839)

MILLS, Barney, and Eliza Gassaway, all of Annap., were married on
Thurs. evening last, by Rev. Mr. Poisal. (April 7, 1836)

MILLS, Major Cornelius, died Mon., 28th inst., in his 68th year.
He was a patriot, and an active participator in our revo-
lutionary struggle. He was Sergeant at Arms to the House of
Delegates for 40 years. (July 31, 1823)

MILLS, Mr. James, merchant, died in St. M. Co., on Sun., 29th ult.,
in his grand climacteric year, after a tedious illness; for
several years a representative and magistrate of the said
county. (Feb. 23, 1764)

MILLS, James, Esq., died at his seat in St. M. Co., on Wed., 9th
inst., in his 58th year. (March 24, 1791)

MILLS, Mr. James, and Mrs. Priscilla Weems, both of A. A. Co., were
married Thurs. evening last, by Rev. Mr. Watkins. (Nov. 15,
1821)

MILLS, James, of A. A. Co., and Mary Winchester, of Q. A. Co., were
married on Tues., by Rev. Blanchard. (June 6, 1833)

MILLS, James, died Sun. last, at his farm near Annap. (May 11,
1837)

MILLS, John L., and Miss Cecilia Elizabeth Pothain, both of Balto.,
were married in Annap. on Sun. last, by Rev. Wells. (Aug.
17, 1826)

MILLS, Capt. Jonas, died Sun. last on board his schooner the Tanta-
mount, in our harbor. He was from Salem, and leaves a wife
and six children. (Aug. 5, 1819)

MILLS, Mrs. Priscilla, consort of James Mills, died at her residence
in Annap., 29th inst. (Aug. 11, 1831)

MILLS, William, and Susan Till, all of Balto., were married in that
city on 27th ult., by Rev. Mr. Thornton. (April 7, 1836)

MINSKIE, Mrs. Maria Catherine, died Thurs. last [Nov. 23], aged 57;
    for 30 years a resident of Annap. She was buried Monday.
    (Nov. 29, 1749) Samuel Soumaien and John Thompson, execs.
    (Jan. 10, 1750)

MITCHELL, Alexander, died in Annap., on Friday morning last [Oct.
    22], in his 23rd year. (Oct. 28, 1819)

MITCHELL, Ann, daughter of Robert Mitchell of St. Jone's [sic]
    Neck, Kent Co., Del., died of hydrophobia, June 28th, in her
    16th year. (July 18, 1833)

MITCHELL, Charles, distinguished Counsellor and Attorney at Law,
    a native of Conn., and son of the Hon. Judge Mitchell of that
    state, died Sat. morning in Annap. (June 16, 1831)

MITCHELL, James, a labouring man of this place, was drowned a few
    days since, when going out of a flat into Rappahannock River
    in Va., got entangled in a great number of sea nettles.
    (July 25, 1750)

MITCHELL, Gen. John, died Sun., Oct. 11th, at his farm in Chas. Co.
    [Long obit tells of his participation in the Revolution, and
    how his application for compensation for his services met with
    no encouragement.] (Oct. 29, 1812)

MITCHELL, John, and Ann Wirl [?], were married in Annap. on Thurs.
    evening last, by Rev. Mr. Watkins. (Sept. 28, 1826)

MITCHELL, Mrs. Mary H., died at Fair Hill Farm, Cecil Co., on Sat.,
    21st inst., in her 35th year, consort of Col. George E.
    Mitchell, late of the U. S. Army, and a Representative in
    Congress from that district. [Long obit is given.] (May
    3, 1827)

MITCHELL, Richard, and Mary Ann Purdy, all of A. A. Co., were married
    Sun., 3rd July, by the Rev. N. J. Watkins. (July 14, 1831)

MITCHELL, Dr. Samuel, died; "New York, Sept. 7." (Sept. 15, 1831)

MOALE, Mrs. Ann M., wife of Col. Samuel Moale of Balto., died Friday
    morning last, in Balto., in her 52nd year. She was the eldest
    daughter of the late Samuel Harvey Howard, Esq., of Annap.
    (Sept. 20, 1827)

MOALE, Mr. John, and Miss Helen North, were married Thurs. last
    [May 25], at Balto. Town. (June 1, 1758)

MONROE, Ex-President James, died. [Long obit.] (July 14, 1831)

MOORE, Col. Nicholas Ruxton, died yesterday [Oct. 9], in Balto., in

his 62nd year, late a member of Congress, and commandant of
a Cavalry Regiment attached to the Third Division of Maryland
Militia. Col. Moore was one of those worthies who so nobly
achieved the independence we now enjoy. He leaves a wife and
four children. (Oct. 10, 1816)

MOORE, Dr. Robert, formerly of Balto., died at Zanesville, Ohio, in
his 68th year. (Feb. 1, 1838)

MORAN, Michael, was killed in a fire in Balto.; "Balto. Chronicle,
Feb. 26." (March 5, 1835)

MORGAN, Mr. Thomas, died in Annap., on Thurs. morning last. He leaves
a wife and several children. (Feb. 2, 1826)

MORGAN, Mr. William, died Sun. last, in his 25th year. He leaves a
widow and two children. (Feb. 9, 1826)

MORRELL, Mr. Samuel, died at Wolfeborough, N. H., aged 87 years. He
was one of the intrepid band who destroyed the tea in Boston
harbor in 1775. (Dec. 19, 1833)

MORRIS, the Hon. Gouverneur, died Wed., 6th March, at his seat at
Morrissania, Westchester Co., N. Y., in his 65th year. (Nov.
14, 1816)

MORRIS, Lewis, died Wed. last [May 14]; Captain General and Governor
in Chief of New Jersey, at an advanced age. ["New York,
May 19."] (June 10, 1746)

MORRIS, Owen, died at Phila., on Thurs., 9th inst., the oldest per-
former in the theatrical line belonging to the American stage.
(Nov. 22, 1809)

MORRIS, Robert, merchant, agent, and Factor of Foster Cunliffe, Esq.,
of Liverpoole, died Wed. morning last [July 12] at his
house in Oxford. [Long obit is given.] (July 18, 1750)

MORRIS, Robert, Esq., died Thurs., 8th inst., whose signal and
important services to his country during our revolutionary
struggle with Great Britain are well known throughout the
United States. (May 22, 1806)

MORRIS, Robert Hunter, Chief Justice of East Jersey and formerly
Governor of Pennsylvania, died suddenly in East Jersey on
Friday evening last [Jan. 27]. ("Philadelphia, Feb. 2.")
(Feb. 16, 1764)

MORRIS, Sarah Ann, daughter of John B. Morris, Esq., of Port Tobacco,
died at the Government House in Annap., on Friday morning
last [May 6], aged 12 months. (May 12, 1814)

MORS, Frederick, and Julia Atkinson were married in Annap. on Sun.
    evening last, by Rev. Mr. Davis. (Dec. 21, 1826)

MORSE, Mrs., died at Woodstock, Conn., aged 99; the grandmother of
    Rev. Dr. Morse of Charleston. She leaves 10 children, 72
    grandchildren, and 219 great-grandchildren, and 14 great-
    great-grandchildren. (July 9, 1801)

MORSELL, Mrs. Anna Maria, died in Balto., 23rd July, in her 26th
    year, wife of James Morsell, Esq., of Cal. Co. (Aug. 3,
    1837)

MORTON, Mrs. Elizabeth, died Friday last, daughter of Judge Done.
    (Nov. 8, 1827). She died Thurs., 1st inst., at the residence
    of her father Capt. John Done, in Annap.; wife of Judge John
    H. B. Morton, in her 30th year. [Long obit is given.] (Nov.
    15, 1827)

MORTON, John, aged 40, died suddenly the night following the funeral
    of a neighbor, Mrs. Compton. (Jan. 26, 1832)

MORTON, Mary Rebecca, daughter of Mr. John H. B. Morton, died Friday
    evening last, 29th ult., in her seventh year, at the house
    of her grandfather, Mr. John Done, of Annap. (Feb. 4, 1830)

MOSS, Mr. James, died at his residence on Hackett's Point, A. A. Co.,
    on the 5th inst. (Sept. 11, 1828)

MOSS, Mrs. Monica, consort of Mr. James Moss of Hackett's Point,
    A. A. Co., died Sat., 17th inst., in her 66th year. (Sept.
    29, 1825)

MOSS, Richard, died Wed., 7th inst., at Hackett's Point, in his 52nd
    year. (Jan. 15, 1829)

MOSS, Robert, and Ruth E. Weedon, daughter of Mr. John Weedon, of
    Broad Neck, A. A. Co., were married Thurs. evening last, by
    the Rev. Mr. Watkins. (Feb. 17, 1825)

MOSSMAN, [Archibald], of Balto. Town, was murdered near Hagerstown
    by four convicts he had bought and was intending to resell.
    (July 29, 1773)

MOUAT, Mr. James, died last Sat. [March 12], at his seat near South
    River, aged 83 years; formerly for a long time, Chief Justice
    of this county. He was pretty hearty a few hours before he
    he expired, and died suddenly without a groan. (March 17,
    1763)

MUIR, Col. Adam, died last Wed. [Nov. 11], in Dor. Co. (Nov. 18,
    1747) Thomas Muir, the exec., advertises for debtors to
    settle their debts. (June 1, 1748)

MUIR, John, died in Annap., on 30th ult. [Aug.]; President of the
Farmer's Bank of Maryland, in his 60th year. He was a native
of Scotland, and came to this country at a very early period
of his life...and took an active part in that struggle which
terminated in the freedom of the country. He was a member of
the Legislature of Maryland for six years. (Sept. 5, 1810)

MULLIKEN, Thomas, on Mon. last week [Aug. 1], as he was riding the
road in P. G. Co., near the western branch, got a fall from
his horse which killed him. (Aug. 11, 1763)

MULLIKIN, Mr. Edward, formerly postmaster of Easton and proprietor
of the Easton Whig, died. (Easton Whig) (Aug. 20, 1835)

MUNN, Jonathan, last Sun. se'ennight [Jan. 29], he, a cabinet-maker,
and Uriah Bond, a blacksmith, were attempting to cross the
Gunpowder River on the ice; both fell in and were drowned.
(Feb. 8, 1749)

MUNROE, Charles, and Ellen Maccubbin, all of Annap., were married
Thurs. evening last by Rev. Vinton. (March 12, 1829)

MUNROE, Grafton, of Annap., and Mary Ann, daughter of the late
Jonathan Edwards, of Balto., were married in the latter place
on Tues. evening last, by Rev. Mr. Davis. (Nov. 23, 1826)

MUNROE, Mr. Horatio G., merchant, died yesterday morning [May 10],
in Annap. (May 11, 1820)

MUNROE, Mr. James, Post-Master, died in Annap. on Sun. evening
last. (Nov. 10, 1825)

MUNROE, John, Post-Master in Annap., died on Mon. morning [Nov. 17],
in his 55th year. (Nov. 20, 1817)

MUNROE, Thomas, died at Nicholaef, on or near the Black Sea, aid-de-
camp of the Emperor of Russia; aged 36 years. (Nov. 27, 1834)

MURAT, Achille, Esq., of Florida, and formerly of Italy, eldest son
of His late Majesty, Joachim Murat, King of Naples, and Mrs.
Catherine Dangerfield Gray, of Tallahassee, late of Fredericksburg, Va., and daughter of Major Byrd C. Willis, were married
at Tallahassee, on July 12th. (Aug. 17, 1826)

MURDOCH, Mrs. Elizabeth, relict of the late Gilbert Murdoch, died
in Annap., on Tues. last. (Dec. 24, 1835)

MURDOCH, Gilbert, died Mon., 9th inst., in his 69th year. He was a
native of Scotland, but came early to this country. He was
a member of the Methodist Episcopal Church. (Sept. 12, 1822)

MURDOCH, Mr. James, and Miss Catherine Peacock were married in Tal.
Co. on 28th ult., by Rev. William Clark. (Nov. 11, 1813)

MURDOCH, Mr. James, died in Annap., on Sun. morning last. (Dec. 29, 1825)

MURDOCH, Miss Margaret, died 11th inst., at the residence of Mrs. Ann E. Hill, of P. G. Co. [Long obit is given.] (Aug. 17, 1826)

MURDOCH, Thomas A., and Mary E. Slicer, all of Annap., were married Tues., 9th inst., by Rev. Mr. Waters. (Oct. 18, 1838)

MURDOCH, William, and Miss Juliet Shepherd, all of Annap., were married on Sun. evening [Oct. 10], by the Rev. Mr. Guest. (Oct. 28, 1819)

MURDOCK, Mrs. Anne, died Thurs. last [Oct. 25], in P. G. Co.; the virtuous consort of Mr. William Murdock, and daughter of the late Col. John Addison. (Nov. 1, 1753)

MURDOCK, William, of P. G. Co., and Mrs. Hamilton, of Annap., were married Sat. last. (Jan. 6, 1757)

MURDOCK, William, died Tues. morning [Oct. 17], at his seat near Queen Anne, P. G. Co., for many years a representative of that county. (Oct. 19, 1769)

MURPHY, John, bearer of an express from the Governor of Penna., which arrived Sun., 14th inst., died suddenly on his journey at Patapsco. (Feb. 17, 1748)

MURRAY, Comm. Alexander, senior officer of the Navy of the U. S., died at his residence near Phildelphia. (Oct. 18, 1821)

MURRAY, Alexander J., of West River, A. A. Co., and Mary, fourth daughter of Jonas Clapham, Esq., of Balto., were married 10th inst., in the latter city, by Rev. Dr. Wyatt. (May 18, 1837)

MURRAY, Daniel of the U. S. Navy, and Miss Mary Dorsey, of Balto., were married 8th inst., at Balto., by the Rev. Mr. Bend. (Dec., 1808)

MURRAY, Henry M., Esq., died in Balto., yesterday morning, a distinguished member of the Bar. He was a native of Annap. His death was occasioned by the bursting of the boiler of the steam boat Eagle, 18th inst., while on her passage from Annap. to Balto. (April 29, 1824)

MURRAY, James, and Miss Charlotte W. Rackliffe, were married on Tues., 29th (Aug.). (Sept. 6, 1809)

MURRAY, Dr. James, died in Annap., on the 17th inst., in his 30th year. (Dec. 30, 1819)

MURRAY, John, attorney-at-law, drowned Mon. last [April 13], with
John Nevitt, merchant, Captain Etherington and his boy, by
the capsizing of a boat while crossing over from Cambridge.
(April 16, 1772)

MURRAY, John, Consul of the United States, died at Glasgow in March
last. (June 6, 1805)

MURRAY, Mrs. Sarah, died yesterday noon, at the advanced age of 87,
relict of the late Dr. James Murray. (Nov. 23, 1837)

MURRAY, Dr. William, died lately at his house in Chestertown, Kent
Co. (April 20, 1769)

MURRAY, William Vans, Esq., died Sun., 11th inst., at his seat in
Dor. Co.; late minister from the United States at the Hague,
and minister plenipotentiary to the French republic. (Dec.
22, 1803)

MUSGROVE, Major N., an officer in the Revolutionary army, was shot
by his son-in-law Alexander Duvall, on the 6th inst., in
Mont. Co. At the time of his death he could have been but
little short of 70 years. (July 17, 1833)

MYERS, Mrs. Anne, died Tues. last [Sept. 24], in child-bed, in Dor.
Co., the consort of Rev. John Myers, late Rector of this
Parish, now of St. Mary's White Chapel Parish in that county.
(Oct. 3, 1774)

MYERS, Rev. John, died last Thurs. [Feb. 21], in Dor. Co.; rector of
a parish in that county. (Feb. 28, 1760)

NAYLOR, Mrs., died in Amwel, N. J., aged about 103 years. She was
born in that neighborhood in its first settlement. For upwards of 50 years past, her whole diet consisted of bitter
tea and a little bread and butter three times a day; and
her amusement was continually smoking tobacco. (Feb. 7, 1805)

NEALE, Mr. Edward, died Sun. last [Dec. 28], after a tedious illness;
of Queens Town, Q. A. Co. The next day Mrs. Neale was suddenly seized with some violent disorder and died also. (Jan. 1,
1761)

NED, negro, was executed pursuant to his sentence, for the murder
of Mr. Vachel Dorsey, son of John, of Elk Ridge, in A. A.
Co. (May 14, 1765)

NEEDLES, John, an inhabitant of Easton, formerly High Sheriff of
Tal. Co., died 14th inst., at the house of Mr. Archibald
Golder of Annap. His remains were conveyed to Indian Spring
for interment. (Dec. 17, 1795)

NELSON, Mr. John M., and Miss Anne Jane Fullerton, all of Harf. Co.,
were married 27th ult., in that county, by the Rev. Mr.
Tydings. (Nov. 10, 1825)

de NERMONT, M. Laurent Truhet [?], Chef d'Escadron in the Royal
Guards, and Knight of the Legion of Honor, died in Philadelphia. (July 2, 1835)

NETH, Mrs. Elizabeth, relict of Lewis Neth, Esq., late of Annap.,
died 14th inst. (April 22, 1830)

NETH, Lewis, Esq., and Harriett, eldest daughter of Samuel Maynard,
Esq., Cashier of the Farmer's Bank of Maryland, were married
Sun., 24th inst., by the Rev. Mr. Blanchard. (June 28, 1832)

NETH, Lewis, merchant, died Friday morning, in his 73rd year. (June
3, 1825)

NETH, Lewis, Esq., of Annap., died yesterday. (Oct. 11, 1832)

NEVETT, Major Thomas, died last Friday [Feb. 10], near Cambridge,
in Dor. Co., for many years chief magistrate of that county.
(Feb. 15, 1749) Sarah Nevett, the administratrix, advertises
for debtors to the estate. (March 15, 1749)

NEVILL, Hon. Samuel, died Sat., 27th ult., at Perth Amboy, Second
Judge of the Supreme Court of New Jersey, aged 66 years.
[Long obit is given.] (Nov. 15, 1764)

NEVITT, John, merchant, drowned Mon. last [April 13], by the capsizing
of a boat while crossing over from Cambridge. (April 16,
1772)

NEWMAN, Mr. George, died last Sat. [April 6] about two miles from
town, in consequence of innoculation for Small Pox. (April
11, 1765)

NEWMAN, Joseph, last Wed. [Feb. 11], was killed by the accidental
discharge of a gun in Q. A. Co. (Feb. 17, 1747)

NEWTON, Monicah, was killed by lightning which struck the house of
Thomas Wheatly, of St. M. Co., Tues. evening last, aged 16.
She was in bed with her sister. (June 13, 1750)

NICHOLLS, Mr. John, died Friday last, in A. A. Co. (Jan. 26, 1826)

NICHOLLS, John, and Mary Hunter, both of A. A. Co., were married
Tues. evening last, by the Rev. Mr. Watkins. (Feb. 21, 1833)

NICHOLLS, Nelson, of Annap., and Miss Elizabeth Grammer, also of
Annap., were married Tues. evening last, by the Rev. Mr.
Griffith. (July 15, 1824)

NICHOLLS, Mrs. Rachel, died Mon. night after a short illness. (March
   20, 1823)

NICHOLS, Allen, died 18th May last, in Montecello, Ala., formerly of
   Annap. He leaves a wife and four children. (Sept. 24, 1835)

NICHOLS, Benjamin, and Mrs. Elizabeth Nichols, both of A. A. Co., were
   married Thurs. evening last by the Rev. Nicholas Watkins.
   (Jan. 2, 1834)

NICHOLS, Rev. Henry, rector of St. Michael's Parish, died Sun. last
   [Feb. 12], at his house in Tal. Co., at an advanced age.
   (Feb. 15, 1749)

NICHOLS, Mr. Jeremiah, died Sun. last [Oct. 7], in the prime of
   life, at his house in Tal. Co. (Oct. 11, 1753)

NICHOLS, Mrs. Mahala, wife of William Nichols, son of William, died
   Sun., 6th inst., at Carroll's Quarter, near Annap. (Sept.
   17, 1835)

NICHOLS, Nelson Reed, died Sun. morning last, in his 37th year.
   (Dec. 11, 1834)

NICHOLS, William, and Margaret E. Watkins, both of A. A. Co., were
   married Thurs. evening last, by the Rev. Mr. Watkins. (March
   23, 1837)

NICHOLSON, Mr. Beale, died here on Tues. last [March 8], in the
   prime of his age. (March 10, 1763)

NICHOLSON, Mr. Joseph, Jr., attorney-at-law, of Kent Co., and Miss
   Elizabeth Hopper, a daughter of Major Hopper, of Q. A. Co.,
   were married Thurs. last [July 28]. (Aug. 4, 1757)

NICHOLSON, Joseph H., Esq., of Annap., and Elizabeth Ann, eldest
   daughter of Peter Hagner, of Washington, D. C., were married
   in the latter place on Tues., 10th inst., by the Rev. Mr.
   Hawley. (April 19, 1827)

NICHOLSON, the Hon. Joseph Hopper, died yesterday, aged 47 years,
   Chief Judge of the Sixth Judicial Circuit, and a Judge of
   the Court of Appeals of Maryland. (March 13, 1817)

NICHOLSON, Lieut. Joseph M., of the U. S. Navy, died at the Navy
   Hospital, Norfolk. He was a native of Maryland. (April 11,
   1833)

NICHOLSON, Mrs. Sarah, died Tues. morning last, at an advanced age;
   for many years a member of the Methodist Church. (Aug. 5,
   1824).

NIXON, John, died in Philadelphia, on Sat., 31st ult. [Dec., 1808],
    aged 75 years; President of the Bank of North America, and
    one of the oldest and most respectable merchants of that
    city. (Jan. 11, 1809)

NORRIS, John, and Miss Susan Coulter, all of Annap., were married
    last evening [July 16], by the Rev. Mr. Ryland. (July 17,
    1811)

OBERSTEUFFER, John C., and Rebecca Ann Pennington, were married Tues.
    last, by the Rev. Mr. Guest. (Aug. 11, 1831)

OBERTEUFFER, Charles A., of Balto., and Mary L. Pennington, formerly
    of Annap., were married in the former city, 24th ult., by the
    Rev. Mr. Heiner. (April 7, 1836)

O'BRIEN, William, of Annap., drowned last Sun. afternoon, when a
    squall upset his boat in the Severn River. A negro man and
    boy were also drowned. (June 28, 1787)

OGLE, Miss Anne, eldest daughter of His Excellency, the Governor,
    died last Wed. night [June 4]. (June 9, 1747)

OGLE, Mrs. Anne, departed this life in Annap., on Thurs., 14th inst.,
    at the advanced age of 94 years. Her remains were interred
    at White Hall, the seat of Horatio Ridout, in the family
    vault. (Aug. 21, 1817)

OGLE, Benjamin, died Friday morning last [July 7], in his 61st year,
    formerly Governor of this State. His remains were privately
    interred the same evening on his farm. (July 21, 1809)

OGLE, Mrs. H., died in Annap., on Mon. morning [Aug. 14], after a
    tedious illness. (Aug. 17, 1815)

OGLE, Mrs. Mary R., died at Bel Air. P. G. Co., on Wed., 4th inst.,
    wife of William C. Ogle, of P. G. Co., and daughter of late
    George Bevans, Esq., of A. A. Co. (Nov. 19, 1835)

OGLE, Gov. Samuel; his wife Anne was delivered of a son on Sun.
    last. (July 21, 1747)

OGLE, Master Samuel, died last Thurs., of the measles, at his father's
    country seat; only son of His Excellency, the Governor, aged
    14 months. (Sept. 21, 1748)

OGLE, His Excellency Samuel, Esq., Governor of this province, died
    last Sun. morning at 4:00, in his 58th year. [Long obit is
    given.] (May 3, 1752) He was buried Tues. [May 5] in the
    church in this city; his coffin was covered with black velvet,
    and the pall supported by five Gentlemen of the Council, and
    the presiding Judge of the Provincial Court. (May 7, 1752)

OLDFIELD, William, and his little son, aged about four years old, were accidentally drowned Thurs. last [Oct. 30], in the Little Choptank River. (Nov. 6, 1766)

O'NEAL, John, "the Hero of Havre de Grace," died Friday, 26th inst., in his 71st year. He was a native of County Antrim, Ireland, and emigrated to the United States in his 18th year. [The obituary tells of his saving Havre-de-Grace during the late War.] (Feb. 1, 1838)

ONION, Mr. Stephen, died Mon. last [Aug. 26], at his house in Balto. Co.; owner of the Ironworks on Gunpowder River. (Aug. 29, 1754)

O'REILLY, Mrs. Letitia, died Sun. evening, 15th inst., at her residence on Herring Bay, A. A. Co., consort of Mr. John A. O'Reilly, in her 28th year. (Feb. 26, 1824)

O'REILY, Dr. Polydore E., died on Wed. last [Dec. 20] in his 32nd year. For several years he pursued his professional vocations on Magothy in the county. (Dec. 21, 1815)

ORME, Rev. Mr. John, for many years the pastor of a dissenting congregation at Upper Marlborough, died April 28th, in P. G. Co., aged 67 years. (May 11, 1758)

ORONO, Madam, relict of Orono, late Chief of the Penobscot Indians, who died a few years since at the age of 110, died on Penobscot River, aged 115 years. (Feb. 1, 1809)

OUTTEN, Mr. William, one of the sub-Sheriffs of Wor. Co., was shot through the body (on 6th inst.) by one John Willie, who it is said, refused to pay his taxes in Maryland. Mr. Outten was shot dead on the spot. Willie surrendered himself. This happened in the upper part of Wor. Co., near the confines of Sussex Co., in Pennsylvania government. (Feb. 15, 1759)

OWEN, ---, a ship carpenter, drowned Sat. last [Sept. 1], in Kent Narrows. (Sept. 4, 1751)

OWEN, Mr. Richard, died at Plinhimmon, Balto. Co., aged 77. For some years he was a teacher at St. John's Coll., Annap. (March 7, 1822)

OWEN, Mr. Thomas, and Miss Matilda C. Goldsborough of this city, were married Tues., 6th inst., by Rev. Mr. Gillis, at Major Ephraim Gaither's in Mont. Co. (Nov. 22, 1832)

OWENS, Alexander, and Mary Wells, all of A. A. Co., were married on May 31, by the Rev. Mr. Gosnell. (June 14, 1832)

OWENS, Dr. James, of A. A. Co., and Eliza Ann, daughter of Robert

Welch, of Ben., Esq., were married on Tues. evening last, by
Rev. Mr. Blanchard. (Dec. 22, 1825)

OWENS, Samuel, of A. A. Co., and Miss Eliza Hopkins, of Washington,
were married on the evening of Tues., 10th inst., by the Rev.
Mr. Ryland. (April 19, 1827)

OWENS, William, son of James, died Sat., 1st inst., at his father's
residence in this county, aged 23 or 24 years. (Oct. 6, 1831)

OWINGS, Mrs. Mary, widow of the late Samuel Owings, of Stephen, of
Balto. Co., died in Annap., on the evening of the 16th inst.,
in her 76th year. [Long obit is given.] (Feb. 19, 1835)

PACA, Mrs., died Sat. last [Jan. 15], wife of William Paca, Esq.,
of Annap. (Jan. 20, 1774)

PACA, Edward T., of Wye Hall, and Mariana E., daughter of Major
Jones, of Annap., were married Tues. evening, 1st Aug., by
Rev. Mr. McElhiney. (Aug. 10, 1837)

PACA, John, died Jan. 2, between one and two o'clock, at Chilberry,
at the seat of James Phillips, Esq., in Harf. Co.; the deceased
was the father of our Governor. (Jan. 13, 1785) An account
of his funeral is given. (Jan. 21, 1785, issue of the
Maryland Journal)

PACA, Mr. William, a young gentleman of the law in Balto. Co., and
Miss Mary Chew were married Thurs. last [May 26]. (June 2,
1763)

PAGE, John, died in Williamson Co., Va.; he committed suicide. He
had a married daughter in S. C. (Aug. 4, 1808)

PAGE, Col. John, died in Va., on 11th inst., in his 65th year; the
Commissioner of Loans, and late Governor of that State. He
was one of our earliest Revolutionary patriots, and for
several years was a Representative in Congress. (Oct. 27,
1808)

PAINE, Mrs., died on Sun. morning, 18th inst., at her father's house
at Cranbrook, in her 68th year, the wife of Thomas Paine,
author of "The Rights of Man." (Sept. 29, 1808)

PARISH, John Henry, and Ellen Hollidayoke, all of Annap., were
married Sun. evening last in Annap., by Rev. Thomas G. Waters.
(May 30, 1839)

PARK, Mungo, the enterprising traveller whose researches in Africa
have been read with so much avidity, has died. (July 17,
1806)

PARKE, Capt. Julius Caesar, died Mon. last, at Upper Marlborough, a
noted master of the sword. (Nov. 4, 1756)

PARKER, Gabriel, died Friday night last [Nov. 29], in P. G. Co., son
to Col. Parker of Cal. Co. His death was occasioned by a
slight wound received from a squib, which hit him on the jugular vein. He was lately married. (Dec. 6, 1745)

PARKER, Col. Gabriel, died last Friday morning in Cal. Co. [Sept.
15]; for many years Chief Justice and Deputy Commissary and
several times High Sheriff of that county, which place he had
held to the time of his death. (Sept. 20, 1749)

PARKER, Mrs. Margaret, died on the 9th inst., at Broad Creek, Kent
Island, Q. A. Co., in her 29th year. She leaves a husband
and five small children. (Dec. 19, 1816)

PARKER, Richard, from Maryland, has been drowned for some time, and
his body was found at the shore at Monument Ponds, Plymouth
[Mass.], on 28th Oct. His friends and relations may inquire
about his possessions at John Draper, printer, Newbury St.;
"Boston, Oct. 3, 1745." (Dec. 31, 1745)

PARKERSON, William, and Miss Sarah Purdy, were married in Annap.,
on 4th inst., by the Rev. Mr. Wyatt. (April 12, 1809)

PARKINSON, Richard, and Miss Susanna Welch, both of Annap., were
married Sunday evening last [July 5], by the Rev. Mr. Guest.
(July 9, 1818)

PARKINSON, Thomas, and Ann Wailes, all of Annap., were married on
Sat. evening last, by Rev. T. Riley. (July 9, 1829)

PARNHAM, Dr. Francis, died a fortnight ago, in Chas. Co. (Dec. 2,
1756)

PARR, Mark, one of those concerned in robbing the store of Dr.
James Walker, and lately escaped from our prison, is said to
have been found dead in the Backwoods a few days ago. (Sept.
21, 1748)

PARRAN, Mr. Young, lately died, one of the Representatives and
Chief Justice of Cal. Co. (Jan. 9, 1772)

PARSONS, William, of the Dist. of Columbia, and Miss Sarah Miller
of Annap. were married in the latter city, Thurs. evening,
by the Rev. Mr. Ryland. (Oct. 24, 1822)

PASCAULT, Lewis, of Balto., and Miss Ann Goldsborough, were married
Thurs. evening last [May 20], at White Hall, the seat of
Horatio Ridout, by Rev. Mr. Bitouzey. (June 5, 1811)

PATTERSON, John B., of Va., and Miss Catherine W. Goldsborough, were
   married at Cambridge, Dor. Co., on Thurs., 3rd inst., by the
   Rev. Dr. Kemp. (Oct. 24, 1811)

PATTERSON, John Barnes, of George-Town, D. C., and Miss Eliza
   McCeney, of A. A. Co., were married Thurs. evening last, by
   Rev. President Humphreys, of St. John's Coll., Annap. (Nov.
   29, 1832)

PATTERSON, Robert, and Miss Mary Caton, were married May 1, by the
   Rev. Bishop Carroll. (May 8, 1806)

PATTERSON, William, Jr., died at Balto., on Thurs., 20th inst., in
   his 29th year; of the House of William Patterson and Sons,
   Balto. (Oct. 27, 1808)

PAUL, John, was drowned last week as he was removing from P. G. Co.,
   and crossing the Patuxent about 15 miles from town with a
   cart load of goods; by some accident he fell off the cart
   into the river. (Dec. 8, 1763)

PEACH, Richard, a lawyer, died 3rd inst. He was elected a delegate
   to the Legislature of Maryland from P. G. Co., soon after he
   reached his 21st birthday. (Sept. 15, 1831)

PEACO, Dr. John W., of the U. S. Navy, and Miss Georgieanne Sprogell,
   of Philadelphia, were married in the latter city on Thurs.,
   13th inst., by the Rev. Dr. Bedell. (May 20, 1824)

PEACO, Dr. John W., of the U. S. Navy, a native of Annap., died at
   Savannah, 24th ult. (June 7, 1827)

PEACO, Margaret, daughter of Samuel Peaco, of Annap., died Tues.
   morning last. [Long obit is given.] (Aug. 25, 1831)

PEACO, Mrs. Mary, died in Annap., Thurs. evening last, after a long
   and painful illness, in her 45th year. She was long a respectable member of the Methodist Church. (July 31, 1817)

PEALE, Mr. Charles, died last week in Chestertown. He was formerly
   Deputy Secretary of the General Post Office in London.
   (Dec. 5, 1750)

PEARCE, Benjamin, died last week; at the Head of South River; as a
   result of a gunshot wound accicentally received. (Nov. 22,
   1753)

PEARCE, Edward W., died Jan. 19th, at Urbana, Ohio, aged 29 years,
   a native of Kent Co., Md. The deceased was a lawyer and a
   soldier. (Feb. 17, 1814)

PECK, Michael, was executed at Frederick-Town, 8th inst., for the
   murder of George Jacob Poe last July. (Oct. 21, 1762)

PEMBERTON, Joseph, son of Israel Pemberton, of Philadelphia,
and Anne Galloway, were married Tues., [June 2], at West
River Meeting. (June 4, 1767)

PENNINGTON, Mr. Elijah, died in Annap. Thurs. night last. He leaves
a widow and several children. (March 31, 1825)

PENNINGTON, Mrs. Rebecca, relict of the late Mr. Elijah Pennington,
died Thurs. night last, in Annap. (May 5, 1825)

PENRICE, Mrs. Anne, died Sun. afternoon, on her return from Church.
(Nov. 29, 1832)

PERRY, Edmund has been missing since the time of the hard frost; a
body presumed to be his was found Sun. last, in the Severn.
(May 23, 1765)

PERRY, William, Esq., died Thurs. last [10th inst.] in Annap., in
attendance on his legislative duties; late President of the
Senate of this State. His remains were interred on Sat.
last. (Jan. 17, 1799)

PETTIBONE, Philip, and Henrietta Brown, all of A. A. Co., were
married Thurs. evening last, by the Rev. Mr. Welch. (June 16,
1825)

PHELPS, Mrs. Catherine, died in Annap., on Tues. morning, Christmas
Day,[widow of Joseph Phelps]. (Dec. 27, 1838)

PHELPS, Mrs. Esther, died in A. A. Co., Wed. last, in her 64th year.
(March 22, 1832)

PHELPS, Mr. Joseph, an old and respectable inhabitant, died Mon.
evening last. (March 7, 1833)

PHELPS, Zacharia, died in Balto., on the 4th inst., in his 28th year.
(July 12, 1838)

PHENIX, Mr. Hugh, died Sun. morning last, at his residence on Kent
Island. He leaves a widow and children. (Feb. 2, 1826)

PHILLIPS, Miss Eleanora, daughter of the late Peter Phillips, of
Annap., died in Balto. on 10th inst. (Jan. 19, 1826)

PHILLIPS, Mr. John, of Annap., and Miss Mary Ann Gibson, also of
Annap., were married Wed., 25th Sept., by the Rev. J. A. Gere.
(Oct. 3, 1833)

PHIPPS, Benjamin, a lad of about 15 years of age, unfortunately lost
his life by a fall off a tree, a few days ago near West River.
(Nov. 10, 1763)

PICKERING, Timothy, aged 84, died in Salem, Jan. 29th. [Obit gives
    details of his career in the Revolutionary War.] (Feb. 5,
    1829) Longer obituary notice appears in issue of Feb. 12.

PIDGEON, John, died 12th inst., at an advanced age. He was one of
    the oldest printers of Balto., and took part in the Battle
    of North Point. On the day of his death he had joined his
    old companions in arms to assist in the ceremonial of the
    laying of the cornerstone of the proposed monument, and had
    returned to the city in the steamboat Carroll. He fell over-
    board and drowned. (Sept. 19, 1839)

PINCKNEY, Miss Ann, sister of the late Hon. William Pinckney, died
    in Balto., 30th April, in her 80th year. (May 7, 1835)

PINCKNEY, Edward C., of the Bar of Baltimore, and editor of The
    Marylander, died 11th inst.; from the Baltimore American.
    (April 17, 1828)

PINCKNEY, Jonathan, of Balto., and Mrs. Rebecca Davidson, of Annap.,
    were married on Sun. evening last [Oct. 28], by the Rev. Mr.
    Higinbothom. (Nov. 1, 1804)

PINCKNEY, Jonathan, Cashier of the Farmer's Bank of Maryland, died
    in Annap., on Tues. night last, after an illness of a few
    hours. He leaves several children. (Jan. 3, 1828)

PINCKNEY, Mrs. Mary, died in Charleston, S.C., on the 4th inst., aged
    60 years, wife of Major-General Charles Cotesworth Pinckney.
    (Jan. 30, 1812)

PINCKNEY, Mr. Ninian, died in Annap. on Thurs. night last, for many
    years Clerk of the Executive Council of this state. (Sept.
    30, 1824)

PINCKNEY, Col. Ninian, of the United States Army, died 16th inst.,
    in Balto. (Dec. 22, 1825)

PINCKNEY, Somerville, and Mary Franklin Deale, were married on Thurs.
    evening last, by the Rev. Mr. Blanchard. (Dec. 11, 1828)

PINCKNEY, Dr. William, died Mon., 10th last, in his 38th year, in
    Annap. [Long obit is given.] (Jan. 13, 1825)

PINDELL, Benjamin, and Miss Juliana Anderson, were married on Sun.
    evening [June 14], at Pleasant Plains, the seat of Mr.
    Frederick Grammer, by Rev. Mr. Hammond. (June 18, 1818)

PINDELL, Mr. Benjamin T., of Annap., and Miss Rebecca Anderson, of
    Balto., were married in the latter city on Sun., 12th inst.,
    by Rev. John Valliant. (June 23, 1825)

PINDELL, Philip, died at his residence in A. A. Co., on Sun. morning at an advanced age. (Sept. 30, 1824)

PINDELL, Philip, and Elizabeth Gray were married 7th inst., in A. A. Co., by Rev. Gibbons. (Aug. 23, 1827)

PINDELL, Rinaldo, of A. A. Co., and Sarah W. Gover, daughter of William Gover, Sr., of P. G. Co., were married Tues., 9th inst., by the Right Rev. Bishop Claggett. (July 24, 1811)

PINDLE, Mrs. Julia Ann, consort of Benjamin T. Pindle, of A. A. Co., died Sun. evening last, in her 26th year. She leaves a husband and two small children. (Nov. 13, 1823)

PINKNEY, Mr., died Mon. night; notice dated 11:00 P.M., from the Washington National Intelligencer. (Feb. 28, 1822)

PINKNEY, Miss Catherine, died Monday morning last [Dec. 6], daughter of Jonathan Pinkney of this place. (Dec. 9, 1813)

PINKNEY, Gen. Charles Cotesworth, died Aug. 16th, at his residence in Charleston; a compatriot in the fields of the Revolution. [Long obit is given.] (Sept. 1, 1825)

PINKNEY, Mrs. Elizabeth, consort of Jonathan Pinkney, Esq., cashier of the Farmer's Bank of Maryland, died Sun. morning last in her 55th year. She leaves a husband and children. (Feb. 20, 1823)

PINKNEY, Elizabeth, died Friday last, in Balto., at the residence of Richard Gill; infant daughter of Somerville Pinkney of this place. (Oct. 22, 1835)

PINKNEY, Jonathan Edward, son of Somerville Pinkney of Annap., died Sat., 5th inst., at the residence of his grandfather, Capt. James Deale, aged 20 months. (May 10, 1832)

PINKNEY, Ninian, and Mrs. Amelia Hobbs, were married in Annap. on Thurs. [May 1], by the Rev. Mr. Higinbothom. (May 8, 1806)

PINKNEY, Mr. Robert, was killed last Sat. [Nov. 13], by a fall from a horse. He leaves a widow and three small children. (Nov. 18, 1773)

PINKNEY, Rev. William, and Elizabeth Lloyd Lowndes, daughter of Richard T. Lowndes, were married 2nd inst., at Blenheim, P. G. Co. (Nov. 1, 1838)

PITT, John R., a member of the Legislature, died in Dor. Co., on Wed., 6th inst. (Dec. 14, 1826)

PITTMAN, Jonathan, aged 81, and Jane Argadine, aged 18, both of

Sycamore Township, were married at Hutchinson's Tavern, Cincinnati, Ohio, on 29th ult. (Dec. 29, 1825)

PLAIN, Mrs. Isabella, died in Annap., Mon. night last, consort of
Mr. George Plain. (Jan. 30, 1823)

PLATER, Madam, consort of Col. George Plater, of St. M. Co., died
Oct. 30 past. (Nov. 14, 1750)

PLATER, George, Esq., and Mrs. Rebecca Bowles, relict of the late
James Bowles, Esq., were married Tues. last [June 10]. (June
17, 1729)

PLATER, Hon. George, Esq., of St. M. Co., and Elizabeth, widow of
Capt. John Carpenter, late of this place, deceased, were
married Mon. last [June 25]. (June 28, 1749)

PLATER, Hon. George, Esq., died Sat. last, May 17, at his seat in
St. M. Co., aged over 60 years; for many years one of His
Lordship's Council of State, Naval Officer of Patuxent, and
lately appointed Secretary of the Province. (May 22, 1755)

PLATER, George, Esq., of St. M. Co., and Hannah, daughter of Richard
Lee, Esq., were married Sun., 5th inst., in Chas. Co. (Dec.
16, 1762)

PLATER, George, Esq., died Friday, 10th inst.; Governor of this
State. His remains were deposited at Sotterly, his seat in
St. M. Co., in the family vault. (Feb. 16, 1792)

PLATER, Mrs. Hannah, died on Tues. morning, 20th inst.; consort of
George Plater, Esq., of St. M. Co., and daughter of Richard
Lee, Esq. She was in the full bloom of life, and had been
not ten months married. (Sept. 29, 1763)

PLATER, William, of St. M. Co., and Mrs. Eliza McElderry, were
married at Glasvar, Chas. Co., on Thurs., 12th inst. (Jan.
19, 1826)

PLOWMAN, Mr. Jonathan, merchant of Balto. Town, and Rebecca Arnold,
eldest daughter of Mr. David Arnold, were married Thurs.
last [Oct. 7], in Cal. Co. (Oct. 14, 1762)

PLUMMER, John, Jr., of P. G. Co., and Miss Anne Worthington, daughter
of John Worthington, of A. A. Co., were married Sun. morning
last [March 25], near Queen Anne, by the Rev. Mr. Weems.
(March 28, 1810)

PLUMMER, Mr. Samuel of P. G. Co., was found dead on Wed., 12th inst.,
in the road near his plantation, and is supposed to have died
in a fit of apoplexy. He was sober, industrious, and above
60 years of age. (Dec. 20, 1759)

PLUMMER, Yate, died Mon. night, 23rd ult., after a short illness, at
his home in A. A. Co., in the 48th year of his age. He leaves
a widow and nine children. (Aug. 2, 1764)

POE, Mr. George Jacob, was shot at his own house, on the 26th of last
month, about eight miles from Frederick-Town. He was shot by
a Dutch servant man of his, with two bullets and five swan shot
through the body, just below the navel, of which he instantly
died. He leaves a widow and several children to lament him.
(Aug. 5, 1762)

POMPILLON, Mr.; some few days ago, at Oxford, as two little girls of
his were sitting by a fireside by themselves, the fire flew
and catched the cloathes [sic] of one of them, and burnt her
to that degree that she died a few hours after. (Feb. 16, 1764)

POOLE, Mrs. Edward, died in Annap., on Thurs. last [Dec. 8]. (Dec.
15, 1808)

PORTER, Capt. David, of Balto., died on June 24, at New Orleans.
(Aug. 11, 1808)

PORTEUS, Edmund, died Thurs. [March 26], in Chas. Co., Clerk of that
county. He is succeeded in the said office by Benjamin Fendall, Esq. (April 2, 1752)

POTTS, Joseph, Attorney-at-law, of Berwick-on-Tweed, died Sat., 7th
inst., in his 29th year, at the house of Mr. John Thomas, in
Fred. Co. His remains were decently interred in the Quaker
burial ground. (Sept. 12, 1776)

POTTS, Richard, died in Frederick-Town. (Dec. 15, 1808)

POWELL, James, was executed near Annap. last Friday for burglary
committed some time ago in Som. Co. He was about 39 years
old and a native of this province. (May 21, 1752)

PRATT, Thomas G., Esq., of Upper Marlborough, P. G. Co., and Adeline
Mackubin Kent, eldest daughter of Col. Robert W. Kent, of
South River, were married Tues., 8th inst., by Rev. Mr. Wright.
(Sept. 17, 1835)

PREVOST, J. B., late minister to South America, died in Upper Peru.
(Sept. 8, 1825)

PRICE, Walter L., a Revolutionary officer, died in Annap. on Tues.
last. He leaves a widow and several children. (April 15,
1824)

PRICE, William, delegate to the General Assembly from All. Co., died
leaving a wife and children. (From the Maryland Republican)
(Jan. 29, 1829)

PRIESTLEY, Edward, cabinet-maker, died Sun. morning last, 12th inst.,
in his 59th year. He was a native of Annap., and came to Balto.
about 1790, a friendless orphan with a helpless mother. He
leaves two sons. [Long obit. is given.] (From the Baltimore
American.) (March 16, 1837)

PRIESTLEY, Mrs. Mary Ann, died Mon., 30th ult., in her 86th year,
mother of Edward Priestley. Formerly a resident of Annap.,
for many years she had been an inhabitant of Balto. (April
2, 1835)

PRIM, Lawrence, a sailor, was drowned on Mon., 2nd inst., by the
capsizing of a canoe near town. (July 5, 1764)

PRITCHARD, Capt. John, master of the ship Cunliffe, bound for Va.,
was killed in action with a French privateer, on Jan. 17,
1744/5, aged 39 years. (July 12, 1745)

PRITCHARD, Mr. Pinkney, formerly of A. A. Co., and Anne Elizabeth
Smith, of Richmond, were married 10th inst., at the latter
place by Rev. Thomas Crowder. (Oct. 17, 1839)

PRITCHARD, William, died at Portland Manor, Mon. morning. (Oct. 3,
1822)

PROSPER, James, of Annap., and Miss Eliza Du Puys of Balto., were
married in the latter city on Tues., 23rd ult., by the Rev.
Mr. Burch. (June 1, 1815)

PRYSE, Thomas, sadler, of Annap., was drowned off the mouth of the
Magothy, Friday last, en route from Annap. to Balto. (Feb.
28, 1793)

PUE, Mrs. Mary, relict of the late Dr. Michael Pue, of Elk Ridge, died
Mon., 29th ult., in her 90th year. (Aug. 8, 1833)

PUGSLEY, John, a stay maker on the North side of Severn, on going
home from a wedding yesterday evening, lost himself in a
violent snow-storm, a few yards from his house, and was
found dead in the morning.)Feb. 21, 1750)

PUMPHREY, Charles, and Eleanor Miller, all of A. A. Co., were married
3rd inst., by the Rev. Watkins. (June 14, 1832)

PURDY, James, died in this city, on Friday, 26th ult., of pleurisy,
in his 59th year. He leaves four children. (Nov. 8, 1832)

QUERY, Thomas, was killed by Indians on Nov. 8, in "the Great Cove,"
in Fred. Co. (Dec. 1, 1763)

QUYNN, Allen, died Tues. morning (Nov. 8), in his 77th year; long a

resident of Annap., and for 25 years a member of the House
of Delegates. (Nov. 10, 1803)

QUYNN, John, and Miss Maria Leakin, of Balto., were married Aug. 26,
at Balto., by the Rev. Dr. Bend. The groom was a resident
of Annap. (Sept. 4, 1806)

RABLING, Thomas, and his wife were killed this day fortnight during
a terrible thunderstorm in St. M. Co., near the head of
Jowles' Creek, when lightning struck the mulberry tree they
were under. Also killed were another man, woman, and three
children. An infant at Mrs. Rabling's breast was unhurt.
(June 7, 1749)

RAFFERTY, Rev. Dr., of Annap., and Miss Catherine Howard, were
married in A. A. Co., on Thurs. evening, 2nd inst., by the
Rev. Mr. Tyng. (Dec. 9, 1824)

RAFFERTY, Dr., Principal of St. John's Coll., died Aug. 8, in Orange
Co., N. Y. (Aug. 12, 1830)

RAFFERTY, Mrs., died Sat., 30th ult., in her 34th year, consort of
Rev. William Rafferty, Professor of Languages in St. John's
College. The deceased had been but a short time among us--
she was lately from New York. (Nov. 11, 1819)

RAFFERTY, Mrs. Catherine, widow of the late Dr. Rafferty, Principal
of St. John's College, died Tues. morning last. (Jan. 27,
1831)

RAITT, Mr. John, died on Thurs. last [June 30], and on Friday was
buried; merchant and late Sheriff of A. A. Co. (July 6, 1758)
Anne Raitt, widow, is administratrix. (July 27, 1758)
Nathan Hammond, Jr., is administrator. (Jan. 10, 1760)

RALLINGS, Miss Rebecca, of Annap., died 10th inst. (March 27, 1834)

RALPH, Rev. George, died at Pomona, Balto. Co., on Mon., 17th inst.,
in his 61st year. His qualifications as an instructor of
youth have long been very generally known. He was a minister
of the Episcopal Church. The last appointment he received,
to the Rhetorical Chair in the University of Maryland, evinces
the confidence reposed in his learning and talents. (May 27,
1813)

RAMSAY, Commander John, of the snow Mary (Capt. Brown), died on his
passage from London. The ship carried 52 felons. (Oct. 26,
1748)

RAMSAY, Col. Nathaniel, died at Balto., on 24th ult. In the Revolutionary War he distinguished himself as a brave, meritorious
and humane officer. [Long obit gives details of military
career.] (Nov. 6, 1817)

RAMSEY, Miss, aged nine or ten years old, the only daughter of Mr.
Ramsey, of Cal. Co., was inhumanly murdered by a thirteen year
old negro boy. (June 13, 1805)

RANDALL, Beale, of Balto. Co., and Miss Martha Robosson, of A. A. Co.,
were married on Thurs. evening, 9th inst., by the Rev. Mr.
Reid. (Nov. 23, 1815)

RANDALL, Henry K., and Emily Munroe, eldest daughter of Thomas Munroe,
Esq., were married in the city of Washington, 23rd inst. (Nov.
30, 1826)

RANDALL, John, Esq., Collector of the Port of Annap., died Mon.
night. (June 15, 1826)

RANDALL, Miss M., of Annap., died Tues. evening, 26th ult. (Aug. 4,
1808)

RANDALL, Dr. Richard, a native and long time resident of Annap., died
April 17th, at Liberia. (July 2, 1829)

RANDALL, Thomas, Esq., of the Superior Court of Middle Florida, and
Laura Henrietta, eldest daughter of William Wirt, Attorney-
General of the U. S. A., were married at Washington, on Tues.,
21st inst., by the Rev. Dr. Laurie. (Aug. 30, 1827)

RANDELL, Charles, on Sat., 5th inst., was found dead in the Road
near Solomon Wooden's in Balto. Co. He is supposed to have
been instantly killed by a fall from his horse the night
before. (Nov. 17, 1763)

RANDELL, Capt. John, died last Sun. morning, at his lodgings in
town, aged 66 years. (Oct. 30, 1755)

RASIN, Mr. William, died on 13th inst., at George-Town, Kent Co.;
formerly one of the Representatives of that county. (Feb.
25, 1762)

RATHBONE, Mrs. E., died in New York, suddenly on Sat. evening, 27th
ult.; wife of Mr. J. Rathbone, merchant of that city, aged
52 years. (Feb. 7, 1810)

RAVENSCROFT, Rt. Rev. John, D. D., Bishop of the Protestant Episcopal Church in North Carolina, died in Raleigh, Friday morning
last, at the residence of Gavin Hogg, Esq., in his 58th year;
"Raleigh, N.C., March 8." (March 18, 1830)

RAWLINGS, Mrs. Elizabeth, died Sun. last, at an advanced age, of
Annap. (Nov. 9, 1837)

RAWLINGS, Gassaway, of A. A. Co., died Wed., 24th inst. Had he
lived one more day, he would have completed his 69th year.
(July 2, 1812)

RAWLINGS, Capt. Jehosophat, of this place, died of small pox. News
    of his death comes by letters from London. (April 6, 1758)

RAWLINGS, Mr. John, departed this life at his farm on South River,
    on the 8th inst., in his 51st year. (Jan. 16, 1812)

RAWLINGS, Joseph, formerly of Annap., died at Centreville, 15th inst.
    (June 28, 1809)

RAWLINGS, Mr. William, and Mrs. Jane Barber, all of Annap., were
    married Thurs. evening last, by the Rev. Mr. Guest. (Nov. 22,
    1832)

RAY, Dr. Hyde, of the U. S. Navy, and Miss Catherine Steele, daughter
    of the late James Steele, Esq., were married Thurs. evening,
    by the Rev. Mr. Blanchard. (Feb. 22, 1827)

RAY, Dr. Hyde, died Mon. last, at his residence in this city, Sur-
    geon in the U. S. Navy, leaving a widow and several children.
    (Sept. 10, 1835)

RAY, Lieut. James H., of the U. S. Navy, died yesterday, 10th inst.,
    in his 28th year. (Nov. 11, 1824)

RAY, Mr. Jesse, died 12th inst., at his residence in this county,
    at an advanced age. (Dec. 17, 1825)

RAY, John, was killed Thurs. morning last, at the door of his house,
    in P. G. Co., about 17 miles from Annap. He was struck by
    lightning. (May 7, 1752)

RAY, Mrs. Mary, died in Annap., on Tues. morning, relict of the
    late Jesse Ray. (Dec. 10, 1835)

READ, Elizabeth, drowned four days ago, when the ice broke at the
    Furnace Pond, at Alexander Lawson's Iron Works in Balto.
    Co. (Dec. 28, 1752)

READING, ---, an ancient and insane woman of Tal. Co., fell into a
    fire and was burnt to death. (Dec. 16, 1762)

REANEY, Dr. William, died at Balto., on the 28th ult., in his 22nd
    year. (Dec. 1, 1825)

REED, Frances, of Fred. Co., died in Annap. on Friday night last
    [May 22]. (May 28, 1807)

REED, Capt. James, of the U. S. Army, died at Phila., on the 11th
    inst., Commandant of Fort Mifflin. (Aug. 26, 1819)

REED, Gen. Philip, died Mon. night at Huntingfield, his residence
    in Kent Co., Md., "another Revolutionary soldier and patriot
    gone." [Long obit is given.] (Nov. 12, 1829)

REID, Upton Scott, died the night of Jan. 26th, and was buried Jan.
28, by his Masonic brethren. (Feb. 14, 1822)

REINAGLE, Alexander, died at Balto., on Thurs. evening, [Sept. 21],
in his 62nd year, one of the managers of the Phildelphia and
Balto. Theatres. (Sept. 27, 1809)

RENNY, Mr. Robert, died yesterday, Rector of St. Margaret's in this
county. (June 23, 1774)

RETALIC, Mr. Simon, died at Fort McHenry, on the 5th inst., an arti-
ficer, aged about 45 years, and a native of Annap. (March
18, 1824)

REVELL, Mr. Martin F., and Miss Mary W. Wirt, were married in Annap.,
on the evening of of the 6th inst., by Rev. Mr. Watkins.
(May 12, 1825)

REVELL, Martin F., and Miss Mary Horne, both of Annap., were married
Thurs. evening last, by Rev. Watkins. (May 6, 1830)

REVELL, Mrs. Mary Elizabeth, died Sat. last, after a lingering illness, consort of Martin F. Revell, of Annap. (April 2, 1829)

REYNOLDS, John, and Miss Ellen R. Dunn, both of Annap., were married
Sun. evening last, by Rev. Mr. Vanquickenborne. (Jan. 30,
1823)

REYNOLDS, Maccubbin, of A. A. Co., was killed in a quarrell with a
neighbor, both of whom lived at Elk Ridge. (Aug. 17, 1748)
Philip Hammond is admin. (March 29, 1749)

REYNOLDS, William, hatter, of this place, lost his two eldest sons,
aged seven and six, on Sun. last [July 12], when they were
accidentally drowned. (July 14, 1747)

RICE, Peter, one of the members of the House of Delegates, from
Caroline Co., died yesterday morning, at the house of Mr.
Lloyd M. Lowe, in this city. (Jan. 31, 1805)

RICHARDS, Clement, and Mrs. Sarah Tucker, were married Sun. evening
last in Annap., by the Rev. Mr. Wyatt. (June 5, 1806)

RICHARDS, Clement, an old Revolutionary soldier, died on Sun. morning
last [Aug. 14]. He was buried on Mon. afternoon, with the
honors of war. (Aug. 11, 1808)

RICHARDS, John S., editor of the Reading Journal, and Nancy D. O'Bryan,
of Phila., were married 1st inst. (Nov. 7, 1839)

RICHARDS, Mrs. Sarah, died Tues. evening, of a pulmonary complaint.
(April 17, 1823)

RICHARDS, Thomas, was executed Friday last at Upper Marlborough for horse stealing. (June 27, 1750)

RICHARDSON, Mrs., of Kent Island, and her three daughters were drowned Sun. last when a small schooner capsized on the Chester River; from the Easton Gazette. (Aug. 9, 1838)

RICHARDSON, Mr. Samuel, departed this life on 19th ult., in the 58th year of his age, of Fred. Co. (March 1, 1764)

RICHARDSON, Samuel R., of Annap., and Miss Johanna F. Weedon, of Broad Neck, A. A. Co., were married Thurs. morning last by Rev. Dr. Hammond. (June 6, 1839)

RICHARDSON, Mr. Thomas, late of Annap., merchant, was killed instantly by lightning on the evening of Friday last [June 17], at the house of Mr. Adair in Balto. Town. [Long account is given.] (June 23, 1768)

RICHARDSON, Mr. William, died at his residence on West River, on the evening of the 6th inst., in his 58th year. (Oct. 14, 1824)

RICHARDSON, William, and Miss Susanna Lavey were married in Annap., on Sun. last, by the Rev. Dr. Davis. (March 24, 1825)

RIDGATE, Thomas How, merchant in Port Tobacco, died Friday, March 26th, in his 56th year. [Long obit is given.] (April 8, 1790) Elizabeth Ridgate is the administratrix. (July 1, 1790)

RIDGAWAY, Richard, Esq., died in Centreville, Q. A. Co., on Friday, 5th inst.; a member of the House of Delegates of Maryland. (Sept. 11, 1828)

RIDGELY, ---, aged two years, the only son of Mr. John Ridgely, of Balto. Co., died last week when he fell into the fire. (Aug. 3, 1748)

RIDGELY, General, died 17th inst., in Baltimore City. [Long obit is given.] (July 23, 1829)

RIDGELY, Absalom, died on Mon. afternoon [July 13], in his 26th year. (July 16, 1818)

RIDGELY, Charles, died on Mon. last [Nov. 25], in Annap., in his 75th year. (Nov. 28, 1805)

RIDGELY, Charles, Jr., of Hampton, and Miss Maria Campbell, of Balto., were married in that city on Thurs. evening last [Sept. 21], by the Rev. Mr. Bend. (Sept. 27, 1809)

RIDGELY, Charles, and Miss Elizabeth Fowler, daughter of William Fowler of Balto., were married in Balto., on Tues., 30th ult., by the Rev. Mr. Wyatt. (Feb. 7, 1810)

RIDGELY, Mr. David, of Annap., and Miss Julia Maria Woodfield, of
   A. A. Co., were married Tues. evening last [April 12], by the
   Rev. Alfred Griffith. (April 14, 1814)

RIDGELY, Mr. David, of Annap., and Miss Maria Sellman, of Balto.,
   were married in the latter city on Tues., 15th inst., by the
   Rev. Mr. Jennings. (Dec. 24, 1818)

RIDGELY, Edward D., died Sat. last. (July 8, 1830)

RIDGELY, Mrs. Harriett, daughter of the late John Callahan, Esq.,
   and wife of Dr. John Ridgely, of Annap., died Sat., 26th
   inst. (Jan. 31, 1828)

RIDGELY, Col. Henry, died last week, at Elk Ridge, formerly Chief
   Justice of A. A. Co., for several years. (Feb. 14, 1750)

RIDGELY, Henry Associate Judge of the Third Judicial District, died
   on 22nd ult., at his residence on Elk Ridge, in his 46th
   year. (June 26, 1811)

RIDGELY, Mrs. Hester F., wife of Dr. John Ridgely, of Annap., and
   daughter of the late Judge Henry Ridgely of Annap., died on
   Thurs., 24th inst. (March 31, 1836)

RIDGELY, Dr. John, and Miss Harriet Callahan, were married Tues.
   evening [Nov. 3], by the Rev. Mr. Addison. (Nov. 5, 1812)

RIDGELY, Dr. John, of Annap., and Miss Hester F. Ridgely, of George-
   Town, D.C., were married in the latter place on Thurs., 26th
   ult., by Rev. Mr. Brookes. (April 2, 1835)

RIDGELY, John Callahan, eldest son of Dr. John Ridgely, of Annap.,
   died yesterday morning, in his 15th year. (Feb. 24, 1831)

RIDGELY, Mrs. Julia M., died on Friday; wife of David Ridgely, in
   her 23rd year. (May 29, 1817)

RIDGELY, Maria Sellman, died in Annap., on Tues. evening, 26th inst.,
   in her 6th year; daughter of David and Maria Ridgely. (Aug.
   28, 1834)

RIDGELY, Mrs. Matilda, relict of the late Judge Henry Ridgely, and
   eldest daughter of the late Samuel Chase, Judge of the Supreme
   Court and Signer of the Declaration of Independence, died in
   George-Town, D. C., on 2nd inst., in her 72nd year. She was
   a native of Annap. (Feb. 12, 1835)

RIDGELY, Nicholas, and Mrs. Jemima Merriken, all of Annap., were
   married on Sun. evening [Jan. 17], by the Rev. Mr. Guest.
   (Jan. 21, 1819)

RIDGELY, Richard, and Miss Mary Jane Brewer, daughter of Mr. Nicholas
   Brewer, all of Annap., were married on Tues. evening [Dec. 14],
   by the Rev. Mr. Guest. (Dec. 16, 1819)

RIDGELY, the Hon. Richard, died at his seat in A. A. Co., Thurs.
   morning, 26th ult., in his 69th year; late an Associate Judge
   of the Third Judicial District of Maryland. During the Revolutionary War he took an active stand in the support of those
   principles, the triumph of which, established the independence of our country. (March 4, 1824)

RIDGELY, Richard, of Annap., died 8th inst., in his 41st year. He
   leaves a widow and children. (Jan. 15, 1835)

RIDGELY, Lieut. Samuel, eldest son of Col. Charles S. Ridgely, of
   A. A. Co., died April 2nd, at New Orleans, in his 21st year.
   The deceased had graduated from West Point. [Long obit is
   given.] (May 31 1827)

RIDOUT, Addison, died early in August at Sulphur Springs, Monmouth
   Co.. Va., aged 31; educated at St. John's College, Annapolis;
   member of the House of Delegates. (Aug. 24, 1826)

RIDOUT, Mrs. H., consort of Horatio Ridout, died 11th inst., at
   White Hall, near Annap. (June 26, 1811)

RIDOUT, Miss Harriett, daughter of Samuel Ridout of Annap., died at
   the Sulphur Springs, Va., early in September. (Sept. 21,
   1826)

RIDOUT, Horatio, Esq., of White Hall, and Miss Ann Weems, were
   married on Thurs. last, by the Rev. Mr. Nind. (Oct. 22, 1812)

RIDOUT, Horatio, of H., and Jemima Duvall, all of A. A. Co., were
   married 12th inst., by Rev. Mr. Hutton. (Sept. 19, 1839)

RIDOUT, John, Esq., died Friday, 6th inst., at his house in Annap.,
   in his 66th year. On Sunday, his remains were interred in
   the family burying ground at White Hall. (Oct. 12, 1797)

RIDOUT, John, of White Hall, and Miss Charlsine C. Nixon, were
   married at Dover, Delaware, on 19th ult., by Rev. Mr. Der-
   borough. (Feb. 11, 1813)

RIDOUT, Dr. John, of Hagerstown, and Miss Prudence Gough Owings,
   daughter of the late Samuel Owings of Stephen, of Balto.,
   were married Thurs. evening, 2nd inst., at West River.
   (Jan. 9, 1823)

RIDOUT, Mrs. Mary, consort of Samuel Ridout, of Annap., died Mon.
   last [March 2]. (March 5, 1807)

RIDOUT, Mrs. Mary, died on Sun. [Aug. 14]. Her remains were conveyed
on Mon. last to White Hall, to be interred there. (Aug. 18,
1808)

RIDOUT, Miss Meliora Ogle, late of P. G. Co., died 14th inst., at
her father's residence. [Long obit is given] (Oct. 20, 1825)

RIGBY, Mrs. Asenath, died Mon., 26th inst., of typhus fever. A resident of Annap., she leaves three children. (Dec. 29, 1831)

RIGBY, Mrs. Elizabeth, died in Annap., Sun. night last, at an advanced age. (May 31, 1827)

RIGBY, James, and Miss Anne Johnson, were married on Thurs. evening
last [April 18], by the Rev. Mr. Wyatt. (April 25, 1805)

RILEY, Mr. James, ship carpenter; his body was taken up on the Eastern
Shore the beginning of last month. (Dec. 13, 1749)

RINGGOLD, James, of Kent Island, and Miss Elizabeth Slemaker of
Annap. were married on Mon. evening last [April 4], by the
Rev. Mr. Wyatt. (April 7, 1808)

RINGGOLD, Miss Mary, of Wash. Co., died in Annap. on Sun. morning
last [Aug. 11]. (Aug. 15, 1805)

RINGGOLD, Peregrine, and Miss Mary Clarke Coe, both of Annap., were
married here Sun. evening last, by Rev. Mr. Vanquickenborne
of White Marsh. (Jan. 2, 1823)

RINGGOLD, Gen. Samuel, of Wash. Co., died Sun., 18th Oct. He was
interred at Fountain Rock. [Long obit is given.] (Oct. 22,
1829)

RINGGOLD, Mr. Thomas, one of the Delegates from Kent Co., died Wed.,
1st inst.; late of Chester-Town. (April 9, 1772)

RISTEAU, Mr. Talbot, Clerk of Balto. Co., died Friday last [Nov. 23],
of a nervous fever. (Nov. 29, 1753)

ROBERTS, Allen, one of several married men with families, was killed
last week in Cal. Co., when a gust of wind blew a house down.
(May 2, 1799)

ROBERTS, John, was executed at Chestertown Friday last, for breaking
open and robbing the store of Capt. Marsh. (May 22, 1755)

ROBERTS, John, was murdered by Joseph James Harris Caulk, who was
tried and sentenced to death; "Easton, June 6." (June 14,
1809)

ROBERTS, Dr. Jonathan, died 15th inst., at his farm on Kent Island,
aged about 65 years. (July 20, 1797)

ROBINS, Mr. Thomas, died Sun., 29th ult., after 10 days' illness,
    at Peach Blossom, in Tal. Co.; in his 22nd year, a young
    gentleman who was but lately returned from Great Britain to
    his native country, and entered into possession of a very
    affluent fortune. (Dec. 10, 1761)

ROBINSON, Capt. Benjamin, of A. A. Co., and Harriett Cromwell, of
    Balto. Co., were married Thurs. evening last, by the Rev.
    David Steele. (March 13, 1834)

ROBINSON, Mrs. Catherine W., consort of Mr. Lyles R. Robinson, and
    daughter of the late Dr. Richard Goldsborough, of Cambridge,
    Md., died Wed., 10th inst., at her residence near Winchester,
    Va., in her 35th year. [Long obit is given.] (Dec. 24, 1828)

ROBINSON, Mr. Edward, formerly of Winchester, Va., died on Tues.
    afternoon, at the residence of his mother. (June 4, 1829)

ROBINSON, Mrs. Elizabeth, of Severn, died in Annap., on Mon. last,
    in her 57th year. (Aug. 20, 1829)

ROBINSON, George, and Mary Ann Welch, both of Annap., were married
    Thurs. evening last by Rev. Mr. Poisal. (Oct. 29, 1835)

ROBINSON, Mr. Jacqueline [sic], died suddenly in Annap., on Sat.
    afternoon. (July 7, 1825)

ROBINSON, Hon. John, President of the Council of Virginia, died.
    (Aug. 30, 1749)

ROBOSON, Mrs. Mary, died Sun. morning last [April 23], relict of
    Col. Elijah Roboson, in her 62nd year. Her venerable mansion,
    situated on the public line from the Severn ferry to Balti-
    more was always a receptacle for the wearied traveller; it
    was under her roof they found repose. (April 27, 1815)

ROE, Mr. H., died at Newburg, N. Y., formerly a teacher in the A. A.
    Co. Free School, and recently appointed teacher of the Primary
    School, about to be opened in Annap. (Sept. 17, 1829)

ROGERS, Benjamin, his wife and seven children, and Edmund Marle,
    all of Fred. Co., were killed or carried off by a party of
    Indians on Wed. [Oct. 1]. (Oct. 9, 1755)

ROGERS, Hon. John, Chancellor of the State of Maryland, died last
    night. (Srpt. 24, 1789)

ROGERS, Commodore John, died Wed. evening, at the Naval Asylum, near
    the Schuylkill, in his 74th year. (Aug. 9, 1838)

ROGERS, Mr. Nicholas, died Sun. evening last [May 7], at Balto. Town,
    after a long and lingering illness. (May 11, 1758)

ROGERS, Thomas, Clerk of the Senate of this state, died in Annap.,
   on Sat. night last [Dec. 15], in his 40th year. (Dec. 20,
   1821)

ROGERS, William, Esq., died here last Sat. morning [July 29] very
   much lamented, in his 50th year, and on Sun. evening was
   decently interred. He was a gentleman born and bred in New
   England, but had long been a worthy inhabitant of this place.
   He enjoyed many posts of honour and trust. He leaves a widow
   and three children. (Aug. 2, 1749)

ROGERS, Mr. William, died last week at Balto. Town, aged about 60,
   one of the first settlers of that flourishing town, one of
   the county magistrates, and an eminent planter. (June 18,
   1761)

ROGERSON, Capt. Thomas, died in Chas. Co., in his 77th year, for
   many years a member of the Legislature of Maryland. He was
   Chairman of the Committee on Military Persons. "Another
   Revolutionary character gone!" (Aug. 1, 1833)

ROHRER, Samuel, of Hagerstown, and Elizabeth, daughter of Conrad
   Schultz, were married in Balto., the 20th ult., by the Rev.
   Mr. Ulhorn. (April 6, 1826)

ROSS, Mrs. Alicia, died Wed. last [July 9], after a short illness,
   wife of John Ross, Esq., of Annap. (July 15, 1746)

ROSS, Dr. David, of Bladensburg, and Ariana, eldest daughter of
   John Brice, of Annap., were married yesterday evening. (Sept.
   5, 1750)

ROSS, John, Esq., died Thurs. evening last [Sept. 18], at his house
   in town, one of the Aldermen of this City, and Lord Baltimore's
   Deputy Agent, in his 71st year. He had been a widower above
   20 years. (Sept. 25, 1766)

ROSS, John, drowned off the mouth of the Magothy Friday last en route
   from Annap. to Balto. (Feb. 28, 1793)

ROSS, John, of Annap., died Friday evening [Oct. 13], last. (Oct.
   18, 1809)

ROSS, Mark, aged 19, and Miss Betsy Freelock, aged 70, were married
   at Ipswich, Mass. (Aug. 30, 1809)

ROUSBY, Mr. John, died last week of a violent fever, aged about 25,
   at his seat on Patuxent River, Cal. Co.; eldest son of the
   late Hon. John Rousby, Esq., Collector of His Majesty's
   Customs for the District of Patuxent. He leaves a widow
   and one child. (Feb. 6, 1751)

ROWLANDSON, John, drowned last month off Poplar Island. (March 6,
     1766)

ROYSTON, James, of Annap., died Sat. morning last, in his 52nd year.
     (Dec. 5, 1805)

RUDGKING, Edward, was executed Friday last for the murder of his
     fellow servant. (Oct. 10, 1765)

RUMSEY, Benjamin, died at Joppa, in Harf. Co., on Mon., 7th inst.,
     for many years one of the Judges of the High Court of Appeals
     in this state. (March 24, 1808)

RUSH, Richard, and Miss Catherine F. Murray, were married on Tues.,
     29th ult., at Piney Grove, by the Rev. Mr. Judd. (Sept. 6,
     1809)

RUSSELL, James, Esq., died on the morning of Aug. 1, at his house in
     Westminster, Eng., at an advanced age. He was long success-
     fully engaged in mercantile pursuits, having for a series of
     years cultivated a correspondence with Virginia and Maryland.
     (Nov. 20, 1788)

RUSSWURM, Mr. Jn. B., editor of the Liberia Herald, and Sarah Eliza-
     beth McGill, were married at Liberia on Jan. 10, 1833. (April
     18, 1833)

RUTLAND, Capt. Edmund, died at Boston on the 13th of last month, of
     a lingering illness; a resident of Annap. (July 4, 1765)

ST. CLAIR, Major-Gen. Arthur, died at his farm on Laurel Hill, Somer-
     set Co., Penna., on Monday, 31st ult. "Another Revolutionary
     Hero gone." (Sept. 17, 1818)

SALTER, ---, was drowned, with his horse, on Friday evening last,
     as he was going over a ferry at Fredericksburg. (Feb. 16,
     1764)

SANDERS, Mrs. Eliza, died Friday morning last, consort of William
     Sanders, of this county, leaving four infant children. (May
     24, 1827)

SANDERS, John, a young man, was drowned one day last week when he
     attempted to cross West River on the ice and he fell in.
     (Jan. 15, 1761)

SANDERS, John, Esq., died in Harf. Co., on Sat. last [May 8]. He
     was a Representative from that county in the Legislature of
     of this state. (May 13, 1813)

SANDERS, Mrs. Rebecca, wife of Robert Sanders, Sr., died Thurs.,

March 19, at her house on South River Neck, aged about 75
years. She was decently interred on Thurs. last. She had
been married for 56 years, and lived to see the fourth generation. (April 2, 1752)

SANDERS, William, and Miss Eliza Smith, were married Thurs. evening
last [Feb. 1] in this county, by the Rev. Mr. Duncan. (Feb.
8, 1816)

SANDERS, William, of A. A. Co., died suddenly, May 26th. (June 3,
1830)

SANDERS, William G., and Mrs. Matilda M'Cartey, daughter of Dennis
Magruder, were married Sun., 19th ult., at Mount Sabentia,
P. G. Co., by the Rev. Mr. McCormick. (March 2, 1815)

SANDS, Mrs., died Thurs. morning last. (Dec. 29, 1831)

SANDS, Mrs. Ariana, died Friday, 7th inst.; formerly of Annap., but
for many years an inhabitant of Balto. (June 13, 1839)

SANDS, Mrs. Charlotte, consort of Dr. William Sands, of A. A. Co.,
died Thurs., 22nd ult. She leaves five small children.
(June 13, 1839)

SANDS, John, of Annap., died this morning, in his 45th year. (July
2, 1807)

SANDS, Joseph, died Sat. morning last, in his 64th year; Collector
of the Port of Annap. (Nov. 8, 1832)

SANDS, Richard, Esq., and Sarah Ann Hardesty, all of this city,
were married Thurs. evening last, by Rev. Mr. Vinton. (April
19, 1838)

SANDS, Samuel, died last evening [Oct. 3], in Annap., in his 38th
year. (Oct. 4, 1809)

SANDS, Miss Sarah, died Friday night last in Annap., in her 59th
year. (April 3, 1823)

SANDS, Mrs. Sarah, died Sun. morning last, consort of Mr. Joseph
Sands, Sr., of Annap., in her 42nd year. (March 27, 1823)

SANDS, Sarah Elizabeth, daughter of Dr. William Sands, of this county,
died Friday last. (July 30, 1829)

SANDS, Thomas, of the U. S. N., and Sarah, daughter of the late
William Whittington, were married in Annap. on Tues. evening,
by the Rev. Mr. Blanchard. (March 30, 1826)

SANDS, Mr. William, died Sun. last [Aug. 12], in Annap., in his 75th
year. (Aug. 15, 1810)

SANDS, Dr. William, and Miss Charlotte Duvall, all of A. A. Co., were
married Thurs., 31st ult. (Feb. 7, 1828)

SAWYER, Charles Conyer, died Friday, 19th inst., of a tetanic infec-
tion, aged six years, four months, and sixteen days, son of
Capt. John Sawyer of the Bohemia Islands. This youth was one
of the unfortunate sufferers taken from the wreck of the Brigantine Dragon. He leaves a grandfather and aunt. [Long obit
is given.] (Aug. 25, 1825)

SCHAEFFER, Miss Ann Maria, died in Annap., on Wed., 1st inst., the
youngest daughter of Baltzer Schaeffer, in her 17th year.
(Aug. 9, 1821)

SCHAEFFER, Rev. George B., died in Balto., on Sun., 25th inst., late
rector of St. Margaret's Westminster Parish, A. A. Co., in
his 28th year. He leaves a wife and two children. (Dec. 29,
1825)

SCHMUCK, Capt., of the U. S. Army, and Miss Ellen A. Kilty, of
Annap., were married Thurs., 15th inst., at Norfolk, by Rev.
Delany. (March 29, 1827)

SCHMUCK, Capt. Jacob, died at St. Augustine, 10th ult., in his 43rd
year; of a U. S. Artillery Regiment. [Long obit gives details
of his military career in the War of 1812. (May 14, 1835)

SCHNEIDER, John, musician, and inhabitant of Annap., died Sat. evening last, after cutting his own throat. (Oct. 31, 1771)

SCHREIBER, Mrs. Anna Maria, died 8th inst., near Hanover, Adams Co.,
Penna.; consort of the late Andrew Schreiber, in her 92nd year.
She lived in a state of matrimony with her husband for 66
years, and resided on the plantation where she died for 70
years. She had 126 descendants at the time of her death.
(May 21, 1801)

SCHWRAR, George, eldest son of Mr. George Schwrar, died Tues. evening
last, aged seven years and six months. (Sept. 11, 1828)

SCHWRAR, Philip, and Miss Sarah Thompson, all of Annap., were married
Sun. evening last, by the Rev. Mr. Ryland. (Nov. 7, 1822)

SCHWRAR, Philip, drowned Sat. last. He leaves a wife and two children. (March 2, 1826)

SCIBLE, Mr. William, died in A. A. Co., on Friday evening last.
(May 4, 1826)

SCIPLE, John Henry, died Tues. night last, at his residence a few
miles from Annap. (Feb. 2, 1826)

SCOLLAY, Dr., and Miss Harriet Lowndes, formerly of Annap., were
     married Jan. 19 last, in Jefferson Co., Va., by the Rev. Mr.
     Smith. (March 20, 1823)

SCOTT, Benjamin, of A. A. Co., died Tues. last. (April 4, 1839)

SCOTT, Mrs. Elizabeth, died in Annap., on Tues. night last [Sept. 7],
     at an advanced age, the venerable relict of the late Dr.
     Scott. (Sept. 9, 1819)

SCOTT, George, Esq., died lately at his house in P. G. Co., farmer
     of the quit rents in Fred. Co., and Deputy Commissary of
     P. G. Co. (Sept. 12, 1771)

SCOTT, John, about 10 days ago, was accidentally shot and killed
     while deer hunting in Q. A. Co. (Aug. 28, 1760)

SCOTT, Lieut. John B., of the U. S. Army, and Rebecca T., daughter
     of Alexander C. Magruder, of Annap., were married Thurs.
     evening last, by Rev. Mr. Blanchard. (Jan. 3, 1833)

SCOTT, Mrs. Sarah Cornish, consort of Leonard Scott, merchant, died
     in her 41st year. (Feb. 26, 1818)

SCOTT, Miss Susan Bruce, died Tues., 1st inst., in Westminster,
     Fred. Co., in her 18th year. (Feb. 10, 1825)

SCOTT, Dr. Upton, and Elizabeth, youngest daughter of John Ross,
     Esq., Esq., were married Sun. evening last. (Sept. 9, 1756)

SCOTT, Dr. Upton, died Wed. evening, 23rd ult., at the advanced age
     of 90 years, a native of Ireland, but for more than 60 years
     a most distinguished inhabitant of Annap. (March 3, 1814)

SCOTT, William, and Miss Eliza Bryan, both of A. A. Co., were married
     on Sun. evening last, by the Rev. Mr. Emory. (Dec. 14, 1820)

SEAGAR, Capt. John, master of the schooner Chester River, which
     arrived yesterday from Antigua, died after two days' illness
     in Antigua. (June 5, 1760)

SEARS, Caleb, died in A. A. Co., Friday last. (May 20, 1830)

SEARS, Charles C., and Miss Juliana M. Saunders, both of A. A. Co.,
     were married Thurs. last, by the Rev. Mr. Watkins. (Jan.
     26, 1832)

SEARS, William, of Tal. Co., and Miss Elizabeth Murdoch of Annap.,
     were married on Thurs. last [Oct. 25], by the Rev. Mr. Davis.
     (Oct. 31, 1816)

SEFTON, John H., and Elizabeth Tydings, both of A. A. Co., were wed
     on Thurs. evening by Rev. Mr. Watkins. (March 23, 1837)

SELBY, Col. John, died in Wor. Co., one of the worthy representatives
of that county. (April 4, 1754)

SELBY, John S., and Margaret, daughter of the Rev. Nicholas Watkins,
all of Annap., were married Thurs. morning last, by Rev. Mr.
Vinton. (Sept. 18, 1828)

SELBY, Mr. Jonathan, died Sat. night last, at his residence on the
north side of Severn. (Dec. 15, 1825)

SELBY, Parker, High Sheriff of Wor. Co., lately died there. (March
4, 1773)

SELLMAN, Alfred, of A. A. Co., and Miss Ann Parran, of Balto., were
married in the latter city, 13th inst., by Rev. William F.
Chesley. (May 22, 1828)

SELLMAN, Mrs. Anne F., died at her residence in A. A. Co., on Sun.
last; relict of the late Jonathan Sellman. (Sept. 2, 1824)

SELLMAN, John, and Miss Elizabeth Selby, were married Thurs. evening,
9th inst., at West River, by Rev. Mr. Morrell. (Jan. 16, 1823)

SELLMAN, John S., died Tues. last at the residence of Major Thomas
H. Dorsey, third son of John S. Sellman, Esq., of A. A. Co.,
aged 19 months. (July 10, 1834)

SELLMAN, John Stevens, and Mary, daughter of the Late Richard Dorsey,
both of A. A. Co., were married Tues. evening last by Rev.
Dr. Rafferty. (Nov. 11, 1824)

SELLMAN, Gen. Jonathan, died Mon. night last [May 21], at his farm
on Rhode River. (May 231, 1810)

SELLMAN, Leonard, and Miss Mary Rankin, were married Sun. evening
last [June 24], by the Rev. Mr. Higinbothom. (June 28, 1804)

SELLMAN, Miss Mary Ann Deborah, died Friday, Aug. 5th, at the residence of her brother, Mr. John S. Sellman, in her 18th year.
[Long obit is given.] (Aug. 11, 1825)

SELLMAN, Samuel Thomas, died Wed. morning, fourth son of John S.
Sellman, of South River, aged three years, five months,
and twenty-two days. (Aug. 23, 1838)

SEVIL, John, an overseer of Mr. Hemsley's, in Q. A. Co., was
stabbed by a negro fellow of Mr. Hemsley. (July 5, 1764)

SEWARD, John A., of Dor. Co., and Eliza Ann Tucker, of A. A. Co.,
were married Thurs. evening last, by the Rev. Mr. Nicholas
Watkins. (Oct. 1, 1829)

SEWELL, Benjamin, and Miss Hester Nicholson, were married on Sun.
[Jan. 5], in Annap., by Rev. Mr. Wyatt. (Jan. 16, 1806)

SEWELL, Benjamin, of Annap., and Mary Smith, daughter of John Smith,
of Balto., were married in the latter city on Sun. evening
last [May 23], by the Rev. Thomas Burch. (May 27, 1819)

SEWELL, Benjamin, died in Annap., Thurs. night last. (Aug. 7, 1823)

SEWELL, Benjamin, and Caroline Davis, all of Annap., were married
on Thurs. evening last, by the Rev. Mr. Watkins. (Dec. 29,
1825)

SEWELL, Mr. Benjamin, died in Annap., on Friday last. (April 17,
1828)

SEWELL, John, died in Annap. on Friday. (Feb. 28, 1828)

SEWELL, Capt. John, and Miss Ellen Brewer, daughter of Brice B.
Brewer, of Annap., were married Thurs. evening last, by the
Rev. Mr. Guest. (Oct. 25, 1832)

SEWELL, Capt. John, died Tues., 1st inst., of congestive fever,
on board the steamboat South Carolina, on her passage from
Norfolk; he was aged 30 years. (Oct. 10, 1839)

SEWELL, John M., a native of A. A. Co., died on the 17th ult., at
Port-Au-Prince. (Aug. 10, 1820)

SHAAF, Arthur, Esq., of Fred. Co., died Thurs. morning, the 15th
inst., in George-Town, in his 49th year. His country seat
was named Arcadia. He was buried Sat. in the Episcopal
Burying Ground. (June 5, 1817)

SHAAF, Arthur, of Annap., and Mary A. Foster, daughter of the Hon.
Judge Forsyth, of Ga., were married in Washington, on Tues.
evening, 16th inst., by the Rev. Walter Addison. (Aug. 25,
1825)

SHAAF, John T., M. D., died at Gisborough, Friday last, aged 56 years.
This distinguished physician, after completing his professional
education in Europe began the practise of medicine in this
city. (May 5, 1819)

SHAAF, Mrs. Mary, departed this life on Friday night last [Aug. 31],
in her 34th year of her age, the amiable consort of Dr.
John T. Shaaf of Annap. (Sept. 5, 1810)

SHARPE, William, Esq., brother of His Excellency the Governor, died.
He was First Clerk of His Majesty's Council in Ordinary.
(Nov. 12, 1767)

SHAW, Mrs. Ann, relict of the late James Shaw, Esq., died in Annap.,
on Friday morning last. (Oct. 5, 1826)

SHAW, Mr. George, and Miss Eliza J. Robinson, were married on Sun.
evening last, by the Rev. H. L. Deane. (April 8, 1819)

SHAW, George, merchant of Annap., died Mon., the 18th, in his 59th
year. (May 21, 1829)

SHAW, James, Attorney, died in Annap., Friday, 10th inst., in his
48th year. (Sept. 16, 1830)

SHAW, Mrs. Jane, relict of the late Dr. John Shaw, of Annap., died
17th Oct., at "Richlands," the seat of Mr. James Cunningham,
near Frederick-Town. (Nov. 1, 1827)

SHAW, Dr. John, and Miss Jane Selby, were married on Thurs. [Feb.
12], by the Rev. Mr. Gibson. (Feb. 19, 1807)

SHAW, Dr. John, died Jan. 10, on his passage from Charleston, S. C.,
to the Bahama Islands, for his health. Dr. Shaw was Professor of Chemistry in the Medical College of Baltimore, and
was 31 years old. (March 22, 1809)

SHAW, Commodore John, U. S. Navy, died at Phila., Wed. evening,
17th inst., after a severe attack of the dysentery; aged
50 years. (Sept. 25, 1823)

SHAW, John, died on Thurs., 26th ult., in his 82nd year; in the
struggle for our independence, he espoused the cause of freedom. He served as Treasurer of the State. (March 5, 1829)

SHAW, Mrs. Margaret, died on July 5, in her 48th year. (July 5,
1806)

SHAW, Thomas, Esq., and Miss Maria Sophia Morris, were married at
Frederick-Town, on the 21st ult., by the Rev. Mr. Shaffer.
The groom is Cashier of the Frederick Branch Bank. (Aug.
4, 1814)

SHAW, Thomas, Esq., formerly Cashier of the Frederick-Town Branch
Bank, died in Balto., on Sat. last. (Sept. 13, 1832)

SHEAD, William, drowned in the Severn recently. (June 19, 1751)

SHECKELLS, Levi, and Martha Day, all of A. A. Co., were married on
Thurs. evening last, by the Rev. Mr. Watkins. (Feb. 21,
1833)

SHEE, Gen. John, Collector of the Port of Philadlephia, died in that
city on Thurs. last [Aug. 4]. (Aug. 11, 1808)

SHEPHARD, Mr. James, and Miss Susan Mace, of Annap., were married
    Sun. evening last, by Rev. Mr. Fechtig. (Dec. 11, 1817)

SHEPHARD, Lucretia, daughter of the late James Shephard, died Mon.
    night, at the residence of Mr. William Bryan, in her 20th
    year. (Oct. 1, 1835)

SHERBERT, Mrs. Margaret, died in Annap., on Sun. morning [Jan. 26].
    (Jan. 30, 1817)

SHEREDINE, Daniel, Esq., died at North East, Cecil Co., on the 12th
    inst., in his 72nd year, a delegate elect to the next Legis-
    lature of this state. (Oct. 16, 1823)

SHEREDINE, Mrs. Tabitha, died Sat., Oct. 21, in Balto. Co., the
    relict of Major Thomas Sheredine, formerly of the same county.
    She was in her 79th year. (Nov. 16, 1769)

SHEREDINE, Thomas, died early this morning, of small pox, at his
    house in Balto. Co., for many years a magistrate and a rep-
    resentative, and at the time of his death, Sheriff. His
    son Thomas will succeed him as High Sheriff. (May 28, 1752)

SHEREDINE, Upton, died at Mid Hill, Fred. Co., on the 14th inst.,
    of yellow fever; first Commissioner in the district of Mary-
    land, under the law of the United States for the direct tax.
    (Jan. 23, 1800)

SHERER, Mrs. Hannah, died at Standing-stone Flat, in Penna., on Mon.,
    Dec. 31, 1804, aged 104. She came to this county 30 years
    ago when it was in the possession of savages. (March 14,
    1805)

SHERMAN, Mrs. Catherine, died in Annap., on Sat. night last, the
    consort of E. Sherman. (Dec. 9, 1824)

SHIPLEY, Jemima, the six year old daughter of Otho Shipley, who
    resides about 23 miles from Balto., died shortly after the
    death of Mr. Shipley's three year old child [unnamed in
    obituary.]; "Baltimore, May 15." (May 17, 1827)

SHIPLEY, Larkin, died 16th inst., in A. A. Co. [Long obit is given.]
    (March 28, 1822)

SHIPPEN, Edward, died in Philadelphia on April 15, late Chief Justice
    of the Supreme Court of Pennsylvania, in his 78th year. (April
    24, 1806)

SHORT, ---, aged about three years old, son of John Short, fell
    into a spring four or five inches deep, a little beyond
    South River, and was drowned. (May 22, 1751)

SIGELL, Mr. Milbourne, printer, departed this life on Mon. last
[Feb. 25], in Annap., in his 41st year. He was a member of
the Protestant Episcopal Church. (Feb. 27, 1811)

SILK, Mr. William, and Miss Lucinda Tow, both of St. Clair Twp.,
were married at Pittsburg on Thurs., 23rd ult., by the Rev.
Francis Herron. (Sept. 20, 1827)

SIM, Mrs., wife of Col. Joseph Sim, of P. G. Co., died 3rd inst.
(April 11, 1776)

SIM, Mrs. Catherine, died on Friday, 29th ult., in her 86th year,
second daughter of William Murdock, Esq., and wife of Major
Joseph Sim, of P. G. Co. (Dec. 5, 1771)

SIM, William, merchant, died Mon. night last [Feb. 3], in P. G. Co.,
near Nottingham. His death is supposed to have been caused
by some ill treatment he met with about six weeks ago.
(Feb. 6, 1751)

SIMMONS, Capt. John, died last week at Lower Marlborough, of the
ship Revolution, now lying at Patuxent. (Oct. 10, 1750)

SIMMONS, John W., a married man with a family, was killed last
week in Cal. Co., when a gust of wind blew a house down.
(May 2, 1799)

SIMMONS, Mr. Joseph, the oldest inhabitant of Annap., died on Sun.
evening last. [Long obit is given.] (Aug. 6, 1829)

SIMMONS, Mr. Knighton, died Thurs., 7th inst., at his house in St.
James Parish, in his 29th year. (July 27, 1774)

SIMMONS, Thomas Henry, died Friday last, at his late residence,
Lilac Hill, in Cal. Co., in his 27th year. (Feb. 21, 1833)

SIMMONS, Col. Thomas T., late Register of Wills for A. A. Co., died
in Annap., Mon. last. [Long obit is given.] (Sept. 13, 1832)

SIMMONS, William, and Miss Matilda Tillard, daughter of Major Thomas
Tillard, were married on Sun., Sept. 23rd, near Herring Creek,
by the Rev. Mr. Compton. (Oct. 4, 1804)

SIMPSON, Mrs. Dulcibella, died yesterday morning in Annap., in her
73rd year. (March 31, 1825)

SIMPSON, Thomas, died on Tues. morning last [July 25], at the residence of Charles Carroll of Carrollton, in Annap. (July 27,
1815)

SISTER Mary Frances, died Thurs., 30th Aug. [Long obit is given.]
(Sept. 13, 1832)

SISTER Mary George, died in Balto., 19th inst., in her 21st year.
(Sept. 27, 1832)

SKELTON, Mrs. P., formerly of Annap., Md., died 3rd inst., in her
67th year, in Cincinnati. (Nov. 15, 1832)

SLEMAKER, Mrs. Elizabeth, consort of Jacob H. Slemaker, Esq., died
in Annap., on Thurs. last. (Dec. 7, 1826)

SLEMAKER, Jacob, of A. A. Co., and Miss Susan Hyde, of Annap., were
married Thurs. last, by Rev. Mr. Vinton. (June 5, 1828)

SLEMAKER, Jacob H., died Mon. morning last at his residence at South
River Ferry. (Dec. 29, 1837)

SLEMAKER, Mrs. Susan, died Thurs. last, consort of Jacob H. Slemaker,
of South River Ferry. (Dec. 18, 1834)

SLICER, Rev. Henry, of the Methodist Episcopal Church, and Elizabeth
C. Roberts, all of Balto., were married in that city on Tues.
morning last, by the Rev. Dr. Roberts. (April 5, 1827)

SLICER, Lewis E., formerly of Annap., and Elizabeth Ann Widderfield,
of Balto. City, were married in the latter place on 26th
inst., by Rev. J. L. Gibbons. (June 6, 1833)

SLIGH, William, died Thurs. last, in Annap., of small pox, aged
22 years, Clerk of the city and of the Provincial Court. He
leaves a widow and one child. (March 10, 1757)

SLOAN, James, Jr., died March 31st. [Long obit is given.] (From the
Baltimore American.) (April 15, 1819)

SLYE, Mr. George, died Thurs., 25th ult., at his seat at Bushwood,
St. M. Co. He leaves a widow and other relatives. (June 10,
1773)

SMALL, George, Jr., and Eunice Chase, were married in Limington, on
14th inst. (Oct. 25, 1827)

SMILIE, John, died in this city yesterday afternoon [Jan. 6], a
Representative in Congress from Pennsylvania, aged about
74 years. (Jan. 7, 1813)

SMITH, Mrs., was murdered by poison in Cal. Co., some years ago.
(July 2, 1761)

SMITH, Dr. Charlton, departed this life on Thurs., 5th inst., aged
near 100 year. Dr. Smith was a native of Durham, Eng., and
emigrated to this state almost 50 years since, and for the
last 10 years has resided at Mirmingham House, A. A. Co., the
seat of Dr. Gerrard H. Snowden. (Jan. 12, 1815)

SMITH, Clement, merchant of Georgetown, Potowmack, and Miss Margaretta Clare Brice, daughter of John Brice, Esq., of Balto., were married on Thurs. evening [Nov. 12], by the Rev. Dr. Whitehead, in Balto. (Nov. 19, 1807)

SMITH, Mr. James, died last week at Chester-Town, in Kent Co., at a good old age, for a great number of years, Clerk of that county. He is succeeded in that office by Mr. Dennis Dulany, late of this city. (March 20, 1760) William Murray is the executor. (June 5, 1760)

SMITH, James, died in Annap., on Tues. evening, after a short illness. (Sept. 12, 1822)

SMITH, Rev. James, of Annap., and Mrs. Mary Childs, of A. A. Co., were married Mon. evening last, by Rev. Battee. (March 16, 1826)

SMITH, Rev. James, of the Methodist Church, died in Balto., on Sun. evening last, in his 42nd year. He was stationed minister in this city during the past year. (April 13, 1826)

SMITH, Mr. John, died in Annap., on Wed., 21st ult., after a long illness, at an advanced age. (April 29, 1824)

SMITH, Joseph, servant to Mr. Reynolds of Annap., drowned last Friday when he went into a creek to wash, and got into deep water. (Aug. 12, 1756)

SMITH, Miss Rachel, died in Annap., at the house of Mr. W. G. Tuck, on Sun. last, in her 69th year; a native of Cal. Co., but recently an inhabitant of P. G. Co. (April 1, 1824)

SMITH, Samuel, died Thurs. last, over South River; who formerly served his county as a representative and a sheriff; for many years a worthy magistrate. (April 20, 1748)

SMITH, Gen. Samuel, died in Balto., in his 87th year. A native of Lancaster Co., Penna., he had resided for 79 years in Balto. He served in the Revolution. (April 25, 1839)

SMITH, Samuel B., died at the residence of his father-in-law, in Philadelphia, on the eve of the 28th ult., in his 50th year. For the last 18 years he had been Assistant Surgeon in the U. S. Army. (Dec. 3, 1834)

SMITH, Sarah Ann, eldest daughter of Anthony and Mary Ann Smith, died Mon., 11 Sept., at Elk Ridge, aged 17 years and seven months. She was a member of the Methodist Episcopal Church. (Sept. 21, 1837)

SMITH, Mr. Walter, died last week in Cal. Co., in his 56th year, a representative of the county for above 30 years. (Sept. 21, 1748) Alethia Smith advertises for debtors and creditors to settle their accounts. (March 22, 1749)

SMITH, William, formerly servant to Mr. Reynolds, was found drowned yesterday in South River. He went out in a canoe Sunday last with another man, who has not since been heard of, so it is supposed his companion suffered the same fate. (July 18, 1771)

SMITH, William Hamilton, died on Monday 1st inst., in his 22nd year. He is supposed to have been poisoned by his own negroes; "Calvert Co., May 15, 1764." (May 17, 1764)

SMITH, William Loughton, of S. C., died suddenly, 19th inst. [Dec., 1812], at his country residence. (Jan. 7, 1813)

SMITHSON, the Hon. William, of the Senate of Md., died lately at his seat in Harf. Co. (Feb. 8, 1809)

SNOWDEN, Charles A., died 5th inst., second son of the late Richard Snowden, who died 3rd inst. (Sept. 11, 1823)

SNOWDEN, Dr. Gerard H., of Birmingham House, A. A. Co., and Arabella Orr, youngest daughter of the late Hugh Montgomery Stuart, of Va., were married April 28th, in Washington, by Rev. Mr. Hawley. (May 6, 1824)

SNOWDEN, John, departed this life on Tues. morning, the 1st inst., at his residence near the Patuxent Iron Works, aged [at least 70] years. (Nov. 3, 1808)

SNOWDEN, Mr. Richard, Jr., died Sun. last [March 18], after a short illness at his house on Patuxent River, near his Father's Iron Works. (March 22, 1753)

SNOWDEN, Mr. Richard, died yesterday morning, at his seat on Patuxent River, near his iron works, in his 76th year. He leaves a widow and numerous offspring. (Jan. 27, 1763) Elizabeth Snowden, Thomas Snowden, Samuel Snowden, and John Snowden are executors. (April 7, 1764)

SNOWDEN, Richard, died at his residence in P. G. Co., 3rd inst., in his 47th year. (Sept. 11, 1823)

SNOWDEN, Samuel, died in Alexandria, Thurs. morning, 14th inst., in his 53rd year; for 30 years proprietor and publisher of the Alexandria Phenix Gazette. (July 21, 1831)

SNOWDEN, Major Thomas, died lately at his seat in P. G. Co., in his 35th year. [Long obit is given.] (Nov. 3, 1803)

SNOWDEN, Thomas, Sr., Esq., of A. A. Co., died at his residence on
Mon. morning last. (Oct. 29, 1835)

SNYDER, Symon, Esq., late Governor of Penna., died at his residence
in Selin's Grove, Union Co., Penna., Tues., 9th inst. (Nov.
18, 1819)

SOLLERS, Mr. James, a young man, broke his arm in a wrestling bout
in Balto. Town last week. The bone protruded, mortification
ensued, and he died soon after. (Sept. 15, 1763)

SOMERVELL, Dr. James, died Friday, 15th inst., in his 57th or 58th
year, at his house in Cal. Co. (Feb. 20, 1751)

SOMERVELL, Mrs. Sarah, died Sun. last [March 23], at her house in
Cal. Co., relict of the late worthy Dr. James Somervell, who
died Feb., 1751. (April 10, 1755)

SOPER, James P., aged 62, died Thurs., 18th inst., aged 62 years,
at his residence in A. A. Co. He leaves a wife. (May 25,
1826)

SOPER, Thomas, overseer of Mr. Cook's, in P. G. Co., on Tues., 6th
inst. He was murdered by a negro belonging to Mr. Gault.
(Nov. 15, 1764)

SPALDING, Benedict, died Sat., 4th inst., at his residence in Leonard-
Town, in his 35th year, leaving a widow and three children.
[Long obit is given.] (Feb. 16, 1832)

SPARKS, Dr. Edward, and Miss Rosetta, daughter of the late Jonathan
Pinckney, all of Annap., were married Tues. evening last by
Rev. Blanchard. (July 27, 1826)

SPARKS, Dr. Edward, and Sophia R., daughter of the late Jonathan
Pinckney, of Annap., were married Thurs. last, by the Rev.
Mr. Humphreys. (Feb. 2, 1832)

SPARKS, Mrs. Rosetta, consort of Dr. Edward Sparks, and daughter of
the late Jonathan Pinckney, died Tues. night. (April 2, 1829)

SPARROW, Mrs. Rachel, consort of Mr. Solomon Sparrow, and daughter
of the late Mr. William Hall, III, died in Annap., on Sun.
morning last. (Sept. 4, 1828)

SPARROW, Mr. Thomas, died Wed. morning last [Feb. 14], after a few
days' illness. For many years he has been Doorkeeper to the
Honourable the Lower House of Assembly, and Cryer of the
Provincial and Anne Arundel County Courts. (Feb. 11, 1753)
Jonas Green is the executor. (March 8, 1753)

SPEED, Major Robert G. H., aged 26, died on Wed., 18th inst., at

Ithaca, N. Y. (of the Bar of the State of New York). He was the son of the late Dr. Joseph Speed, of Caroline Co., and a brother of J. J. Speed, of Annap. (Dec. 10, 1829)

SPENCE, Capt. Robert T., died at his residence near Balto. on 26th ult.; a distinguished officer of the U. S. Navy. (Oct. 5, 1826)

SPENCER, Mrs., consort of Nicholas Spencer, died in Annap. on Tues. evening last. (Sept. 22, 1825)

SPENCER, Rev. Archibald, M. D., died Sun. evening last [Jan. 13], aged 62, rector of All Hallows Parish in this county; well known in many parts of this continent for his lectures in Experimental philosophy. (Jan. 17, 1760)

SPENCER, Nicholas, and Mrs. Susanna Kirkland, all of Annap., were married Thurs. evening last, by Rev. Davis. (March 29, 1827)

SPENCER, William, Esq., died lately at his residence, Kent Co., Md. He served as a Delegate in the State Legislature from that county. In the fall of 1815, he was chosen a member of the State Senate, and unanimously appointed President of the Senate. (April 11, 1822)

SPRIGG, Capt., died in the powder magazine explosion at Fort Cumberland. (Oct. 19, 1758)

SPRIGG, Col. Edward, died Sat. last [Nov. 30], in P. G. Co., after a short illness of 20 hours, who has for more than 22 years past one of the Representatives of that county; for several years the Honourable Speaker of the House; presided as Chief in the Commission of the Peace for some years. (Dec. 4, 1751) Mary Sprigg is the extx. (23 April, 1752)

SPRIGG, Mrs. Margaret, wife of Richard Sprigg, Esq., died 13th inst., at his seat on West River. (July 14, 1796)

SPRIGG, Osborne, Esq., died Mon. last, Jan. 7, High Sheriff of P. G. Co. (Jan. 10, 1750) Rachel Sprigg, extx., advertises. (April 11, 1750)

SPRIGG, Mr. Richard, of West River, and Margaret, only daughter of John Caille, were married on Thurs. last [Aug. 1], in Dor. Co. (Aug. 8, 1765)

SPRIGG, Richard, Esq., died Sat., 24th inst., at his seat on West River, in his 59th year. (Nov. 29, 1798)

SPRIGG, Richard, died on March 20th, at Charleston, S. C., where he he had gone for his health, in his 37th year, Chief Justice of the First Judicial District of this State, and late a Judge of the General Court. (March 27, 1806)

SPRIGG, Thomas, Esq., discharged the great debt of nature last Sat. evening, at his seat on West River, in his 67th year. (Jan. 3, 1782)

STALLINGS, Mr. John, and Miss Pamela L. Key, all of this city, were married Tues. evening, by the Rev. Mr. Griffith. (June 10, 1824)

STALLINGS, Mrs. Rebecca, died Thurs. last, in her 80th year. (Aug. 9, 1832)

STANSBURY, Mr. Daniel, died last week very suddenly in Balto. Co., a native of that place, in his 85th year. He had eat a hearty supper [sic] the evening before he died. He leaves a twin brother. (April 7, 1763)

STANSBURY, Ezekiel F., of Balto., and Rebecca Ann Munroe, of Annap., were married Thurs. evening last, by the Rev. Jonathan Munroe. (March 26, 1829)

STANSBURY, Joseph, of A. A. Co., died on the 21st of this month, in his 76th year. (Dec. 28, 1820)

STANSBURY, Capt. Tobias, died a few days ago in Balto. Co. (Oct. 20, 1757)

STARK, General, died 8th inst., at his residence in Manchester, on the bank of the Merrimack, aged 93 years [eight?] months, and 24 days. (May 23, 1822)

STARK, Wilson M., and Matilda Green, only daughter of the late Lewis Green, formerly of this city, were married at Lower Sandusky, Ohio, on 11th April, by the Rev. Leonard Hill. (May 3, 1838)

STEARNS, Samuel, L. L. D., died at Brattleborough, Vermont, the most celebrated astronomer in the United States. (Sept. 6, 1809)

STEEL, Miss Isabella, daughter of the late James Steel, died Sat. night last, in Dor. Co. (Aug. 11, 1825) Memorial verses on her death appear in the issue of Sept. 1, 1825.

STEELE, Mrs. Ann, died Sat. last in Annap., wife of John N. Steele, Esq., of Dor. Co., and daughter of Judge Buchanan of Wash. Co. (April 25, 1839)

STEELE, Dr. Charles, and Charlotte, daughter of James Murray, all of Annap., were married Tues. evening last, by the Rev. Mr. McElhiney. (April 13, 1837)

STEELE, Henry M., Esq., of Dor. Co., and Maria Lloyd, second daughter of Francis S. Key, of the Dist. of Col., were married Tues. evening, by Rev. Dr. Davis. (June 5, 1823)

STEELE, James, Esq., of Annap., died Sat., 21st Sept., at Boones-
borough, on his return from the Springs, in his 37th year.
(Oct. 9, 1816)

STEELE, John M., of Annap., and Miss Ann O. Buchanan, daughter of
the Hon. Thomas Buchanan, were married near Hagerstown.
(Oct. 14, 1819)

STEPHEN, Benjamin M. H., eighth son of the Hon. John Stephen, of
Bladensburg, P. G. Co., died 6th inst., in his eighth year.
(Dec. 11, 1828)

STEPHEN, John, Esq., Attorney at Law, of Balto., and Miss Juliana
Brice, of Annap., were married on Tues. evening last [Nov. 1],
by the Rev. Mr. Judd. (Nov. 3, 1808)

STEPHEN, Mr. John, son of Judge Stephen, died at Bladensburg, on the
17th inst., in his 14th year. (Dec. 24, 1828)

STERLING, Rev. Mr. James, died Thurs. last [Nov. 10], in Kent Co.,
after long enduring the excruciating pain of the stone in the
bladder, rector of St. Paul's Parish, in that county. (Nov.
17, 1763)

STERRETT, Capt. Andrew, late commander of the ship Warren, of Balto.,
and a captain in the U. S. Navy, died on his passage to Lima,
Peru, on Jan. 9th, after an illness of 28 days. (Feb. 25, 1808)

STERRETT, Mr. David, of Balto., was killed in a duel, by Thomas Had-
field, on the 29th ult. (May 5, 1791)

STERRETT, Mr. John, died on Friday last [April 28], at Balto. (May
3, 1809)

STEUART, Mr. Leslie, died at Greenwich, near New York, on the 23rd
inst. (May 30, 1816)

STEUART, Mr. William, died Tues. morning, at the seat of Mr. Clement
Hill, in P. G. Co., Register of the Land Office. (Sept. 15,
1774)

STEUART, William, and Miss Sarah Miller, were married Sun. last, at
Mount Steuart, by the Rev. Mr. Gosnell. (Jan. 30, 1823)

STEUART, William, Esq., of Mount Steuart, in A. A. Co., died in
Balto., yesterday morning, in his 86th year. (Nov. 1, 1838)

STEVENS, Mrs. Eliza, wife of Samuel Stevens, former Governor of this
state, died at Compton, Mon. night, 8th ult. (Dec. 25, 1834)

STEVENS, Vachel, late Examiner-General of the Western Shore of Maryland, died Sat. morning, in his 58th year. (Jan. 9, 1811)

STEWART, Mr. Anthony, merchant of Annap., and Jane, youngest daughter
of Mr. James Dick, merchant of London Town, were married.
(March 22, 1764)

STEWART, Charles, was killed by Indians in the "Great Cove," Fred.
Co., on Nov. 8. (Dec. 1, 1763)

STEWART, Charles, and Alicia Ann Thompson, eldest daughter of the
late John Thompson, were married in Annap., on Thurs. evening
last, by Rev. Mr. Watkins. (April 28, 1825)

STEWART, Charles, son of David, died Thurs., 23rd inst., at his residence, in A. A. Co., at an advanced age. He had several times
been elected to the Legislature. (Aug. 30, 1827)

STEWART, Charles, and Mrs. Henrietta Morgan, all of Annap., were
married Sun. evening last, by Rev. Mr. McElhiney. (Jan. 26,
1837)

STEWART, David, son of Caleb, and Miss Elizabeth Ginn, both of A. A.
Co., were married Thurs. evening, 27th ult., by the Rev. Mr.
Watkins. (Feb. 10, 1825)

STEWART, Leslie, Esq., of Balto., and Miss Maria E. Brenton, of
Harlem, were married on Wed., 29th ult. [April], at St.
Michael's Church, Bloomingdale, N.Y., by the Rev. Mr. Jarvis.
(May 7, 1812)

STEWART, Richard, of South River, died Sept. 7. (Sept. 18, 1806)

STEWART, Robert W., of Som. Co., Md., and Miss Nancy Jones Warren,
of Sussex Co., Del., were married on the 17th ult., by the
Rev. Mr. Bell. (Nov. 7, 1810)

STEWART, Mrs. Sarah, relict of the late Capt. David Stewart, died
Sat. night last, at the residence of Jos. N. Stockett, A. A.
Co. (Oct. 15, 1829)

STEWART, Mrs. Sarah A., died Sun. last, in her 57th year, relict
of the late Dr. John Stewart, of A. A. Co. (Dec. 5, 1833)

STEWART, Thomas, died Sat. last, at his residence on Patapsco, in
his 58th year. (May 7, 1835)

STEWART, Mr. Vincent, died last week in Balto., of injuries received
during a frolic at a tavern. He leaves a wife and six children.
(April 19, 1749). Robert Stewart, his brother, mentioned in
issue of May 3, 1749.

STINCHCOMBE, Mrs. Sarah, died at this city, on Sat. night last, after
a severe illness, at the advanced age of 72. (April 8, 1824)

STINCHCOMB, Mr. William, died Sat. night last, on the North side of
Severn, in his 35th year. (Nov. 12, 1829)

STITH, Rev. William, A. M., President of William and Mary College,
died Friday se'ennight [Sept. 26]; "Williamsburg, Oct. 3."
(Oct. 16, 1755)

STOCKETT, Mrs. Ann, consort of Joseph N. Stockett, Esq., died Mon.
night, on the south side of Severn River. (July 22, 1824)

STOCKETT, Mrs. Anne Caroline, died Thurs., 22nd inst., at her husband's residence in South River Neck, wife of Mr. Joseph N.
Stockett, in her 18th year. (Dec. 29, 1814)

STOCKETT, John S., and Miss Ann Grayson, were married on Sun. evening
[April 19], by the Rev. Mr. Nind. (April 23, 1812)

STOCKETT, Dr. John Shaaf, died at his residence in A. A. Co., on Sat.
morning last. (May 12, 1825)

STOCKETT, Joseph N., and Miss Sophia Watkins, were married in A. A.
Co., Thurs. last, by the Rev. Mr. Blanchard. (Nov. 24, 1825)

STOCKETT, Manilla, only daughter of Dr. Richard G. Stockett, of
Elk Ridge, died Friday, 13th inst., aged 22. (Aug. 19, 1830)

STOCKETT, Mrs. Mary, died 14th inst., in her 63rd year. She lived
at South River. (June 15, 1815)

STODDERT, Benjamin, died at Bladensburg, last Friday [Dec. 23], in
his 62nd year. He was buried on Sun. evening, by the side
of the mother of his children, at Addison's Chapel. Raised
up under the unfavorable circumstance of a want of fortune
arising from the death before his birth of his father, Capt.
Stoddert, of Maryland, who commanded and gave name to Fort
Stoddert, of the West, before the Revolution, he owed every-
thing to the native strength of his mind. He engaged in the
holy struggle for independence. He entered as a Captain in
the particular regiment officered by General Washington, and
was in several encounters. [Long obit gives details of his
military career, his public offices as first Secretary to
the Board of War, and as Secretary of the Navy.] (Dec. 29,
1813)

STODDERT, John T., Esq., of Chas. Co., and Miss Elizabeth Gwinn, of
Annap., were married Tues. evening [May 23], by the Rev. Mr.
Duncan. (May 25, 1815)

STODDERT, Mr. Truman, died about a fortnight ago in Chas. Co., one
of the representatives for that county. (Feb. 7, 1765)

STOLKER, Mr. Robert, died in Annap. on Mon. morning last. (April
17, 1823)

STONE, Mr. David, died Thurs., 18th ult., at his seat in Chas. Co.,
in his 65th year. (April 1, 1773)

STONE, General John Hoskins, departed this life on Friday last [Oct.
5], in his 54th year of age. During the American Revolution
he appeared as a captain the celebrated regiment of Smallwood,
and highly distinguished himself at the battles of Long Island,
White Plains, and Princeton. At the battle of Germantown, he
received a wound that deprived him of bodily activity for the
remainder of life. As a representative of his native Charles
Co., and as a member of the Executive Council, he continued
to serve his country [sic]. In 1794 he was elected Governor
of Maryland. (Oct. 11, 1804)

STONE, Mrs. Margaret, wife of the Hon. Thomas Stone, died June 1st.
(June 7, 1787)

STONE, Mrs. Mary, wife of John Hoskins Stone, Esq., of Annap., died
Sun. evening, 4th inst., aged 32. (March 8, 1792)

STONE, Mrs. Mary, died on Mon. evening last [March 19], in Annap.,
in her 29th year. (March 21, 1810)

STONE, Robert Coulden, and Miss Mary Mann, both of Annap., were
married on Tues., evening last [July 23], by the Rev. Mr.
Higinbothom. (July 25, 1805)

STONE, Thomas, died 1st inst., at his seat at Nanjemoy, Chas. Co.,
in his 75th year. Upwards of 40 years a magistrate of the
county, for a long time before his death [he had been] Chief
Justice of the County Court. (April 22, 1771; May 2, 1771)

STONE, Mr. Walter, of Chas. Co., Md., merchant, died on the 6th ult.,
at the Sweet Springs, Botetourt Co., Va. (Oct. 6, 1791)

STONE, William Murry, D. D., died Mon., 26th ult., at his residence
near Salisbury, Som. Co., Md., Bishop of the Protestant
Episcopal Church in Maryland. (March 8, 1838)

STONER, ---, the 10 or 12 year old son of Jacob Stoner, died when his
father's house at Manockosy [sic] burned to the ground, Mon.
se'ennight. (May 11, 1748)

STONESTREET, Dr. James E., died Wed. night last, at the house of
Mr. Charles Waters, on the north side of Severn, in his 25th
year. (Sept. 27, 1804)

STONESTREET, Thomas, died last week in P. G. Co., a native of this
county, aged beyond all doubt 98 years, but more probably
105 or 106 years old. (Sept. 12, 1771)

STORKE, Miss Catherine, died at the seat of Col. Baily Washington

in Stafford Co., Va., on Sun., 14th ult., the daughter of
William Storke, Esq., of Bellieffe, in King George. (Aug.
15, 1805)

STRICTLAND, ---, a little girls, daughter of Joseph Strictland, of
Cal. Co., who could but just go alone, a few days ago, got by
itself some distance from the house, where the oven was, and
fell down on a heap of coals just drawn, and lay there till
it was burnt so much that it died soon after. (July 24, 1760)

STRINGER, Dr. Samuel, died last Wed. [Aug. 19], at Elk Ridge, formerly Mayor of Annap. (Aug. 25, 1747)

STUART, Gen. Philip, a distinguished officer of the Revolution and
a native of Maryland, died. During the late war he again
served his country in the field, and for several years he
represented his native state in Congress. During the last
12 years he lived in Washington, D. C., where he died on
Sat., 14th inst.; from the National Intelligencer. (Aug.
19, 1830)

STURGES, Daniel, was shot dead by a person unknown some weeks ago
at Matapony Hundred, Wor. Co. (April 25, 1750)

SUDLER, Mrs. Charlotte, relict of William Sudler, Esq., late of
Q. A. Co., dec., died Mon., 2nd inst., at Belfield, the residence of her father James Mackubin, Sr. (May 5, 1825)

SUDLER, Philemon Hopper, died Sat. morning last, aged two years and
nine months, son of Col. T. E. Sudler, Professor at St.
John's Coll., and Mrs. Mary Sudler. (Oct. 24, 1839)

SUDLER, Mr. William, of Q. A. Co., and Miss Charlotte Mackubin,
eldest daughter of James Mackubin, of Severn, were married
at Bellefield, on Tues. evening, 11th inst., by the Rev. Mr.
Judd. (April 19, 1809)

SUET, John, a native of St. Mary's, Md., died in Phila., on the 10th
inst.; a mariner, he was 93 years. (Oct. 27, 1808)

SULLIVAN, James, Esq., Governor of Mass., died at Boston, 17th inst.,
in his 65th year. (Dec. 22, 1808)

SULLIVAN, Mr. John, died 17th ult., an old inhabitant of Annap.
(Dec. 1, 1825)

SULLIVAN, John, and Mary Brigdall, both of Annap., were married in
Balto., Sat. last, by the Rev. Mr. Valliant. (July 21, 1831)

SULLIVAN, Lemuel, and Miss Willy Gardner, all of Annap., were married
on Sun. evening last [Dec. 10], by the Rev. Mr. Watkins.
(Dec. 14, 1820)

SULLIVAN, Mr. Lemuel, died on Sun. (Feb. 28, 1828)

SULLIVAN, William, and Matilda Hall, both of Annap., were married
Thurs. evening last, by Rev. Watkins. (March 16, 1826)

SUMMERFIELD, Rev. John, died in N. Y., on the 13th inst. (June 23,
1825)

SUMMERFIELD, Mr. William, aged 54, died 19th inst., at Bloomingdale.
This gentleman was the father of the late admired Rev. John
Summerfield. (Sept. 29, 1825)

SUTTON, Josias, of Cecil Co., about a month ago, being at work
digging some gravel, to mend his mill-dam, cav'd [sic] and
undermined the bank so much that the earth fell down and
killed him on the spot. (Dec. 10--Dec. 17, 1728)

SWAN, Mr. Robert, merchant, died here on Friday last [May 4], in
his 44th year; one of the Common Council of this city, and
on Sun., his remains were very decently interred. (May 10,
1764)

SWANN, Thomas, Esq., and Ann Jane Charnley, all of Annap., were
married Tues. last, May 15th, by the Rev. President Humphreys.
(May 17, 1832)

SWANN, Mr. Thomas, died Sun. morning last, proprietor of the City
Hotel. (Jan. 31, 1833)

SWEARINGEN, George, was executed by hanging on the gallows in the
flat on the west side of Wills Creek. Mr. Beall, the Sheriff,
performed the duties of his office. (Oct. 8, 1829)

SWEETSER, Mrs. Ann, died at the Middle Ferry, about six miles from
Balto., on the 9th inst., in her 58th year, consort of Seth
Sweetser, formerly of Annap. (Sept. 18, 1823)

SWEETSER, Seth, Sr., of A. A. Co., died in Balto., on the 19th inst.,
aged 66 years. (July 24, 1828)

SWIFT, Mrs. Mary, widow, died Sept. 26 last, at her seat near Port-
Tobacco, in Chas. Co., aged about 90 years. She attributed
her good health in a great measure to the Peruvian bark which
she at first took by the advice of the late Dr. Gustavus
Brown, and continued to take in a small dose every day for
the last 40 years. (Oct. 6, 1773)

SWIFT, Rev. Mr. Theophilus, rector of Port Tobacco Parish, in Chas.
Co., died about a fortnight ago, in Phila., of consumption.
(May 13, 1762)

SWORMSTEDT, Mr. Samuel L., and Margaret Boone, all of this county,

were married Thurs. evening last at Stony Creek, by the Rev.
Mr. Welch. (April 28, 1825)

SYBELL, Mrs., died in Annap., on Wed. last [Oct. 10], consort of Mr.
Henry Sybell. (Oct. 17, 1810)

SYBLE, Mr. Henry, and Miss Mary Stallions, were married on Thurs.
last, by the Rev. Mr. Duke. Both bride and groom were of
Annap. (Feb. 7, 1805)

SYDEBOTHOM, Mrs. Margaretta Augustina, died Friday, Oct. 5, 1781,
in her 26th year. (Oct. 11, 1781)

SYMMER, Mr. Alexander, merchant of Upper Marlborough, and Miss Margaret Lee, youngest daughter of the late Hon. Philip Lee, Esq.,
were married Sun. evening last [Feb. 18]. (Feb. 22, 1759)

SYMMES, Capt. John Cleves, a native of New Jersey, and author of the
theory of the Open Poles, and Concentric Spheres, died in Hamilton, Butler Co., Ohio, on Thurs., 19th ult. (June 18, 1829)

TALBOT, Mrs., a venerable matron now living in P. G. Co., has
lived to see her fifth generation. (March 11, 1762)

TANEY, Hon Octavius C., of Cal. Co., died in Balto., on Tues. last.
He was a meber of the Maryland Senate. (March 8, 1832)

TANEY, Roger B., and Miss Ann P. C. Key, were married on Tues. evening
[Jan. 7], at Frederick-Town, by the Rev. Mr. Zocchey. (Jan.
16, 1806)

TASKER, Hon. Benjamin, Jr., died here on Friday evening last [Oct.
17], in his 40th year: Secretary of the Province, and one of
His Lordship's Council of State. [Long obit is given.]
(Oct. 23, 1760)

TASKER, Hon. Benjamin, President of the Council, died on Sun. last
[June 19], in his 79th year. (June 23, 1768)

TAYLOE, John, Jr., Esq., only son of the Hon. John Tayloe, Esq.,
one of H. M. Council of this Province, and Rebecca, daughter
of the Hon. George Plater, Esq., one of His Lordship's
Council of Maryland, were married 11th inst., at the house
of Ralph Wormly, Esq., in Middlesex; "Williamsburg, Va.,
July 23." (Aug. 11, 1747)

TAYLOR, Benjamin, and Margaret Jane, eldest daughter of Richard
Parkinson, all of Annap., were married Thurs. evening last,
by Rev. Mr. Davis. (Jan. 1, 1835)

TAYLOR, Mr. Edward, was murdered in Cecil Co., by one of his runaway

slaves, the beginning of this month. The (murderer) is a
brother to one who was hanged some years ago for shooting
Mr. Aquila Hall, in Balto. Co. Anne Taylor offers a reward
for the capture of the slave. (Dec. 19, 1750) The negro
Joe [q.v.] broke out of Cecil Co. jail, where he was imprisoned
for murdering his master Edward Taylor, at Elk Ferry. (Dec.
19, 1750)

TAYLOR, Elisha, and Harriet Hart, were married on Wed. morning, by
Rev. Mr. Vinton. (Dec. 27, 1838)

TAYLOR, Mrs. Elizabeth, died June 24th, at the residence of Capt.
Samuel Gover, near Friendship, A. A. Co., in her 76th year.
(June 27, 1833)

TAYLOR, Lieut. Francis, of the U. S. Army, and Sarah, daughter of
Gen. Richard Harwood, were married Thurs. evening last, by
Rev. Mr. Blanchard. (Sept. 17, 1829)

TAYLOR, Gamaliel, of Annap., and Miss Euphen Bruce, also of Annap.,
were married Sun. evening last [Oct. 28], by Rev. Mr. Willis-
ton. (Nov. 8, 1804)

TAYLOR, James, who lived in the northwest fork of Nanticoke River,
Dor. Co., was killed some time last June, by a rattlesnake.
(Aug. 9, 1749)

TAYLOR, Capt. John, was found dead after the wreck of the sloop
Betsy, on March 4. (March 5, 1812)

TAYLOR, Lemuel G., of Balto., and Miss Anne Rawlings, of Annap.,
were married Thurs. morning last, by the Rev. Mr. Fechtig.
(Nov. 13, 1817)

TAYLOR, Mrs. Mary E., died suddenly in Annap., on Sat. evening last.
(May 13, 1830)

TAYLOR, Thomas, and Miss Maria Hutton, all of Annap., were married
here on Thurs. evening last, by the Rev. Mr. Smith. (Aug.
25, 1825)

TAYLOR, Capt. William, of the Brigantine Raleigh, was knocked overboard by the boom and was drowned on Thurs. last [Oct. 6],
at Sandy Point. (Oct. 21, 1746)

TAYLOR, William, Sr., an old inhabitant of Annap., died Thurs. night
last. (July 8, 1824)

TAYMAN, Thomas W., and Mary R. Watson, all of A. A. Co., were married
Tues. morning last, by Rev. Mr. Waters. (June 14, 1832)

TEAL, ---, daughter of Emanuel Teal, aged about 13 years, accidentally
drowned with one Fell [q.v.]. (July 11, 1754)

TELKIN, Mr. Telk, a baker, died in Annap., on Friday night last. He
    was a native of Germany and came to this city from Balto.
    (Aug. 28, 1823)

TERRY, Miss Sally, died Thurs. evening last, in Annap. (Oct. 27,
    1831)

TERRY, William, died Friday last. (Oct. 25, 1821)

TERRY, Mr. William, died in Annap. on Sat. evening last, after a
    short but severe illness, leaving a widow and two children.
    (Oct. 14, 1824)

THISTLE, Mr. Bayard, died in Cumberland on Thurs. morning last, at
    the house of his grandfather (Major John H. Bayard), in his
    24th year, son of Mr. George Thistle, of this county. The
    unfortunate youth was shot in the back by the late Dr. Charles
    V. Swearingen, on 17th ult. (From a Cumberland paper.)
    (Oct. 17, 1833)

THOMAS, Elizabeth, daughter of John Thomas, Esq., died at Lebanon,
    on West River, on 26th inst., in her 13th year. (May 31, 1838)

THOMAS, Ellis, eldest son of Ellis Thomas, Esq., of A. A. Co., died
    24th ult., in his 39th year. (Sept. 13, 1827)

THOMAS, Isaiah, a native of Mass., died in Balto., a few days since,
    aged c.70, son of the late Isaiah Thomas, known as the Father
    Printing in the United States. (July 2, 1835)

THOMAS, Mrs. Jane, died in Balto., on Sat., 10th inst., in her 77th
    year, widow of Luke Thomas, late of Balto. (Oct. 19, 1820)

THOMAS, John, died Mon. last, Jan. 1, in Fred. Co., High Sheriff
    of that county. (Jan. 3, 1750)

THOMAS, John, died Sun. evening last, at West River, formerly
    President of the Senate of this state. (Feb. 7, 1805)

THOMAS, John, of West River, Md., and Miss Elizabeth Murray, daughter
    of Commodore Alexander Murray, were married in Phila., on
    Wed. evening, Dec. 31st, 1817, by the Rev. Mr. Wilson. (Jan.
    15, 1818)

THOMAS, John Hanson, and Mary L. Colston, daughter of Rawleigh Col-
    ston, of Berkley Co., Va., were married Thurs. evening, 5th
    inst. (Oct. 18, 1809)

THOMAS,, John Hanson, one of the most eminent legislators of this
    state, died at Frederick-Town, Tues., 2nd inst., of typhus.
    (May 11, 1815) [Long obit is given in issue of May 18.]

THOMAS, Nicholas, Judge of the General Court, died. Robert Goldsborough, Jr., was appointed Judge in his place. (March 4,
1784)

THOMAS, Philip, Jr., son of the Hon. Philip Thomas, and Mrs. Galloway,
a widow, were married last week at West River Meeting. There
were upwards of 100 guests who partook of the wedding dinner.
(May 9, 1754)

THOMAS, Hon. Philip, one of the members of His Lordship's Council of
State, died on Tues. last [Nov. 23], at his seat at West
River, in his 70th year. (Nov. 25, 1762)

THOMAS, Philip, died at Rockland, Cecil Co., on the evening of the
3rd inst. (April 12, 1809)

THOMAS, Philip H., died Mon. last, much regretted at his residence
in the county. (Dec. 22, 1825)

THOMAS, Philip W., and Miss Julia Chisholm, both of A. A. Co., were
married Thurs. last [Nov. 10], at West River, by the Rev.
Mr. Compton. (Nov. 17, 1803)

THOMAS, Philip W., and Miss Rebecca Waters, of A. A. Co., were
married on Tues. last, by the Rev. Mr. Compton. (Sept. 25,
1806)

THOMAS, Mrs. Rebecca, relict of Philip W. Thomas, Esq., late of A. A.
Co., died Friday last, leaving seven children. (July 20, 1826)

THOMAS, Robert, died at his residence in the county, on Sun. last.
(Oct. 3, 1822)

THOMAS, Mrs. Sarah, relict of the late John Thomas, died Sun., 19th
inst., in her 77th year. (Sept. 23, 1824)

THOMAS, William, died last week, formerly a representative, and at
the time of his death, a magistrate for Tal. Co. (April 16,
1767)

THOMPSON, Mr. Charles, a young man formerly of this place, died
Sat. night last, in Balto. (Oct. 17, 1833)

THOMPSON, Edward, of Annap., and Miss Sarah Camden, of A. A. Co., were
married Tues. evening last, 16th inst., by Rev. John Decker.
(April 25, 1839)

THOMPSON, Henry, of Annap., and Miss Mary West, of Balto., were
married in that place on Sun. last [Nov. 13]. (Nov. 17, 1803)

THOMPSON, James W., and Miss Anne Maria K., eldest daughter of John
M'Feeley, were married Thurs. evening last, in Centreville,
by Rev. Mr. Decker. (Dec. 24, 1835)

THOMPSON, Mrs. Jane, relict of the late Richard Thompson, one of the
    oldest inhabitants of Annap., died Thurs. night last. (June
    7, 1827)

THOMPSON, John, and Eleanor Thompson, were married on Sun. [April 6],
    by the Rev. Mr. Wyatt. (April 10, 1806)

THOMPSON, John, printer, and Miss Eleanor Glover, both of Annap.,
    were married Sun. evening last [March 29], by the Rev. Mr.
    Davis. (April 2, 1818)

THOMPSON, John, a tailor, and a native of Annap., died Sun. last.
    (May 23, 1822)

THOMPSON, John, printer, died Friday morning last, in Annap. A mem-
    ber of the Protestant Episcopal Church, in his 56th year, he
    leaves a widow and several children. (Feb. 23, 1832)

THOMPSON, John Joseph Speed, son of the late John Thompson, printer
    of Annap., died in Balto., 6th inst., in his fourth year.
    (June 13, 1833)

THOMPSON, Joseph R., and Harriett Harwood, were married Sun. evening
    last, by Rev. Mr. Smith. (Dec. 29, 1825)

THOMPSON, Miss Louisa, died Sun. evening last, third daughter of
    Henry Thompson, of Annap., about 14 years of age. (March 11,
    1824)

THOMPSON, Richard, died in Annap., on Sat. morning, in his 63rd year,
    an old inhabitant of this city. (Sept. 6, 1809)

THOMPSON, Solomon, was murdered on the night of 12th ult., near
    Clarksville, Mont. Co. (April 10, 1823)

THOMPSON, William G., aged seven, son of John Thompson, printer,
    died Mon. night. (Jan. 22, 1829)

THOMPSON, William R., and Miss Eliza Weedon, all of Annap., were
    married Sun. evening, 8th inst., by the Rev. Mr. Watkins.
    (March 12, 1818)

THOMSON, Dr. Adam, of this province, a gentleman eminent for his
    medical abilities, died lately in New York, of the flux.
    (Oct. 1, 1767)

THORNTON, Rev. Mr. John, rector of Christ's Church Parish, Q. A. Co.,
    died Mon. morning last [Dec. 2]. (Dec. 6, 1753)

THORNTON, William, died Friday last [Feb. 3], at Balto. Town, formerly
    Sheriff of this [A. A.] Co. (Feb. 9, 1769)

TIFFIN, Capt. William, died suddenly last Sun. [Jan. 21], being seized
with a violent pain in one of his eyes, at Balto. Town, in
Balto. Co. He sailed several voyages out of this province.
(Jan. 25, 1749)

TILDEN, Mrs. Louisa Harvey, wife of Dr. Tilden of Kent Co., Md.,
and third daughter of Samuel Harvey Howard of Annap., died
at Balto., on Sun. evening last [April 28]. (May 2, 1805)

TILGHMAN, Mrs., died Mon., Oct. 24, wife of James Tilghman, and daughter of the Hon. George Steuart, of Annap. (Nov. 10, 1774)

TILGHMAN, Col. Edward, of Q. A. Co., and Julianna Carroll, were
married last. week. (May 10, 1759)

TILGHMAN, James, III, Attorney-at-Law, and Susanna, eldest daughter
George Steuart, Esq., of Annap., were married last Thurs.
[Jan. 19]. (Jan. 26, 1769)

TILGHMAN, Hon. James, late Chief Justice of the Second District, and
one of the Judges of the Court of Appeals of this state, died
Wed., 18th ult., in Chestertown. (May 3, 1809)

TILGHMAN, John, of Tal. Co., and Miss Maria Gibson, daughter of John
Gibson, Esq., of this city, were married on Tues. evening last
[Dec. 27], by the Rev. Mr. Judd. (Dec. 24, 1807)

TILGHMAN, Master Matthew Ward, a very hopeful youth, eldest son to
Mr. Matthew Tilghman, one of the representatives of Tal. Co.,
[met with] a very melancholy accident a few days ago. He was
running just behind a cart, when one of the wheels run [sic]
over the end of a piece of wood, which flung it around with
such force that it broke one of his legs, of which he soon
after died. (March 29, 1753)

TILGHMAN, Col. Richard, died last Tues. [Sept. 9], at his plantation
in Q. A. Co., eldest brother of a very respectable family;
for many years Clerk of that county, and one of the Judges of
the Provincial Court. (Sept. 11, 1766)

TILLARD, Capt. William S., died. (March 16, 1815)

TILLEY, Mr. Jasper, of A. A. Co., died suddenly, on Sat. (March 6,
1817)

TILLOTSON, John, died very recently in Q. A. Co., formerly a representative of that county. (April 16, 1772)

TILTON, Lieut. Edward Gibson, U. S. N., and Josephine, daughter of
H. H. Harwood, of Annap., were married Thurs. evening last,
by the Rev. Mr. Blanchard. (Jan. 10, 1833)

TILTON, Thomas, in his 70th year, and Mary Lucar, in her 13th year,
the daughter's daughter of Thomas Tilton's former wife, were
married 15th inst., at Middleton (Monmouth); from the Trenton
Federalist. (March 13, 1800)

TINLEY, Alexander, of Hancock Town, Wash. Co., attached to a militia
company now here, was drowned Mon. morning in a creek near
the encampment while bathing. His remains were interred Tues.,
in the burial ground, with military honors. (Aug. 11, 1814)

TIPTON, Mr. Jonathan, died at the beginning of this month, in Balto.
Co., aged 118 years. He was born in Kingston, Jamaica, which
place he left while young, and lived almost ever since in this
province. He had his perfect senses to the last, especially
a remarkable strength of memory. His youngest sons are reckoned
among the oldest men in the county. (Jan. 27, 1757)

TISH, Frederick, and Clarissa Philips, all of Annap., were married
here on 15th inst. (Sept. 20, 1827)

TODD, Alexander, and Mrs. Margaret Mace, all of Annap., were married
Thurs. evening last, by the Rev. Mr. Watkins. (Aug. 1, 1822)

TOLLEY, Mr. James, died lately at his father's house in Balto. Co.,
a student-at-law in this city. (Nov. 10, 1768)

TOMPKINS, Daniel D., late Vice-President of the United States, died
Sat., 11th inst., at his residence on Staten Island. (June
23, 1825)

TOMLINSON, Nathaniel, was killed lately by Indians in the "back
country." (April 29, 1762)

TONEY, a mulatto, was executed at Annap. for the murder of Capt.
Curtis. (Aug. 8, 1754)

TONEY, negro, the "poison doctor," was executed Friday last at Port
Tobacco for poisoning the late Mr. Chase. (July 10, 1751)

TOOTELL, Mrs. Helen, was decently interred here on Thurs. last [Sept.
22], widow, aged 73, one of the oldest inhabitant of this
town. (Sept. 29, 1763)

TOOTELL, Mr. James, Purser, of the U. S. Navy, died yesterday, in
Annap. (Sept. 13, 1809)

TOOTELL, Richard, died Wed. morning [Sept. 25], in his 25th year.
(Sept. 27, 1745)

TOY, Rev. Joseph, a minister of the Methodist Episcopal Church, died
in Balto. on Sat. afternoon, 28th inst. (Feb. 2, 1826)

TRACEY, Uriah, died 18th inst., at the city of Washington; a Senator
in the United States Senate from the state of Conn. (July
30, 1807)

TRAPNELL, Rev. Joseph, of Upper Marlboro, and Miss Emily Watkins, of
Annap., were married Tues. evening last, by Rev. Dr. Humphreys.
(June 20, 1839)

TRAVERS, Col. Henry, representative for Dor. Co., died. Col. John
Henry is elected in his place. (March 6, 1766)

TRAVERS, Mr. Matthew,a young man of Dor. Co., skipper of a Bay
Schooner, fell of the bowsprit, and was drowned in the Nanticoke River, on 6th inst. (Nov. 18, 1762)

TREACKLE, James, and Henrietta H. Cromwell, both of A. A. Co., were
married Thurs., 10th inst., by the Rev. Mr. Larkins. (May
17, 1832)

TRENCHARD, Capt. Edward, of the U. S. N., died at New York suddenly,
3rd inst. (Nov. 11, 1824)

TRETCHER, Thomas, died at Alexandria, Va., on the 22nd ult., in his
53rd year. He had the honor of circumnavigating the globe
with the celebrated Capt. Cook. (Nov. 4, 1813)

TRIPPE, Major Henry, of Dor. Co., died last month, for many years
a member of the House of Delegates and Deputy Commissary for
that county. (Jan. 17, 1745)

TRIPPE, Lieut. J., died on board the U. S. Brig Vixen, of which he
was Commander, on his voyage to New Orleans. (Sept. 5, 1810)

TRUEMAN, Capt. John, died in this city on Sat. last. He was an old
Revolutionary officer. His remains were interred on Mon.,
with military honors. (Feb. 8, 1809)

TRUMBULL, Jonathan, Esq., Governor of the State of Connecticut,
departed this lis life on Mon., 7th inst., at Lebanon, in
his 70th year. (Aug. 16, 1809)

TRUXTON, Commodore Thomas, late of the U. S. Navy, died in Philadelphia, Sun. last, 5th inst., in his 68th year. (May 16, 1822)

TUCK, Rachel Ann, died Mon. last, in Annap., in her 6th year, daughter
of Mr. Washington G. Tuck. (March 20, 1823)

TUCK, Washington, of this city, and Miss Elizabeth Lee, of A. A. Co.,
were married on Sun. evening last [Oct. 16], by the Rev. Mr.
Judd. (Oct. 20, 1808)

TUCK, Washington G., of Annap., and Miss Rachel Whittington, were

married on 17th inst., in Cal. Co., by the Rev. Mr. Smith.
(March 24, 1814)

TUCKER, Abel, and Miss Mary Tydings were married Sun. evening last,
at South River, by Rev. Mr. Lane. (July 26, 1804)

TUCKER, Mr. Francis, died in Annap. on Sat. last [June 8], in his
26th year. (June 12, 1811)

TUCKER, John, of Annap., was unfortunately drowned last Sat., when
a sudden gust of wind upset his small sloop, off the mouth
of South River. (June 9, 1803)

TUCKER, Capt. Seely, died Thurs. last [Dec. 8]. (Dec. 15, 1808)

TURNER, John B., and Ann Stone, both of Port Tobacco, were married
in that place on Sun., [May] 20th, by Rev. Mr. Weems. (June
6, 1810)

TURNER, Mrs. Maria, departed this life on Wed., 1st inst.; wife of
Mr. Thomas Turner, and daughter of Augustine Gambrill. (Nov.
9, 1815)

TURVEY, John, last Sun. evening [Oct. 16], a lad about 18 years of
age, belonging to the Winchester, lying in Severn River,
having a dish with a rump of beef in it in his hands, fell
out of the window into the river and was drowned. (Oct. 19,
1748)

TYDINGS, Mr. Ferdinando, a member of the Methodist Episcopal Church,
died yesterday in Annap., at an advanced age. (Nov. 10, 1831)

TYDINGS, Horatio, died in Annap., on Thurs. morning last. (April
13, 1826)

TYDINGS, John, and Mrs. Sarah Ann Stewart, both of the county, were
married Thurs. last, by Rev. Watkins. (Sept. 14, 1826)

TYDINGS, Mr. John, died in Annap. on Thurs. morning last. (Sept.
9, 1830)

TYDINGS, Mr. Joseph, of A. A. Co., and Sarah Tydings, of Annap., were
married Tues. evening last, by Rev. Mr. Poisal. (Dec. 29,
1836)

TYDINGS, Lewis, of Annap., and Miss Louisa Davis, of the county,
were married Thurs. evening last, by Rev. Mr. Griffith. (Jan.
8, 1824)

TYDINGS, Lewis, and Elizabeth Deale, both of this place, were married
Thurs. evening last, by the Rev. Mr. Slicer. (Aug. 25, 1825)

TYDINGS, Mrs. Louisa, consort of Mr. Lewis Tydings, of Annap., died
Mon. morning last. She leaves a husband and a father. (Dec.
30, 1824)

TYDINGS, Mr. Richard, and Miss Rebecca Watts, were married on Tues.
evening, 9th inst., by the Rev. Mr. Watkins. (Nov. 15, 1832)

TYDINGS, Roger, and Mary Ann Nicholson, all of A. A. Co., were married
Thurs. evening last, by Rev. Mr. Waters. (July 3, 1834)

TYLER, Dr. Grafton, and Mary Bowie, all of P. G. Co., were married
Tues. evening, 19th inst., by Rev. Mackenheimer. (Jan. 28,
1836)

TYLER, Samuel, an overseer, was found dead Sun. morning last [Jan.
4], in the snow near the Head of Severn. (Jan. 8, 1761)

TYLER, Truman, Esq., late Cashier of the Planters' Bank, and Register
of Wills for P. G. Co., died at the Banking House, 13th inst.,
in his 57th year. (Aug. 20, 1829)

UNCLES, Frederick, and Pamelia Verlinda Tucker, all of A. A. Co., were
married Tues. evening, 19th inst., by the Rev. Mr. Wright.
(Jan. 28, 1836)

UPSHUR, Mrs. Ann B., relict of the late Arthur Upshur, Esq., died
Mon., 2nd inst., at the residence of Daniel Lloyd, Wye Heights,
Tal. Co. (March 12, 1835)

USHER, Mr. Noble Lee, and Mrs. Hariett Anna Snowden, both parties
of the theatre, were married at Balto. on Sat. evening last,
by the Rev. Mr. Richards. (May 3, 1804)

VALLEIN, Joseph, and Miss Mary Ann Norman, all of Annap., were married
on Thurs. evening last [Jan. 27], by the Rev. Mr. Watkins.
(Feb. 3, 1820)

VAN HORN, Archibald, a member of the State Senate, and formerly a
Representative in Congress from the Second District, died at
his seat in P. G. Co. (March 13, 1817)

VAN QUICKENBORNE, Rev. Charles J., S. J., a Catholic priest, died
17th ult., at Portage des Sious, St. Charles Co., Mo. (Sept.
14, 1837)

VAN WOMER, L. H., died in P. G. Co., on the 16th inst., of a typhus
fever. A native of New York or Vermont, he formerly resided
in this city, in which he superintended a grammar school.
(Oct. 23, 1823)

VESSELLS, Widow, was found murdered at her house in St. M. Co., a

few weeks ago. She was 30 or 35 years of age. (April 4,
1754)

VICARS, Matthew, was found dead in the woods in Dor. Co., with some
rum by his head; 'tis supposed he had drank an over quantity,
which put a period to his existence. (March 21, 1771)

VICKERS, Mr. Clement, died at his residence in Easton, Tal. Co., on
Wed., 17th inst., in his 52nd year. He was late commander
and part owner of the steam-boat Maryland. (Aug. 25, 1825)

VICKERS, William, of Tal. Co., was drowned when the Kent Island
ferryboat capsized. (June 8, 1748)

W---E, J---, of this county, was choked to death by the string he
had round the feet of the hog he had stolen, and slung around
his neck. (Dec. 5, 1750)

WAGGAMAN, Major Henry, died lately in Som. Co., for many years and
at the time of his death, one of the representatives for
that county. (Dec. 11, 1760)

WAGNER, Jacob, died in Balto., on the 17th inst., in his 52nd year.
(Jan. 20, 1825)

WALDEN, Richard, of this place, a few days ago fell overboard in
Bohemia River, and was drowned. (Aug. 14, 1751)

WALKER, Dr. James, died last week at his house at Elk Ridge. (Jan.
18, 1759)

WALKER, Mrs. Rebecca, wife of Col. Thomas Walker, died Sat. evening
after a few hours' illness. On Mon., her remains were interred according to the mode prescribed by Congress. (Jan.
26, 1775)

WALL, Balsar, accidentally drowned last Thurs. [June 7], at noon;
he was a German butcher. (June 14, 1764)

WALLACE, Mrs., died Sat. last [Aug. 31], in her 64th year, in Annap.
(Nov. 5, 1795)

WALLACE, Charles, Esq., departed this life on Thurs. last [Feb. 13],
in his 84th year, at the seat of Mr. Leonard Sellman. (Feb.
20, 1812)

WALLACE, Mrs. Eleanor, wife of Dr. Michael Wallace, died 26th inst.,
at her father's residence, near Nottingham, Patuxent. (Aug.
2, 1787)

WALLACE, Mrs. Mary, relict of Charles Wallace, Esq., died Mon. evening
last, at the age of 87. (April 3, 1834)

WALTER, John, was found lying dead [on Aug. 21], on the road within
   a mile from Elk Ridge Landing. It is evident he was most barbarously murdered. He was a resident of Howard St. (Balto.),
   a tailor, and leaves a wife of three children. (Aug. 24, 1797)

WALTERS, Mrs. Sarah, consort of Capt. Jacob Walters, died on Wed.
   last [Sept. 29], at Patapsco, in her 38th year. (Oct. 7, 1762)

WARD, Capt. Henry, one of the representatives for Cecil Co., died
   there, lately, of the small pox. (July 17, 1760)

WARD, Madam Margaret, died leaving a will. (April 26, 1753)

WARD, William, and Sarah Jane, daughter of Capt. Samuel Gover, of
   A. A. Co., were married Thurs., 16th inst., by Rev. J. Bowen.
   (Jan. 23, 1834)

WARD, the Hon. William H., one of the Associate Judges of the Sixth
   Judicial District of this state, died at eight o'clock, Thurs.
   morning, 26th ult., in Balto. (Aug. 2, 1827)

WARDER, Susanna, formerly the wife of Virgil Warder, who was one of
   the house servants of William Penn, Proprietor of Pennsylvania, died in Phila., on the 30th inst. [June], in her 109th
   year. This aged black woman, a daughter of one of his [Penn's]
   cooks, was born at his mansion house in Pennsbury Manor, in
   March, 1701, the same year he left the Province to return to
   England. The Penn family, respecting her faithful services
   in the time of her youth, allowed an annual sum to support
   her comfortably, when she was not able to work, to the end of
   her days. (July 19, 1809)

WARDROP, Mr. James, died on Feb. 29, at New York, after a long and
   lingering illness; merchant of Upper Marlborough in this
   Province. (March 13, 1760) Lettice Wardrop, Alexander
   Symmer, and Joseph Belt, Jr., are execs. (Aug. 7, 1760)

WARFIELD, Capt. Allen, died in Annap., on Mon., 28th inst.; formerly
   of A. A. Co. He leaves a wife and three children. He was a
   professor of religion. [Long obit is given.] (May 31, 1827)

WARFIELD, Dr. Anderson, died Tues. morning, in his 53rd year; from
   the Balto. American. (Feb. 28, 1828)

WARFIELD, Dr. Charles Alexander, died Friday, 29th ult., at his seat
   in A. A. Co., in his 62nd year. He was among the earliest
   who espoused the cause of independence. In arduous course of
   practice for upwards of 42 years, his skill and benevolence
   as a physician were equally attested and approved. He had
   been a member of the Board of Examiners of the medical faculty
   since the second year of its organization. (Feb. 18, 1813)

WARFIELD, Mrs. Elizabeth, died on Thurs. morning, the 8th inst.;
  consort of Dr. Charles Alexander Warfield, of A. A. Co.
  (Sept. 22, 1808)

WARFIELD, Evan, son of Lancelot Warfield, died at the Havanna, 15th
  ult, in his 19th year. (Nov. 17, 1803)

WARFIELD, Hon. Henry, was found dead in his bed in Frederick on
  Mon. morning last. He had represented this state in Congress;
  from the Balto. Chronicle. (April 21, 1839)

WARFIELD, John, Sr., died April 30th, at Philipsville, A. A. Co.,
  in his 71st year. (May 7, 1835)

WARFIELD, Mrs. Louisa, late consort of Allen Warfield, of A. A. Co.,
  died on the evening of 26th inst. [Dec.], aged 26. (Jan. 2,
  1823)

WARFIELD, Nathan, and Caroline B. Hammond, both of A. A. Co., were
  married Tues. evening last, at the residence of Dr. Newbern
  by Rev. Mr. Kalbfus. (Feb. 14, 1833)

WARFIELD, Philemon, of A. A. Co., and Miss Ann Wright, of Annap.,
  were married on Sun. evening last [Oct. 24], by the Rev. Mr.
  Watkins. (Oct. 28, 1819)

WARFIELD, Mrs. Rachel, died 13th inst., in her 64th year, at the
  residence of Dr. William Hammond. (Aug. 26, 1824)

WARFIELD, Richard, died Sun. last [Feb. 23], of pleurisy, at his
  plantation about nine miles from this town, on the Patapsco
  Road, in his 79th year; a representative and a magistrate.
  (Feb. 27, 1755)

WARFIELD, Singleton, died on Mon. morning [March 8], son of Thomas
  Warfield. (March 11, 1819)

WARFIELD, Thomas, died on Sun. morning [March 7], at his residence
  in this county, in his 74th year. (March 11, 1819)

WARFIELD, William, of Annap., and Miss Mary Worthington, of A. A. Co.,
  were married Tues. evening last, at the seat of John Worthington, Esq., by Rev. Mr. Davis. (Sept. 19, 1816)

WARFIELD, William, died in Annap., Friday morning last, in his 40th
  year. (Oct. 3, 1822)

WARING, Major Francis, died lately at his house in P. G. Co., Chief
  Justice and one of the Representatives of his county. (Feb.
  23, 1769)

WARREN, Mrs. Ann, consort of William Warren, manager of the Baltimore and Philadelphia Theatres, died at Alexandria, on the 28th ult. (July 7, 1808)

WARREN, William, and Mrs. Ann Wignell, both of the Balto. and Phila. Theatres. were married on Thurs. last, Aug. 28, by the Rev. Dr. Rattoone. (Sept. 4, 1806)

WARREN, William, died Friday evening, in his 65th year, for many years manager of the Balto. and Phila. Theatres. He was a native of England, and for more than 30 years a resident of this country. He leaves a widow and a large family. (Oct. 25, 1832)

WARRICK, William, was killed some time last November by Obed Griffith, aged 17, who has been brought to trial in Balto. Co. [Details of case have been given.] The boy was sentenced to six years in the penitentiary. (April 8, 1819)

WARRING, William, died June 8th, at the residence of his mother, Mrs. Elizabeth Warring, of Brotherton, in his 15th year. (June 26, 1834)

WASHINGTON, the Hon. Bushrod, one of the Justices of the United States Supreme Court, died Thurs. He was in his 71st year. [Long obit is given.] (Dec. 3, 1829)

WASHINGTON, George, died: Resolutions of the General Assembly of Maryland on the occasion of his death. (Dec. 19, 1799) An account of his funeral is given. (Dec. 26, 1799)

WASHINGTON, George S., Esq., nephew of the late President Washington, died suddenly on Tues. night, 16th ult. [Jan.], in Augusta, in his 37th year. His remains were deposited in St. Paul's Churchyard. (Feb. 8, 1809)

WASHINGTON, Mrs. Martha, departed this life at Mount Vernon, on Sat., [May 22], consort of General George Washington. (May 27, 1802)

WASHINGTON, Gen. William, died at Sandy Hill, S. C., on the 16th ult. (April 18, 1810)

WATERS, Charles A., and Miss Beard, of A. A. Co., were married Tues. evening last, by Rev. Mr. Waters. (June 13, 1839)

WATERS, Col. Jacob, Esq., died Mon. morning at his residence on South River, A. A. Co. (Aug. 15, 1833; Aug. 22, 1833)

WATERS, Dr. James W., of A. A. Co., and Elizabeth, daughter of Thomas Waters, Esq., of Mont. Co., were married Tues., 17th inst., by Rev. Mr. Waters. (Oct. 26, 1837)

WATERS, Capt. John H. D., member-elect of the State Legislature, died at his residence in Som. Co., 3rd inst. (Nov. 18, 1824)

WATERS, Jonathan, died in Annap., Sat. last, in his 63rd year. (May
8, 1823)

WATERS, Ramsay, Esq., Register in Chancery, and Miss Anne Marriott
were married in Annap., on 4th inst., by the Rev. Mr. Ryland.
(July 25, 1822)

WATERS, Mrs. Sarah, relict of the late Jonathan Waters, died Thurs.
last at an advanced age. (Nov. 29, 1832)

WATERS, Thomas G., of Annap., and Miss Anna E. Beard, daughter of
Mr. Stephen Beard, of Head of South River, were married Thurs.
evening last, by the Rev. Mr. Watkins. (March 28, 1822)

WATERS, Mr. Walter W., of Mont. Co., and Elizabeth Ann Warfield, daughter of the late James Warfield, and step-daughter of Nicholas
Worthington of Thomas, of Elk Ridge, were married 3rd inst.,
by the Rev. Mr. Waters. (Jan. 19, 1826)

WATERS, Mr. William Montgomery, died Mon. last, of a pulmonary
affection, at the residence of his father, Dr. Wilson Waters,
of this county. (Oct. 9, 1828)

WATKINS, Dr. Benjamin, of A. A. Co., and Lucinda Hodges, of Annap.,
were married Tues., 27th ult., by Rev. Blanchard. (Dec. 6,
1827)

WATKINS, Dr. Benjamin, and Mary, daughter of Thomas Hodges, both of
A. A. Co., were married Tues., 16th inst., by Rev. Thomas
Foreman. (Nov. 25, 1830)

WATKINS, Mrs. Elizabeth, of West River, died on Sun., 20th [Nov.],
at the seat of her father, William Hall, III. (Dec. 1, 1808)

WATKINS, James F., of Balto., and Miss Ellen Merriken, of A. A. Co.,
were married at West River, on 30th ult., by Rev. Mr. Chesley.
(April 4, 1833)

WATKINS, James H., of Esq., of Annap., and Martha Ann Iglehart, of
A. A. Co., were married Wed., 23rd ult., by Rev. Mr. Wright.
(Oct. 1, 1835)

WATKINS, John, son of Stephen, died Tues., the 14th, at West River.
(Feb. 23, 1815)

WATKINS, John Nicholas, and Matilda Green, all of Annap., were
married Thurs. evening last, by Rev. McElhiney. (Jan. 28,
1836)

WATKINS, Col. Joseph, died at his seat on the south side of South
River, on the 8th inst. (Feb. 20, 1823)

WATKINS, Major Nicholas, died Dec. 14, 1794; lines on his decease are printed. (Jan. 8, 1795)

WATKINS, Nicholas, of Thomas, died at his residence in this county, on Tues. morning last, leaving a widow and several children. (Aug. 24, 1826)

WATKINS, Nicholas Edwin, and Mary Thomas, all of this city, were married on Tues. evening, by Rev. Mr. Davis. (Dec. 18, 1834)

WATKINS, Nicholas J., and Miss Margaret Todd, were married on Sun. [Aug. 24], at Broad Neck on the Severn, by Rev. Mr. Welch. (Aug. 28, 1806)

WATKINS, Nicholas J., Jr., second son of the Rev. N. J. Watkins, died in Balto. on Mon. last, in his 19th year. His remains were brought to Annap. on Tues., on the steamboat Maryland, and interred in the family burial ground on the south side of Severn. (Sept. 15, 1831; Sept. 22, 1831)

WATKINS, Richard, third son of the Rev. N. J. Watkins, died in Annap., Sun. last, aged 10 years. (Sept. 22, 1831)

WATKINS, Richard G., Esq., and Lucretia Margaret, daughter of Col. Richard Harwood, were married at West River, A. A. Co., on Thurs. evening last, by the Rev. Mr. Gosnell. (Feb. 12, 1824)

WATKINS, Thomas, of A. A. Co., and Anne P. Wheeler, of P. G. Co., were married in the latter county, on Tues., 1st inst., by the Rev. Mr. Watkins. (Nov. 10, 1825)

WATKINS, Thomas, Jr., and Amanda F., daughter of Col. Gassaway Watkins, all of Elk Ridge, were married Thurs., 19th ult., by the Rev. S. Linthicum. (March 12, 1835)

WATSON, Charles, died in A. A. Co., on Sat. last, leaving a numerous family. (May 4, 1826)

WATSON, William, on Tues. last, a hopeful lad, about 12 years old, was knocked overboard by the boom of a schooner and drowned at Greenberry's Point. (Aug. 16, 1745)

WATSON, William, died on Mon. evening last [March 20], in his 26th year. (March 22, 1809)

WATTS, Mrs. Anne, died in Annap. on Mon. night last [Sept. 8]. (Sept. 10, 1818)

WATTS, Edward, aged 10, son of Richard B. Watts, was killed Tues. afternoon, by the accidental discharge of a gun, set off by

his brother Charles, aged seven or eight. [Long account is
given.] (Dec. 13, 1827)

WATTS, Mrs. Elizabeth, consort of Mr. Richard B. Watts, died on Oct.
10. (Oct. 17, 1810)

WATTS, Miss Elizabeth, daughter of the late Richard B. Watts, died
in Annap., on Sun. morning last, in her 19th year. (Nov. 3,
1825)

WATTS, Mr. George, and Miss Sarah Stockett, were married in Annap.
on Thurs. evening last. by the Rev. Mr. Hammond. (Nov. 16,
1826)

WATTS, Mrs. Mary, consort of Mr. Richard B. Watts, of Annap., died
Tues. night, after a lingering illness. (Sept. 26, 1822)

WATTS, Mrs. Rachel, consort of George Watts, died in Annap., on Sat.
night last. (Sept. 28, 1826)

WATTS, Richard B., and Miss Mary Watson, were married Tues. evening
by Rev. Mr. Wyatt. (April 2, 1812)

WATTS, Thomas, a simple young man, was so abused a few weeks ago by
people at a private tippling house on Chester River, Q. A.
Co., Md., that he died. (Jan. 31, 1754)

WATTS, William, of Cumberland, and Matilda Ann Nichols, of Annap.,
were married Sun. evening last, by Rev. Mr. Hank. (April 5,
1838)

WAYMAN, Thomas, of A. A. Co., and Miss Elizabeth Cratchley, of Annap.,
were married Sun. evening last [Jan. 16], by the Rev. Mr.
Guest. (Jan. 20, 1820)

WAYMAN, Thomas, died on the North side of Severn River, on Sat. last.
(Jan. 12, 1826)

WEBSTER, John, died Friday last in Balto. Co., aged 91 years; a native
of Kent Island, he lived all his days in this province.
Among many other virtues he enjoyed temperance, which doubtless
contributed greatly to his longevity. He lived to see 108 of
his posterity, 22 of which died before him. (April 12, 1753)

WEBSTER, William H., the celebrated songster and comedian, and Miss
Rebecca Merriken, of Phila., were married Sun. morning last,
by Rev. Joseph Pilmore, D. D. (from a Philadelphia paper).
(Oct. 25, 1809)

WEEDEN, William, and Miss Margaret Nichols, all of A. A. Co., were
married Thurs. evening last, by Rev. Mr. Vinton. (Aug. 10,
1837)

WEEDON, Clement, and Miss Ann Davis, were married in A. A. Co. on Sun. evening last, by Rev. Mr. Watkins. (Dec. 29, 1825)

WEEDON, Clement, and Mrs. Mary Warfield, both of A. A. Co., were married Sun. last, by Rev. Watkins. (Dec. 6, 1827)

WEEDON, Jonathan, and Miss Margaret Hutton, all of Annap., were married on Thurs. evening last [July 29], by the Rev. Mr. Guest. (Aug. 5, 1819)

WEEDON, Mrs. Rebecca, consort of Jonathan Weedon, of Annapolis Neck, died Mon. morning last. (April 3, 1834)

WEEDON, Samuel T. See Samuel T. Wright.

WEEMS, Mrs. Alice, wife of John Weems, and daughter of the late President Lee, died July 25, at "Weems' Forest," in Cal. Co. (Sept. 3, 1789)

WEEMS, James, and Eleanora Holland, of Annap., were married Tuesday evening last, by Rev. Mr. McElhiney. (Feb. 8, 1838)

WEEMS, Rev. John, died 2nd inst., in his 57th year, late rector of Port Tobacco Parish, Chas. Co., in which he was officiating minister for more than 30 years. (Nov. 22, 1821)

WEEMS, John, departed this life on Tues., Sept. 7th, at his residence near Louisville, in the state of Kentucky, in his 77th year. He was formerly a resident of A. A. Co., Md. (Oct. 21, 1813)

WEEMS, John B., and Miss Priscilla Harwood, daughter of Col. Richard Harwood, were married Sun. last [Jan. 5], at South River, by the Rev. Mr. Compton. (Jan. 9, 1806)

WEEMS, Mr. John B., died Thurs. night last [June 22], at his residence in A. A. Co. (June 23, 1814)

WEEMS, Nathaniel C., died Sun. night 13th inst., by an attack of the gout in his stomach, at his seat near Billingsley, near Upper Marlborough. (March 24, 1808)

WEEMS, Mrs. Rachel A. H., died 12th inst., while on a visit to her sister, Mrs. Mary Allein, of Pig Point, in her 22nd year; consort of David G. Weems, of Tracey's landing. She leaves a husband and son. (Sept. 26, 1833)

WEEMS, Sutton I., delegate to the General Assembly, from Cal. Co., died in Annap., Sun. morning last. (March 24, 1825)

WEEMS, William, died Sat. evening, 15th inst., at his residence, Portly Manor, A. A. Co., in his [40th?] year. (Aug. 27, 1829)

WELCH, A. G., M.D., and Emily, youngest daughter of the late W. T.
Bedford, were married in Balto., Sun. morning last, by the
Rev. Dr. Wyatt. (Dec. 24, 1835)

WELCH, Edward Augustus, eldest son of Robert Welch of Ben, Esq., died
Sat., 13th inst., not yet 19 years old. [Long obit is given.]
(Feb. 18, 1830)

WELCH, Mr. Francis, died in Annap., on Sat. morning last, for many
years past, warden of A. A. Co. jail. (Sept. 26, 1839)

WELCH, Miss Henrietta, died in Annap., on Tues. morning last. (July
16, 1829)

WELCH, Joseph, died on Friday morning [Oct. 13]. (Oct. 17, 1810)

WELCH, Mr. John, departed this life, at his dwelling near the Head
of Severn, on Sun. last, in his 57th year. He leaves a widow
and family. (March 7, 1816)

WELCH, Mr. John, died at his residence in the lower part of A. A. Co.,
on Thurs. last, leaving a widow and five children. (Jan. 26,
1826)

WELCH, Peregrine, late clerk to the City Commissioners of Baltimore,
died in Balto. on the 23rd ult. (Feb. 2, 1826)

WELCH, Mr. Richard, and Miss Margaret Cromwell, both of A. A. Co.,
were married Sun. last, on the north side of Severn, by the
Rev. N. J. Watkins. (Dec. 15, 1831)

WELCH, Rev. Robert, died at his residence on the north side of Severn
on Sun. last. (July 6, 1826)

WELCH, Mrs. Sarah, wife of Benjamin Welch, of South River, died
Thurs., 3rd inst., in her 34th year. (May 17, 1787)

WELCH, Mrs. Sarah, relict of the late Rev. Robert Welch, died Friday
last, on Magothy River, in her 54th year. (April 23, 1829)

WELCH, Thomas, Esq., and Miss Elizabeth Sellman, were married in
A. A. Co., on the evening of 24th ult., by the Rev. Dr. Rafferty
(Dec. 1, 1825)

WELHAM, Mrs. Emily, consort of John Welham, died Sun., 3rd inst.,
aged about 37 years. (May 7, 1835)

WELLES, Mr. Samuel, died Sat. morning last, in Annap., an aged servant of Christ, more than 40 years a member of the Methodist
Church. [Long obit is given.] (April 2, 1829)

WELLS, Anne, infant daughter of George and Eliza Wells, died Tues.
afternoon. (Aug. 9, 1838)

WELLS, Mrs. Augusta, relict of the late Rev. George Wells of Annap., died Mon. morning at an advanced age. (Nov. 8, 1832)

WELLS, Daniel, Sr., died Friday morning [May 28], in his 75th year. (May 29, 1817)

WELLS, George, Jr., Esq., of Annap., and Miss Janetta C. Sellman, of A. A. Co., were married on the evening of the 10th inst., by Rev. Dr. Rafferty. (May 17, 1827)

WELLS, Rev. George, of the Associated Methodist Churches, died Sat. evening, 11th inst., in his 55th year. A native of England, he was a resident of Annap. for many years. (Dec. 16, 1830)

WELLS, George, Esq., and Catherine Eliza, third daughter of the late Judge Harwood, were married Tues. evening last, by the Rev. Blanchard. (June 12, 1834)

WELLS, Mrs. Janetta, consort of George Wells, Esq., died Tues. morning last, in her 22nd year. (Sept. 2, 1830)

WELLS, John, and Miss Hannah Mayo, all of Annap., were married at West River on Thurs. evening [Oct. 25], by Rev. Mr. Pitts. (Oct. 31, 1810)

WELLS, Dr. John Bloodgood, of Annap., and Ann, second daughter of Richard Iglehart, Sheriff of the county, were married Thurs. evening last, in A. A. Co., by the Rev. James Sewell. (Feb. 18, 1830)

WELLS, Richard, and Catherine Hohne, were married the 4th inst., by Rev. Mr. Ryland. (July 25, 1822)

WELLS, Richard, died Sat. last, at his residence near Annap., an aged and respectable inhabitant, and for many years a member of the Methodist Church. (May 28, 1829)

WELLS, Richard, son of Richard Wells, died in Annap., 22nd inst., in his third year. (Sept. 29, 1831)

WELLS, Richard, died in George-Town, on Wed., 26th April, formerly of Annap., and for many years an old and respectable inhabitant of George-Town, aged 50 years. He leaves a widow and four children. (May 4, 1837)

WELLS, Mrs. Susan, consort of William Wells, merchant of Annap., died Thurs., 4th inst., in her 48th year. (Feb. 11, 1808)

WELLS, Mrs. Susanna, died in Annap., yesterday morning, in her 75th year. (Nov. 22, 1821)

WELLS, Miss Susanna, daughter of William Wells, of Annap., died Tues. night last. (Oct. 14, 1824)

WELLS, Violetta, second daughter of Richard Wells, died on the 26th
    inst., in her fifth year. (Sept. 29, 1831)

WELLS, William, died 16th inst., at the residence of Winbert Tschudy,
    Q. A. Co., in his 64th year; the deceased was lately a resident
    of Annapolis. (Dec. 24, 1828)

WELLS, William, Esq., and Mrs. Isabella Nicholson, both of P. G. Co.,
    were married Sun. last, 14th inst., in Queen Anne, by Rev.
    Mr. Marshall. (June 18, 1829)

WELSH, Mrs. Ann S., died 11th inst., at the Head of South River, the
    consort of Thomas Welsh, Esq. (Sept. 18, 1823)

WEST, Capt. John, died Friday night last [March 7], at his house in
    Herring Bay; one of the Magistrates for this county. (March
    12, 1752)

WEST, Stephen, died Sun. last [Jan. 5], at his house in London Town,
    aged over 70; the oldest inhabitant of that town. (Jan. 9,
    1752) Stephen West, executor of the estate, advertises for
    creditors and debtors to settle accounts. (June 25, 1752)

WEST, Mr. Stephen, merchant, and Hannah, only daughter of the late
    Capt. Williams, at the Wood Yard, were married Mon. last
    [March 5]. (March 8, 1753)

WEYLIE, Rev. John V., A. M., died on Sun. last (Jan. 26), in his 41st
    year; professor of the Latin and Greek languages in St. John's
    College. He was born in Cecil Co., in this state, and was in-
    debted for his education to the benevolence of the virtuous
    Washington. At an early period of his life he devoted him-
    self to the study of Divinity, and was ordained to the office
    of Deacon in the Protestant Episcopal Church, by Bishop Madi-
    son, of Va. (Jan. 30, 1817)

WEYLIE, Mrs. Martha M. J., eldest daughter of Mrs. M. Robinson of
    Annap., and relict of the late Rev. John V. Weylie, departed
    this life on Tues. evening, 28th inst. (April 30, 1818)

WHEAT, Jesse, and Mrs. Ann Burnett, both of A. A. Co., were married
    Tues. last, by the Rev. T. S. Walker. (June 12, 1834)

WHEELER, Daniel, overseer of Mrs. Wootton's plantation, missed his
    way late on Tues. night last week [Feb. 23], or rather Wed.
    morning, it being very dark, when he was going from a tavern
    in Queen Anne's Town, P. G. Co. He fell down head foremost
    into a dreadful gully there, where it is about 25 feet, almost
    perpendicular, and never stirred after. He was a widower and
    leaves 10 children. (March 4, 1762)

WHEELER, Thomas, and Miss Anne Hutton, were married on Sat. evening
    last [Feb. 23], by the Rev. Mr. Wyatt. (Feb. 28, 1805)

WHETCROFT, Burton, Esq., died at Utica, N. Y., on the evening of the
20th inst., in his 69th year. A native of Ireland, he came to
America about 10 years of age, and settled in Maryland. He
was Clerk to the Court of Appeals, and served as Mayor of
Annap. Since 1813, he has lived in Washington, with his only
daughter, the lady of Major Satterlee Clark, of the U. S.
Army. (May 2, 1822)

WHETCROFT, Mrs. Elizabeth, died on Wed. evening [Oct. 25], in her 50th
year, consort of Burton Whetcroft, Esq., of Annap. (Nov. 1,
1809)

WHETCROFT, Henry, Esq., died in Washington City, in his 72nd year,
formerly of Annap., and for many years an active and faithful
clerk in the office of the Third Auditor. (May 11, 1837)

WHETCROFT, Mr. James, of Annap., died yesterday morning, in his 80th
year. (Sept. 20, 1804)

WHITE, Benjamin, died (the following morning), when last Sat. evening,
near Patuxent, he was shot in the thigh, by Richard Clark,
who was committed to prison. He alleged that White was to
marry his (Clark's) mother. Clark used this means to prevent
the match. (Nov. 18, 1756)

WHITE, Gideon, died Thurs. evening last, Chief Justice of the Orphans
Court of A. A. Co. (May 5, 1836)

WHITE, Dr. Gideon, formerly of the U. S. Navy, died Tues. morning
last, in the prime of life, second son of the late Gideon
White, Esq. (May 5, 1836)

WHITE, Joseph, who was subject to fits, drowned Thurs. last in South
River. (July 20, 1758)

WHITE, James, of Annap., and Miss Eliza Sifton, of A. A. Co., were
married on Sun. evening last [Feb. 25], by the Rev. Mr. Watkins.
(March 1, 1821)

WHITE, Capt. K., of Balto. City, and Miss Elizabeth Ross, of Annap.,
were married Tues. last [May 2], by the Rev. Mr. Watkins.
(May 4, 1820)

WHITE, Mrs. Rebecca, died at Carlisle, Penna., on the 30th ult.,
consort of Elisha White, Esq., late of Annap. (Dec. 6, 1832)

WHITE, Samuel, died at his lodgings this morning [Nov. 4]. He has
for several years represented this state in the U. S. Senate.
(Nov. 15, 1809). (NOTE-This is prob. Samuel White, 1770 -
1809, Senator from Delaware.)

WHITE, Miss Sarah, daughter of the late Francis White, died on the

10th inst., in the 37th year of her age, at the residence of her mother, in A. A. Co. (Aug. 18, 1825)

WHITE, Mrs. Sarah, aged 84 years, died Tues., 10th inst., at her late residence on Head of South River. (Sept. 19, 1833)

WHITE, Thomas, and Mary Atkinson, were married on Thurs. evening last [Oct. 13], by the Rev. Mr. Guest. (Oct. 21, 1819)

WHITE, Mr. Thomas, died Tues. evening last, in Annap. (July 29, 1830)

WHITE, William W., and Mary Ann Phillips, all of Annap., were married Thurs. evening last, by the Rev. Mr. Riley. (Dec. 31, 1829)

WHITEFIELD, ---, a sailor belonging to Capt. Spencer, and a relation of the Rev. George Whitefield, was drowned in Patuxent. (March 26, 1752)

WHITEFIELD, Rev. James, Roman Catholic Archbishop of Baltimore, died Sun. morning. (Oct. 23, 1834)

WHITEHEAD, Charles, about 10 days ago, with two of his sons, and a woman set off, in a small canoe from the mouth of the Magothy River for Patapsco. The boys and the woman were thrown out of the canoe, and drowned, and the poor old man was found next day in the canoe, dead. (Feb. 9, 1769)

WHITEWOOD, Mrs. Elizabeth, died in George-Town, Columbia, on the 28th ult. (Aug. 30, 1809)

WHITFIELD, Rev. George, the celebrated Methodist preacher, died at Tottenham, Eng., Dec. 24, aged 79. (March 14, 1833)

WHITTINGTON, Mr. Clement, formerly a midshipman in the U. S. Navy, died Mon. morning, while engaged in superintending the operation of a windmill on South River Neck. He became entangled in a cog wheel and was instantly killed. (Nov. 1, 1827)

WHITTINGTON, Mr. Edward, who for the last year had been engaged to carry the mail from Annap. to St. Leonard's Creek, in Cal. Co., died Thurs., 21st inst., near Friendship, in A. A. Co., in his 23rd year. (March 28, 1833)

WHITTINGTON, John W., and Hannah, daughter of Gideon White, all of Annap., were married Thurs. evening last, by the Rev. Mr. Guest. (Oct. 4, 1832)

WHITTINGTON, Miss Mary Ann, died Mon., 19th inst., at South River. (July 22, 1830)

WHITTINGTON, Peter, and Miss Mary Nichols, all of A. A. Co., were

married on Thurs. morning last, by the Rev. Mr. T. Waters.
(June 27, 1839)

WHITTINGTON, Mr. William, and Miss Sally Welch, of South River, were
married Sun. morning, 19th inst., by the Rev. Mr. Wyatt.
(Aug. 23, 1804)

WHITTINGTON, William, son of John, on Thurs. night last, 7th inst.,
was knocked overboard by the main boom on his own vessel, on
his passage from Balto. to Annap., and was drowned. He leaves
a wife and two children. (June 13, 1810)

WHITTINGTON, William, of Cal. Co., died Friday morning last, in this
city. (March 24, 1825)

WIGGINGS, Daniel H., and Wilhelmina Welch, daughter of Francis Welch
of A. A. Co., were married Thurs. evening last, by Rev. Mr.
Watkins. (Jan. 26, 1826)

WIGGINS, Mrs. Jemima, consort of Mr. Daniel Wiggins, died in Annap.
on Mon. last, aged about 40 years. (Sept. 2, 1824)

WILKERSON, Mr. Young, aged 85, died at the residence of Augustine
Gambrill, on 15th inst. He was a Lieutenant in the Revolutionary Army. (Sept. 27, 1827)

WILKINS, John, of Balto., and Miss Elizabeth Dorsey, daughter of Major
Edward Dorsey, of A. A. Co., were married on Thurs., 19th inst.,
by the Rev. Mr. Roberts. (Nov. 1, 1809)

WILKINS, Miss Mary, only daughter of William Wilkins, merchant of
this city, died 10th inst., in her 16th year. (Aug. 15, 1793)

WILKINS, Mrs. Sarah, died in Balto., on Sat. morning last [April 23],
aged 72, consort of William Wilkins, Sr. (April 28, 1814)

WILKINS, Thomas, ship carpenter, of Kent Co., was accidentally drowned.
(March 1, 1753)

WILKINS, William, died here on Sat. last [Feb. 28], after a long
indisposition, aged 61 years. For a great many years he was
a Prosecutor in the Mayor's Court, and a very useful clerk
to many committees in the Lower House of Assembly. On Tues.
his remains were decently interred. (March 5, 1761) Deborah
Wilkins is executrix. (Aug. 20, 1761)

WILKINSON, Rev. Mr. Christopher, of St. Paul's Parish, Q. A. Co., died
last Friday [April 11]. (April 15, 1729)

WILLIAM, Duke of Cumberland, died October 31st past, suddenly, while
sitting in a chair. He was uncle of His present Majesty.
(Jan. 30, 1766)

WILLIAM HENRY, H. R. H., the Duke of Gloucester, died in London the
25th of August last. (Oct. 17, 1805)

WILLIAMS, ---, the only daughter of Benjamin Williams, drowned Sun.
on the South River. (July 2, 1767)

WILLIAMS, Mr. Alexander, son of Mr. Francis Williams, of Cal. Co.,
died Mon. morning, 20th inst., in his 23rd year. His remains
were interred on the evening of the same day in the burying
ground of this city, attended by the students of St. John's
College. (July 23, 1795)

WILLIAMS, Edward, died Sun. last, in his 76th year, in Annap. (May 7,
1835)

WILLIAMS, Elisha, servant to John and Hannah Sanboufe, was found
drowned yesterday. [The notice contains editorial comment
on the treatment of servants by their masters.] (Aug. 4,
1747)

WILLIAMS, Mrs. Eliza, wife of James Williams, Esq., of Annap., died
16th inst. (April 17, 1794)

WILLIAMS, Henry, of Magothy, and Miss Louisa Wheedon, of Annap.,
were married on Sun. evening last [April 30], by the Rev. Mr.
Welch. (May 4, 1820)

WILLIAMS, James, died on Sat., 18th inst., aged 77 years. (April 23,
1818)

WILLIAMS, Mr. John, on Sun. morning last [Sept. 30], was found lying
dead in the road a few miles from town. He is supposed to
have been hurt in falling from his horse. (Oct. 10, 1754)

WILLIAMS, John, and Miss Maria Selby, all of A. A. Co., were married
on Sun. evening last [Nov. 4], by the Rev. Mr. Welch. (Nov.
8, 1821)

WILLIAMS, John, died Sat. morning last, at his residence on Greenberry's Point, leaving a widow and several infant children.
(Sept. 3, 1835)

WILLIAMS, Mrs. Maria Anne, consort of the late Mr. John Williams
of Greenberry's Point, died Sun. night last, at the residence
of her sister, in Annap. (Jan. 7, 1836)

WILLIAMS, Gen. Osborn, died at his farm near this city on the 27th
inst. (Dec. 30, 1819)

WILLIAMS, Capt. Richard, died Thurs. last [March 26], after a lingering illness at his house at the Wood Yard, P. G. Co. He was
formerly a commander in the Guiney Trade. (April 2, 1752)

WILLIAMS, Theodore, and Caroline Gover were married on the evening
of Tues. last, by the Rev. Mr. Watkins, near the Head of South
River. (July 25, 1822)

WILLIAMS, Mr. Thomas, Jr., of Alexandria, and Miss Eliza Thomas, eldest
daughter of James Thomas, Esq., of Annap., were married Sun.
evening last, by the Rev. Mr. Higinbothom. (Feb. 25, 1802)

WILLIAMS, Thomas, and Mrs. Elizabeth Lowe were married on Sun. evening
[Nov. 8], by the Rev. Mr. Guest. (Nov. 19, 1818)

WILLIAMS, Mr. Thomas N., died at his seat near Berlin, Wor. Co., on
July 30th, in his 59th year; formerly a member of the Maryland
Legislature. [Long obit is given.] (Aug. 16, 1827)

WILLIAMS, Capt. William F., of Balto., and Ann Maria, second daughter
of Brice B. Brewer, of Annap., were married Mon. morning, 18th
inst., by Rev. Job Guest. (Nov. 21, 1839)

WILLIAMS, Zachariah, an old coloured man, died yesterday. (Dec. 29,
1831)

WILLIAMSON, Alexander, Esq., died in Kent Co., on the 6th inst., aged
48, one of the Representatives of that county, and once Speaker
of the Lower House of Assembly. His son Mr. Alexander Williamson, Jr., died about a week before his death, which so greatly
affected him that he died of grief. (Aug. 21, 1760)

WILLIAMSON, Capt. Charles, died in Cal. Co., on Jan. 25, in his 59th
year. (Jan. 29, 1807)

WILLIAMSON, Mr. Henry, died in this city, on Friday morning, in his
26th year. (Aug. 25, 1814)

WILLIAMSON, James, and Miss Maria Tuck, all of Annap., were married
Thurs. evening last, by the Rev. Mr. Higinbothom. (Dec. 27,
1804)

WILLIAMSON, James, and Miss Sarah Ann Mayo were married in Annap.
last evening, by the Rev. Mr. Judd. (Sept. 27, 1809)

WILLIAMSON, James, died in Annap. on Friday evening last, a delegate
elect to the Legislature of Maryland from that city. (Oct.
25, 1832)

WILLIAMSON, Mrs. Mari, died on Mon. last [Oct. 14]; a resident of
Annap. (Oct. 17, 1805)

WILLIGMAN, Charles Henry, and Miss Catherine Jackson were married
Thurs. evening last [Aug. 25], by the Rev. Mr. Wyatt. (Sept.
1, 1808)

WILLING, Charles, died last Sat. [Nov. 23], in his 45th year; Mayor
of Philadelphia; "Phila., Nov. 28." (Dec. 12, 1754)

WILLSON, Mr. Elisha, died Sun. evening, in his 34th year. He was a
native of Vermont, and formerly an officer in the South American service. (Aug. 28, 1823)

WILMER, Jonathan, died at Balto. on Tues. [Aug. 22], a native of this
State. He had returned a few weeks since from Charleston,
S. C., for his health. (Aug. 29, 1805)

WILMORE, Mr. Thomas, died in Annap. on Sun., 16th inst., in his 69th
year. (Aug. 27, 1812)

WILMOT, Mr. Henry, died suddenly, on Tues. last, in Annap. (April
16, 1829)

WILMOT, John, of Annap., died Mon. evening last [June 22], in his 54th
year. (June 25, 1807)

WILMS, Mr. H. A., of Balto., and Miss Eliza Grammer, of Annap., were
married Sun. evening last, by Rev. Mr. Higinbothom. (Nov. 4,
1802)

WILSON, ---, a carpenter, died about a month ago, when he fell off
the top of a house he was building in Annap. (Dec. 10 -
Dec. 17, 1728)

WILSON, George, died lately in Kent Co., where the people made
choice of him in many successive elections to represent them
in Assembly, he being one of the oldest members in the late
House. (Nov. 30, 1748)

WILSON, George W., editor of the Marlbro' Gazette, and Miss Mary A.
E. Lynch, all of P. G. Co., were married Tues. evening last,
near Upper Marlboro, by Rev. Coombs. (Dec. 29, 1837)

WILSON, John, of Fell's Point, Balto., died July 19th, at his brother'
in East St., Balto. (July 29, 1802)

WILSON, Capt. Josiah, late commander of the ship Planter, of Liverpool
died on Tues. last week [Dec. 9], at Mr. Hawkins', on the
Patuxent. (Dec. 18, 1760)

WILSON, Robert, a caulker, on Tues. last [Sept. 16], being somewhat
disordered in his senses, walked into the Dock and was drowned.
(Sept. 23, 1746) His widow Elizabeth advertises that she
still keeps the ferry from Broad Creek to Annapolis. (Dec.
9, 1746)

WILSON, Samuel, a young man about 17 years old, was shot and scalped about three weeks ago, near the house of George Pow, not far from Anti-Eatem. (Aug. 4, 1757)

WILSON, William, died Friday, 9th inst. (Jan. 15, 1835)

WINCHESTER, Mr. Jacob, died in Annap. on Sat. night last, in his 20th year. (Jan. 19, 1826)

WINCHESTER, Jacob, of Kent Island, and Mary, eldest daughter of Horatio Ridout of White Hall, A. A. Co., were married Thurs., 9th inst., by the Rev. Mr. Aisquith. (June 30, 1831)

WINDER, Edward S., Esq., and Elizabeth, eldest daughter of the Hon. Edward Lloyd, were married June 1, at Wye House, Tal. Co., by the Rev. Mr. Hubbard. (June 8, 1820)

WINDER, Gen. Levin, late Governor of this State, and R. W. Past Grand Master of the Grand Lodge of the State of Maryland, who died on the 1st inst., in the 63rd year of his age,....entered the armies of our countries at the early age of 18, at a period when every heart throbbed with anxiety for the fate of the Republic. (July 8, 1819)

WINDER, Gen. William, died at Balto., on Mon., May 24th, at 1:00 A. M., in his 50th year; an eminent lawyer and a distinguished citizen. (May 27, 1824)

WINDSOR, Jacob, was executed last Wed., in Q. A. Co. He had been transported from Eng. to America for 14 years, and had been four times since whipped and pilloried, once for stealing a Bible. (June 12, 1751)

WINTER, Miss Catherine, died in Annap., Thurs. night last, after a long indisposition. (Oct. 27, 1825)

WIRL, Mr. William, died yesterday afternoon; tailor, of Annap. At the time of his decease, he was a member of the Methodist Church. (Feb. 27, 1823)

WIRT, Uriah; on Tues. last week [April 13], just after sunset, he, an elderly man of 65 years of age, and his son, were travelling from Virginia to Frederick-Town, in Fred. Co., when they were attacked by a highwayman, who mortally wounded the elder Wirt with a pistol. (April 22, 1762)

WOART, Rev. J. Loring, and his wife, were lost in the sinking of the Pulaski. (July 26, 1838)

WOLFOLK, Mr. Joseph B., died at Orleans, on Jan. 16th. (Feb. 11, 1830)

WOOD, Mr. Benjamin, died last Friday [July 27], after a long and

illness at the house of Jonas Green, where he had lived upwards of 11 years. The next day he was decently interred.
A printer, aged 38, he was born at Tattershall, Eng. He had
a good education, and well understood the learned languages.
He was an ingenuous and skilled artist. (Aug. 2, 1753)

WOOD, Peter, died yesterday morning, one of the Delegates for P. G.
Co. (Dec. 8, 1803)

WOOD, Samuel, died in Friendship on Tues., 3rd inst., aged 78 years,
9 mos.; he was a member of the Methodist Church for 44 years.
(April 26, 1832)

WOODALL, Mr. Abraham, of Annap., was drowned about five or six
weeks ago, and his body was found about 10 days ago. (April
17, 1751) Catherine Woodall offers a reward to anyone who
will raise the boat. (May 22, 1751)

WOODCOCK, Mr. Henry, died Friday, 6th inst., in his 56th year, in
Annap. He was a native of England, but had resided in America
since early manhood. (Jan. 19, 1792)

WOODFIELD, Mrs. Sarah, relict of the late Thomas Woodfield, died on
Tues. morning, at her residence in A. A. Co., at an advanced
age. (April 10, 1823)

WOODFIELD, Thomas, and Miss Catherine Plain, were married on Thurs.
evening last [Nov. 4], by the Rev. Mr. Wyatt. (Nov. 11, 1813)

WOODFIELD, Thomas, died on Thurs. evening last [Nov. 12], at his seat
on the south side of South River. (Nov. 18, 1813)

WOODHOUSE, Dr. James, died at Phila., 4th inst., in his 39th year;
he was late Professor of Chemistry in the University of Pennsylvania. (June 14, 1809)

WOODWARD, Henry, of this place, and Mary Young, daughter and heiress
of the late Richard Young, and granddaughter of the late Hon.
Samuel Young, were married yesterday afternoon. (Jan. 9,
1755)

WOODWARD, Mr. Henry, died Sat. night last [Sept. 16], at his plantation near town, in the 28th year of his age, a few years
since one of the Representatives for this city. He leaves a
widow and four young children. (Sept. 24, 1761)

WOODWARD, Capt. Henry H., died 27th ult., in A. A. Co. (Nov. 7,
1822)

WOODWARD, Henry W., and Mary E., eldest daughter of Jas. Webb, Esq.,
all of A. A. Co., were married Tues., 24th inst., by the Rev.
Mr. Poisal. (March 5, 1835)

WOODWARD, Mrs. Jane, died Mon., April 21st, at the residence of her
son, near Head of Severn, in her 78th year, relict of William
Woodward. (May 8, 1817)

WOODWARD, William, aged about 15, son of Francis Woodward, of Rock
Creek, in Fred. Co., died Sun., 14th inst., when he slipped
and fell and was crushed by a log he was carrying to the
house for firewood. (Jan. 22, 1767)

WOODWARD, William, Sr., died on Feb. 5th, at his farm in A. A. Co.,
in his 68th year. (Feb. 12, 1807)

WOOLFORD, Dr. Thomas, and Miss Margaret Lecompte, all of Cambridge,
Dor. Co., were married on Tues. evening, 6th inst., by the
Rev. Mr. Weller. (Jan. 15, 1818)

WOOTTON, Mrs. Anne, died Sat., 18th inst., in her 25th year; wife of
Mr. William T. Wootton, of P. G. Co. She is survived by her
husband and two children. (Nov. 24, 1774)

WOOTON, John; by a letter from Providence comes an account of his
death; he was a native of this province. He left here very
young. (Oct. 6, 1774)

WOOTTON, Singleton, died 1st inst., merchant, of Queen Anne, Patuxent
River. (Nov. 6, 1788)

WOOTTON, Turner, Esq., died 12th inst., in his 27th year, at his seat
near Queen Anne, P. G. Co. His remains were respectfully
deposited in the family burying ground when a suitable and
pathetic sermon was elegantly delivered by the Rev. Mr. Ralph.
(Jan. 19, 1797)

WORRELL, Robert, of Annap., sailed in the sloop Betsy, which was
found wrecked on March 4. His body was not found and he is
supposed to have been lost. (March 5, 1812)

WORRELL, Thomas, died in Chestertown, Kent Co., on the 1st inst.,
after a short illness. He was Clerk of the County Court of
that county. (Oct. 13, 1825)

WORT, ---, the little Pedler, well known by the name of Capt. Wort,
who kept a store at Fort Frederick, and three of his Associates,
were lately all killed by the enemy near Loyalhannon. (May
24, 1759)

WORTHINGTON, Mrs. Anne Lee, consort of Mr. Brice J. Worthington, died
Mon., 28th inst., at Summer-Hill. (Sept. 30, 1824)

WORTHINGTON, Beale M., and Miss Elizabeth R. Rocketts, were married
on Thurs. evening last [March 7], at the seat of Mr. John
Worthington, near Annap., by the Rev. Mr. Judd. (March 13, 1811)

WORTHINGTON, Dr. Beale M., died at his residence in A. A. Co., on
Thurs. last. He leaves a widow and several children. (April
15, 1824)

WORTHINGTON, Brice J., Esq., died Tues. evening, at his residence,
Summer Hill, near Annap. (Nov. 16, 1837)

WORTHINGTON, Mr. Brice J. B., died on the evening of 16th inst., at
his residence on Elk Ridge, in his 37th year. (Nov. 23, 1826)

WORTHINGTON, Hon. Brice T. B., died Thurs., 17th ult., at his seat
near the city of Annap., a member of the Senate of this state,
aged 67 years. (Aug. 7, 1794)

WORTHINGTON, Mrs. Catherine, relict of Col. Nicholas Worthington,
died Wed., 18th ult. [Dec., 1793], in his 62nd year. (Jan.
16, 1794)

WORTHINGTON, Miss Elizabeth, daughter of Col. Nicholas and Catherine
Worthington, died in Annap., on Sat., 29th of April last.
(May 4, 1820)

WORTHINGTON, George Fitzhugh, of A. A. Co., and Elizabeth, third
daughter of the late Gen. R. Harwood, of Thomas, of Annap.,
were married Thurs. last, by Rev. Mr. McElhiney. (Oct. 1,
1835)

WORTHINGTON, John, died at his farm near Annap., on Friday morning
last [June 4], in his 65th year. (June 5, 1817)

WORTHINGTON, John G., died 14th inst., aged 33, at Summer Hill, the
seat of Mr. Brice J. Worthington. His remains were deposited
in the family burying ground on the following day. (Feb.
23, 1797)

WORTHINGTON, Mary Dulaney, daughter of Brice J. Worthington, Esq.,
died Sat., 2nd inst., aged 19 years. (May 7, 1835)

WORTHINGTON, N. B., Esq., of A. A. Co., and Sophia Kerr, only daughter of Dr. Joseph E. Muse, of Cambridge, were married on Wed.
morning, May 1st, in the latter place, by Rev. James McKenney.
(May 9, 1839)

WORTHINGTON, Col. Nicholas, died Friday, 1st ult., at his seat near
Annap., in his 60th year. (Dec. 5, 1793)

WORTHINGTON, Nicholas, son of Thomas, died at his residence on Elk
Ridge, on Thurs., 26th inst., in his 54th year, leaving a
wife and an only daughter. [Long obit is given.] (April
9, 1829)

WORTHINGTON, Mr. Thomas, died last Mon. morning [March 12], at his

plantation about five miles from town, in the 63rd, or grand
climacterical year of his age. For many years past, and at
the time of his death, he was one of the Representatives for
A. A. Co., in the Lower House of Assembly. (March 15, 1753)
Brice T. B. Worthington, exec. (April 12, 1753)

WORTHINGTON, Thomas, and Miss Eliza Baldwin were married on Tues.,
    6th inst., by the Rev. Mr. Wyatt. (Dec. 15, 1808)

WORTHINGTON, Thomas, of Nicholas, died 18th inst., at his seat on
    Elk Ridge, A. A. Co., after a long and severe illness, in his
    69th year. (March 27, 1823)

WRIGHT, Capt. James, of Balto., and Miss Anne F. Wier, of Balto.,
    were married on Tues. evening last [June 9], by the Rev. Mr.
    Wyatt. (June 11, 1807)

WRIGHT, Judgematical, of Westmoreland Co., Va., aged 73, and Miss
    Lucy Pursle, of Richmond Co., aged 53, were married on Tues.,
    Nov. 18th, near Middletown Cross Roads, two hours before day-
    break, by Rev. Thomas C. Braxton. (Dec. 25, 1834)

WRIGHT, Lucien B., Rector of All Hallows Par., A. A. Co., and Jane
    Alexander, of Annap., were married Thurs., 25th inst., by
    the Rev. Dr. Humphreys. (Oct. 2, 1834)

WRIGHT, Mr. Robert, died in Annap., on the 15th inst., in his 18th
    year. (March 23, 1826)

WRIGHT, the Hon. Robert, Associate Judge of the Second Judicial
    District of Md., died at his residence in Q. A. Co., on Thurs.
    last. (Sept. 14, 1826)

WRIGHT, Samuel T., Esq., [Called Samuel T. Weedon in Martin's
    abstracts], died Sat., June 30th, after a long illness, Clerk
    of Q. A. Co., and Adjutant-General of this state. (July 11,
    1810)

WRIGHT, William, a sea-faring man, fell overboard from a sloop's
    bowsprit, near our dock, and was drowned last Thurs. [July
    19]. (July 24, 1751)

WRIGHT, William, was drowned on Tues. last week [June 1], attempting
    to swim across Magothy River after a canoe; he was aged 75.
    (June 10, 1762)

WYATT, Mrs. Margaret, died Tues. morning last [Oct. 17], consort of
    the Rev. Joseph Wyatt of Annap. (Oct. 19, 1815)

WYTHE, George, Esq., Judge of the High Court of Chancery for the
    Richmond District, died Sun. last; "Richmond, June 10."
    (June 19, 1806)

WYVIL, Edward, of Cal. Co., and Mary P. Davis, of Nottingham, P. G. Co., were married Nov. 29th last, by the Rev. Mr. Edmondson. (March 14, 1833)

WYVILL, Miss Susan, died in Annap., to which she had removed from her residence near Herring Bay, for her health on Thurs. last [Oct. 25], in the 28th year of her age. (Oct. 31, 1810)

WYVILL, Dr. Walter W., of A. A. Co., and Miss Margaret Murdoch, of Annap., were married on Tues. evening last [Feb. 28], by the Rev. Mr. Guest. (March 2, 1820)

YATES, Mrs. Frances, died Tues. [June 20], of the prevailing epidemic. (June 22, 1815)

YIELDALL, Robert, a prisoner in A. A. Co. gaol, was killed in a fight with another prisoner over their dinner. He leaves a widow and eight children. (Aug. 23, 1764)

YEWELL, Mr. Basil, and Miss Eliza Hall, were married in this county on the evening of the 8th inst., by the Rev. Mr. Hammond. (Dec. 15, 1825)

YEWELL, Mr. Basil, died Mon. last, on the North side of Severn. (Aug. 27, 1829)

YOUNG, Hon. Benjamin, Esq., died of the gout on Friday last [Feb. 8], at his seat on Potowmack, one of His Lordship's Council of State, Judge of the Admiralty Court, Chief Justice of the Provincial Court. and one of the Judges of the Land Office, and formerly one of the Commissioners of the Paper Currency Office. (Feb. 14, 1754)

YOUNG, Col. Benjamin, son of the late Hon. Benjamin Young, and Mary, youngest daughter of the late Hon. Daniel Dulany of Annap., were married Wed. last week [Aug. 10]. (Aug. 18, 1757)

YOUNG, John, Esq., of Caroline Co., and Mary Turnbull, of Annap., were married Tues. last [Feb. 13], by the Rev. Mr. Higginbotham. (Feb. 15, 1798)

YOUNG, Peter, died Friday, Dec. 15, 1775, at his seat near Upper Marlborough, P. G. Co. (Jan. 11, 1776)

YOUNG, Richard, died Mon., at his plantation near Annap.; formerly Clerk of Cal. Co. (Nov. 9, 1748)

ADDENDA

ALLEN, Rev. Thomas D., of the Methodist Episcopal Church, died in
Annap., on 25th inst., having labored in the Ohio and Baltimore Annual Conferences, more than six years. (July 2, 1835)

AGUISTUS, John, died in Annap., a native of Portland, Mass. (Feb.
28, 1810)

BOONE, Mrs. Anne, relict of the late James Boone, of Severn, died
16th inst. (Feb. 24, 1831)

BOYD, Mrs. Mary, wife of Dennis Boyd, died in A. A. Co., on Mon.,
30th ult., in her 63rd year. (Dec. 16, 1830)

BROWN, Rezin, and Miss Priscilla Jenkins, were married by Rev. C.
Davis, on Thurs., 24th ult. (Feb. 7, 1828)

MITCHELL, Col. George E., died in Washington City on June 28th,
late of the U. S. Army, and a member of the House of Representatives from Md. Born in Cecil Co., he was educated to
the profession of medicine; at the outbreak of the late war
with Great Britain he entered the army. [Long obit is given.]
(From the Daily Chronicle) (July 19, 1832)

NOTES ON MARYLAND CLERGY

The following list of clergymen contains the names of those ministers mentioned in the text as having performed marriages. Wherever possible, the denomination and churches served by a particular clergyman are given, to enable the genealogist to locate the church where the marriage was performed. Unfortunately not every clergyman could be identified. A list of the sources consulted is given following the notes on the clergy.

ADDISON, Rev. Walter Dulany; Protestant Episcopal; 1805, St. John's Par., P. G. Co.; 1809, George-Town Par., Wash., D. C.; 1821, Addison Chapel Par., P. G. Co., and Rock Creek Church, Wash., D. C.; 1823, George-Town Par.; went blind in 1827, and resigned his parish; died 1848, aged 79.

AISQUITH, Rev. Henry; Prot. Ep.; 1826, Westminster Par., A. A. Co.; 1838, Severn Par., A. A. Co.; 1851, King and Queen Par., St. M. Co.; d. 1855.

BACON, Rev. Thomas; Prot. Ep.; 1745, came to Tal. Co.; 1747, St. Peter's, Oxford, Tal Co.; 1759, reader, All Saints', Fred. Co.; 1762, rector of All Saints'; d. 1768. age 68.

BAIN, Rev. [John], fl.1814, Dor. Co.; m. Mary, daughter of James Fookes and Nancy (Pattison) Skinner; not further identified.

BARCLAY, Rev. Francis; Prot. Ep.; 1801, came from Eng.; 1804, Old Wye Par., Tal. Co.; 1805, St. Paul's Par., Q. A. Co.; 1806, All Hallows Par., A. A. Co.; 1808, William and Mary Par., St. M. Co.; 1810, went to Va.

BARTOW, Rev. John V.; Prot. Ep.; native of New York; 1815, Trinity Ch., Balto.; d. 1836.

BATTEE, Rev. Dennis, Methodist Episcopal; Agent of Balto. Bible Society; d. March 8, 1865, at Oakland, Balto. Co., in his 81st year.

BELL, Rev. ---, fl.1810; prob. Thomas Bell; Meth. Ep.; minister in 1795; 1797, prob. in Caroline Co.; d. Feb. 26, 1810.

BEND, Rev. Joseph Grove John; Prot. Ep.; native of New York; 1791, St. Paul's, Balto.; d. 1812, age 50.

BITOUZEY, Rev., fl.1811; prob. Germain Bitouzey, Roman Catholic;
    1823, at White Marsh Plantation, formerly Jesuit property,
    in Balto. Co.

BLANCHARD, Rev. John; Prot. Ep.; native of Mass.; 1825, St. Anne's
    Par., Annap.; d. 1834, in Balto., age 35.

BOND, Rev. Dr., fl.1811, in Balto.; not further identified.

BORDLEY, Rev. W. H., fl.1834; prob. William H. Bordley; Methodist
    Protestant; 1843, assistant in Queen Anne Charge; 1844, Kent;
    1845, East Balto.; d. Oct. 9, 1846.

BOWEN, Rev. John; Meth. Ep.; d. Nov. 18, 1864, age 72, at "Greenwood,"
    Balto. Co., having entered the ministry in 1823.

BOWER, Rev. George C.; Prot. Ep.; 1786, All Saints' Par., Fred. Co.;
    1788, Queen Caroline Par., A. A. Co.; 1789, Frederick Par.,
    Wash. Co., and All Saints', Fred. Co., d. 1814.

BROOKES, Rev.; fl.1835; not further identified.

BROWN, Rev. O. B., fl.1834; prob. Rev. Obediah Brown; Baptist;
    1821, Pastor of First Bapt. Ch., Wash., D. C.

BROWN, Rev. Richard; Meth. Ep.; 1822, entered the ministry; 1835,
    in the Balto. Conference; d. Aug. 5, 1859, age 61, in Howard
    Co., Md.

BURCH, Rev., fl.1815, Balto.; prob. Rev. Thomas Burch; Meth. Ep.,
    in records of First Methodist Episcopal Church, Balto.

CAREY, Rev., fl.1838; possibly Rev. John Baptiste Car(e)y, S. J.;
    Roman Catholic; 1831 to 1840, at St. Joseph's Mission, Tal.
    Co.

CHAMBERS, Rev. Mr. Nicholas; fl.1808; not further identified.

CHESLEY, Rev. William F.; Prot. Ep.; 1827, All Saints' Par., Cal.
    Co.; 1830, St. James Par., A. A. Co.; native of Cal. Co., he
    d. 1843.

CLARK, Rev. William, fl.1813, Tal. Co.; not further identified.

CLAXTON, Rev.; fl.1828, Tal. Co.; not further identified.

CLAY, Rev. [Jehu] Curtis; Prot. Ep.; native of Penna.; 1817, St.
    John's Par., Hagerstown; 1822, went back to Penna.

COFFIN, Rev.; fl.1838, Cal. Co.; not further identified.

COLEMAN, Rev. Bishop, fl.1819; not further identified.

COLLIER, Rev. William; Meth. Prot.; 1832, assistant at Anne Arundel
    Charge; 1833, Queen Anne; 1834, East Balto.; 1836, Alexandria;
    1837 to 1838, at Deer Creek.

COMFORT, Rev.; fl.1808; not further identified.

COMPTON, Rev.; fl.1805; possibly John Wilson Compton; Prot. Ep.;
    native of Chas. Co.; 1787, ordained by Bishop White, and
    rector of William and Mary Par., Chas. Co.; 1797, St. James',
    A. A. Co.; 1806, All Saints', Cal. Co.; d. 1813, age 53.

COOKMAN, Rev. George G.; Meth. Ep.; native of Eng.; 1829 to 1831,
    Ebenezer Ch., Easton, Tal. Co.; he was lost in the sinking
    of the President, while on a visit to Eng. He had a son
    Alfred who was also a Meth. minister.

COOMBS, Rev. Mr.; fl.1837, P. G. Co.; not further identified.

CROSBY, Rev.; fl.1839; not further identified.

DASHIELL, Rev. George; Prot. Ep.; native of Som. Co.; 1791, ordained
    by Bishop White and rector of Somerset Par., Som. Co.; 1793
    to 1797, in Del.; 1797, South Sassafras Par., Kent Co.; 1800,
    Chester Par., Kent Co.; 1804, St. Peter's Par., Balto. City;
    1816, left the Prot. Ep. Ch. and organized the Evangelical
    Episcopal Ch.; d. 1852, age 72.

DAVIS, Rev. Benjamin; fl.1835; prob. Meth., as he is described as
    a member of the Balto. Conference.

DAVIS, Rev. Charles A.; fl.1828; Meth. Ep.; found in records of
    First Methodist Episcopal Church, Balto.

DAVIS, Rev. Henry L.; Prot. Ep.; native of Chas. Co.; 1796, ordained
    by Bishop Clagett, minister of All Faith's Par., St. M. Co.;
    1801, King and Queen Par., St. M. Co.; 1802, Trinity Par.,
    Chas. Co.; 1804, North Sassafras Par., Cecil Co.; 1816, St.
    Anne's, Annap.; 1826, moved to Del.; d. 1836.

DEANE, Rev. H. L.; fl.1819; not further identified.

DEANS, Rev.; fl.1759; possibly Rev. Hugh Deane, Prot. Ep.; 1739,
    St. John's Par., Balto. Co., until 1776.

DECKER, Rev.; fl.1838; possibly Rev. John Decker, formerly of Orange
    Co., N. Y., who d. Feb. 9, 1857, at Annapolis.

DORSEY, Rev.; fl.1831; possibly Rev. Thomas J. Dorsey; Meth. Ep.;
    entered the ministry in 1819; d. June 3, 1838, in Balto. Co.,
    age unknown.

DORSEY, Rev. T. B.; fl.1830; not further identified.

DOUGHERTY, Rev.; fl.1825; not further identified.

DUKE, Rev. William; Prot. Ep.; native of Balto. Co.; 1785, ordained
by Bishop Seabury; rector, Queen Caroline Par., A. A. Co.;
1787, St. Paul's Par., P. G. Co.; 1791, St. Paul's Chapel,
Balto. Co.; 1792, North Elk Par., Cecil Co.; 1796, Westminster Par., A. A. Co.; 1804, St. Ann's Par., A. A. Co.; d.
1840, age 83.

DUNCAN, Rev.; fl.1822, in Balto.; prob. Rev. John Mason Duncan;
Presbyterian; Pastor of Associate Reformed Presbyterian
church after March, 1812. He d. April 30, 1851.

DUNCAN, Rev. William; Meth., later Prot. Ep.; native of Kent Co.;
1808, ordained by Bishop Clagett; rector of Durham Par.,
Chas. Co.; 1813, All Hallows Par., A. A. Co.; b. c.1764;
d. 1819.

EDMONDSON, Rev.; fl.1833; not further identified.

EMORY, John; Methodist; entered the ministry in 1810; was in Tal!
Co., by 1812; died Dec. 16, 1835, in Balto. Co.; Bishop
of the Meth. Ch.

FECHTIG, Rev. Louis R.; Meth. Ep.; entered the ministry in 1812;
Presiding Elder of the Meth. Ep. Ch., Balto. Conference, at
the time of his death, died in Wash., D. C., on Sept. 25,
1823.

FINLEY, Rev. John; fl.1826; Baptist; from Albany, N. Y.; elected
Pastor of the First Baptist Church in 1821; 1834, resigned.

FLEMING, Rev., fl.1806; not further identified.

FOREMAN, Rev. Thomas; fl.1830; not further identified.

FRENCH, Rev.; fl.1828; prob. Rev. John C. French; Meth. Prot.;
married Mary Paul on Nov. 19, 1816, by Rev. Hemphill.

GERE, Rev. J. A.; fl.1834; Meth. Ep.; name is found in the records
of the First Meth. Ep. Ch., Balto.

GIBBONS, Rev. John L.; fl.1827; Meth. Ep.; found in records of the
First Meth. Ep. Ch., Balto.; d. June 23, 1871, age 70.

GIBSON, Rev.; fl.1819; prob. Rev. William Lewis Gibson; Prot. Ep.,
later Meth.; native of Kent Co.; 1804, ordained by Bishop
White; 1806, St. Ann's, A. A. Co.; 1807 to 1811, in Va.;
1811, St. John's Par., P. G. Co.; 1812, Havre de Grace Par.,
Harf. Co.; 1813, St. Peter's Par., Mont. Co.; 1814, Queen
Anne's Par., P. G. Co.; 1819, All Hallows Par., A. A. Co.;
1820, resigned his ministry and joined the Meth. Ch.; d. 1848.

GILLIS, Rev.; fl.1832; prob. Rev. Levin I. Gillis, Prot. Ep.; native
of Som. Co., ordained by Bishop Kemp in 1818; 1818, Queen
Anne's Par., P. G. Co.; 1822, St. Paul's Par., P. G. Co.;
1830, Prince George's and St. Bartholomew's Par., Mont. Co.;
1844, Ascencion Par., Wash., D. C.

GLENDY, Rev., John, aged 77, formerly pastor of the Second Presbyterian Church in Balto., died on October 4, 1832, in Philadelphia.

GOLDSBOROUGH, Rev.; fl.1838; possibly one of two Prot. Ep. clergy-
men of this family: Robert William Goldsborough, Prot. Ep.;
native of St. Michael's, Tal. Co.; 1829, St. Paul's Par.,
Q. A. Co.; 1836, All Hallows Par., A. A. Co.; 1844, St.
John's Par., Caroline and Q. A. Co.; also Robert Lloyd Golds-
borough, Prot. Ep.; native of Tal. Co., 1834, St. Paul's Par.,
Balto.; 1834, St. George's and Havre de Grace Par., Harf.
Co.; 1842, Trinity Par., Elkton, and North Elk Par., Cecil Co.

GOSNELL, Rev.; fl.1824; not further identified.

GRIFFITH, Rev.; fl.1824; prob. Rev. Alfred Griffith, Meth. Ep.;
entered the ministry in 1806, died April 15, 1871, age 88,
at Alexandria, Va.

GRIGG, Rev. John; Prot. Ep.; native of New York, ordained prior to
1820 by Bishop Hobart; 1830, St. Paul's Par., P. G. Co.;
1836, returned to N. Y.

GUEST, Rev. Job; Meth. Ep.; entered the ministry in 1806, died on
Dec. 15, 1857, age 72 years.

HAMILTON, Rev.; fl.1838; possibly Rev. G. D. Hamilton; Meth.; in
Queen Anne's Circuit, Q. A. Co., 1837 to 1838.

HAMMOND, Rev.; fl.1826; possibly Rev. W. S. Hammond; Meth.; assistant
minister in Queen Anne's Circuit, Q. A. Co., 1851.

HANK, Rev.; fl.1838; possibly Rev. William Hank; Meth. Ep.; entered
the ministry in 1820, died March 31, 1869, at Middleway,
W. Va., age 73.

HARRIS, Rev. Matthias; Meth., later Prot. Ep.; native of Q. A. Co.,
raised Meth.; ordained in Prot. Ep. Church by Bishop Kemp
in 1826; 1826, missionary in Q. A. and Caroline Counties;
1830, Christ Church, P. G. and Chas. Cos.; 1833, Christ
Church Par., Cal. Co.; 1837, Emmanuel Par., All. Co.; 1842,
Dorchester Par., Dor. Co.; 1844, Chaplain in U. S. Army.

HATCH, Rev. Frederick W.; Prot. Ep.; ordained by Bishop Claggett
in 1811; 1816, All Saint's Par., Fred. Co.; 1820, went to

Va.; 1830, Washington Par., Wash. D. C.; 1836, went to New
York; died in California in 1860, age over 70.

HAWLEY, Rev. William; Prot. Ep.; native of Vermont, ordained in
1814 by Bishop Hobart; 1817, St. John's Par., Wash., D.C.;
died January 23, 1845.

HEINER, Rev. Elias; German Reformed; Pastor of Germ. Ref. Church in
Balto. from November, 1835, until his death on October 20,
1863.

HENSHAW, Rev. John Prentice Kewley; Prot. Ep.; native of Conn.; ordained by Bishop Griswold in 1813; 1817, St. Peter's Par.,
Balto.; 1843, became Bishop of Rhode Island and moved there;
died in 1852 age 60.

HIGINBOTHOM, Rev. Ralph; Prot. Ep.; native of Ireland where he was
ordained in 1774; 1784, St. Anne's Par., Annap.; died 1813.

HODGKISS, Rev. Henry N.; Prot. Ep.; native of New York; 1824, St.
Michael's Par., Tal. Co.; 1827, North Sassafras Par.; 1829,
William and Mary Par., St. M. Co.; died 1829, age 29.

HOSKINS, Rev.; fl.1827, in Balto.; not further identified.

HUBBARD, Rev. Reuben; Prot. Ep.; native of Conn.; orig. Meth.; ordained by Bishop Jarvis in 1812; 1819, St. Michael's Par.,
Tal. Co.; 1823, went to New York, where he died, 1859.

HUMPHREYS, Rev. Dr. Hector; Congregationalist; Prot. Ep.; native
of Conn.; ordained in 1824; 1831, President of St. John's
Coll., Annap.; died 1857, age 60.

HUTTON, Rev. Orlando; Prot. Ep.; native of Annap., ordained in 1837;
1837, Assistant at St. Paul's, Balto.; 1839, Rector of Westminster Par., A. A. Co.; 1844, St. Bartholomew, St. John's
Par., Mont. Co.

INGLIS, Rev. Dr. James, Pastor of the Presbyterian Church in Balto.
since 1802 died Aug. 15, 1819.

JAMES, Rev.; fl.1834; not further identified.

JENNINGS, Rev. Dr.; fl.1824; possibly Rev. S. K. Jennings, M. D.,
former professor of Washington College, who died October 9,
1854, age 81.

JOHNS, Rev. Henry; fl. 1828 in A. A. Co.; probably Rev. Henry Van
Dyke Johns; Prot. Ep.; native of Delaware, ordained in 1826;
1827, Trinity Par., Wash., D. C.; at the time of his death
on April 22, 1859, in his 56th year, he was rector of Emmanuel
Ch., Balto.

JUDD, Rev. Bethel; Prot. Ep.; native of Conn., ordained in 1798;
1807, St. Ann's Par., Annap.; 1811, returned to Conn.; died
1858, age 82.

KALBFUS, Rev. Charles; fl. 1833, in Balto.; not further identified.

KELSEY, Rev.; fl.1825; prob. Rev. William Kesley, Meth. Prot.

KEMP, Right Rev. James; Prot. Ep.; native of Scotland; ordained by
Bishop White in 1798; 1805, Great Choptank Par., Dor. Co.;
1808, Dorchester Par., Dor..Co.; 1812, St. Paul's Par., Balto.;
1814, Suffragan Bishop; 1816, Bishop of Diocese of Maryland.

LANE, Rev. Nicholas; Prot. Ep.; native of A. A. Co., ordained in
1794; 1794, St. Peter's Par., Mont. Co.; 1798, All Saint's
Par., Cal. Co.; 1800, All Hallow's Par., A. A. Co.; 1806,
Christ Church Par., Cal. Co.; d. c.1813.

LARKINS, Rev.; fl.1832; possibly Rev. Jacob Larkin; Meth. Prot.;
entered the ministry in 1819 and died March 29, 1858, age
66, in Balto.; also: Rev. Edward Larkins; Meth.; in Queen
Anne's (later Centreville) Circuit, Q. A. Co., in 1807.

LINTHICUM, Rev. S.; fl.1828; not further identified.

LIPSCOMB, Rev.; fl.1832; there were three ministers of this name
in the Meth. church: Rev. William Corrie Lipscomb, born
Sept. 13, 1792, died Dec. 2, 1879, elected to honorary mem-
bership in the Balto. Conference of the Meth. Prot. Church;
also Rev. Philip D. Lipscomb; Meth. Ep.; entered the ministry in 1822, died in January, 1870, in Balto. Co., age 72;
also Rev. Robert M. Lipscomb; Meth. Ep.; entered the minustry
in 1832; died Feb. 5, 1890, in Balto., age 83.

McCORMICK, Rev. Thomas; Prot. Ep.; native of Ireland, ordained in
1794; 1794, Assistant in Queen Anne Par., P. G. Co.; 1798,
Washington Par., Wash., D. C.; died 1840, age 70.

McELHINEY, Rev. George; Prot. Ep.; native of Ireland, ordained in
1820; 1821, St. James' Par., Balto. and Harf. Cos.; 1826,
Trinity Par., Chas. Co.; 1827, returned to St. James' Par.;
1828, Somerset Par., Som. Co.; 1834, St. Ann's Par., Annap.;
died 1841, age 42.

McKENNEY, Rev. James Asbury; Prot. Ep.; native of Kent Co., ordained
by Bishop Hobart in 1829; transferred from New York to Md. in
1831, and had parishes in Cecil, St. M., and Chas. Co. In
1839 he was at Great Choptank Par., Dor. Co. He later had
parishes in Balto. City, P. G. Co., and Howard Co., Md.

McMULLIN, Rev. S.; fl.1837; possibly Rev. Solomon McMullen; Meth.
Ep.; entered the ministry in 1832; died Nov. 20, 1863, age
55, at Shepherdstown, W. Va.

McPHERSON, Rev. Walter; fl.1791, in Chas. Co.; not further identified.

MACKENHEIMER, Rev. George Lindenberger; Prot. Ep.; native of Balto.,
    ordained in 1827; 1827, Christ Church, St. John's Par., P. G.
    Co.; 1831, Queen Anne Par., P. G. Co.; 1853, St. Thomas' Par.,
    Hancock, Wash. Co.; 1857, Christ Church, Cal. Co.; 1859,
    moved to Va.

MAGRUDER, Rev.; fl.1825; not further identified.

MALCOLM, Rev. Alexander; Prot. Ep.; settled at Annap. from 1749 to
    1754; St. Paul's Par., Q. A. Co., from 1754 to 1763; Chap-
    lain, Md. Assembly; d. 1763.

MANN, Rev. Charles; Prot. Ep.; native of Annap., ordained in 1817;
    1817, William and Mary Par., Chas. Co.; 1831, removed to
    Virginia.

MARR, Rev.; fl.1828, Chas. Co.; not further identified.

MARSHALL, Rev. William; fl.1829, P. G. Co.; may have been the Rev.
    William Marshall who was Prot. Ep. Rector of St. James' Par.,
    A. A. Co., in 1827.

MASON, Rev. Dr. Henry M.; Prot. Ep.; native of Barbadoes, W. I.,
    ordained by Bishop White in Phila., 1823; came to Tal Co.,
    from N.J., in 1837; 1837, Rector of St. Peter's Par., Tal.
    Co.; author of a history of the church; d. 1862.

MAUD, Rev.; fl.1833; not further identified.

MERRIKEN, Rev. Richard H.; fl.1835 in Balto.; not further identified.

MUNROE, Rev. Jonathan; Meth. Ep.; entered the ministry in 1825;
    d. Dec. 4, 1869, age 68, at Westminster.

MURPHY, Rev. Mr.; fl.1823; not further identified.

NEVINS, Rev. William; Presb.; came from Norwich, Conn.; Pastor of
    1st Presb. Church in Balto. from Oct., 1820, until his death
    in Sept., 1835.

NIND, Rev. William; Prot. Ep.; native of N. Y.; ordained in 1808
    by Bishop Claggett; 1808, Westminster Par., A. A. Co.; 1812,
    St. Ann's, Annap.; 1818, North Sassafras Par., Cecil Co.;
    d. 1822, age 45.

PINCKNEY, Rev. William; Prot. Ep.; native of Annap., ordained in
    1835; 1835, Somerset Par., Som. Co.; 1836, Addison Chapel
    and Zion Par., P. G. Co.; 1857, Ascension Par., Wash., D. C.

PITTS, Rev.; fl.1810; prob. Rev. John Pitts; Meth. Ep.; born c.1770,

died in Fred. Co., Md., age 51; entered the Methodist ministry
in 1795; d. Feb., 1821.

POISAL, Rev. John; Meth. Ep.; publisher of the Baltimore Episcopal
Methodist; b. 1807; d. 1882.

RAFFERTY, Rev. Dr. William; Prot. Ep.; native of Ireland, raised
Presb.; ordained Prot. Ep., 1820; 1820, All Hallows Par.,
A. A. Co., also Vice-Principal and then Principal of St.
John's Coll., Annap.; 1829, resigned his parish.

RALPH, Rev. George; Prot. Ep.; native of Eng., ordained in 1791;
1791, in Balto.; 1793, North Sassafras Par., Cecil Co., and
South Sassafras Par., Kent Co.; 1795, Washington Par., Wash.,
D. C.; 1797, Queen Anne Par., P. G. Co.; 1800, Trinity Par.,
Chas. Co.; 1801, All Faith's Par., St. M. Co., 1810 to 1812,
Trinity Ch., Balto.

READ, Rev.; fl.1811; also REID, Rev.; fl.1815; not definitely identified, unless one or both are Rev. Nelson REED, who died Oct.
20, 1840, in his 89th year. He was the oldest member in
connection with the Methodist Episcopal Church, and was to
be buried in the Whatcoat Burial Ground.

REIS, Rev. Edmund J.; Bapt.; 1815, came to First Baptist Church,
Balto., from St. John's, New Brunswick; later formed the
Ebenezer Baptist Church, Balto.

RICHARDS, Rev. Lewis; Baptist; native of Wales, came to Balto. in
1784; elected Pastor of First Baptist Church, and served for
30 years, until 1818.

RIDGELY, Rev.; fl.1805; not further identified.

RILEY, Rev. T.; fl.1829; possibly Rev. Tobias Reiley, Meth. Ep.;
entered the ministry in 1810; d. April 19, 1843, in Cumberland, age 55.

ROBERTS, Rev. Dr.; fl.1827; possibly Rev. R. R. Roberts, or George
Roberts, both Meth. Ep.; both found in records of First
Methodist Episcopal Church, Balto., prior to 1810; Rev. Dr.
George Roberts, President of the Free Schools, died Dec.
2, 1827, in his 63rd year; also Rev. Dr. George Roberts,
L. L. D., of Meth. Ep. Church, who died June 15, 1870,
in his 64th year.

RYLAND, Rev.; fl.1811; possibly William Ryland, Meth. Ep.; b. c.1770,
d. Jan. 19, 1846; entered the ministry in 1802.

SCAHEFFER, Rev. George B.; Prot. Ep.; native of Penna., ordained in
1819; 1819, Grace Church, Balto.; 1823, St. Margaret's Westminster Par., A. A. Co.; d. 1825.

SCOTT, Rev.; fl.1809; not further identified.

SENTHEN, Rev.; fl.1825, in Frederick-Town; probably Rev. Nicholas
   Snethen [sic]; Meth. Prot.; b. 1769; d. May 30, 1848.

SEWELL, Rev. James; fl.1830, A. A. Co.; prob. James Sewell, Meth.
   Ep.; entered the ministry in 1814, d. Nov. 27, 1866, in Balto.,
   age 75.

SHAEFFER, Rev.; fl.1815, Frederick-Town; not further identified.

SHANE, Rev. Joseph; Meth. Ep. minister after 1806.

SLICER, Rev. Henry; Meth. Ep.; entered the ministry in 1822, d.
   April 23, 1874, age 73, in Balto.

SMITH, Rev.; fl.1825; possibly Rev. James Smith; Meth.; d. in Balto.
   in 1826.

SMITH, Rev.; fl.1827; possibly James Smith; Meth.; 1812 to 1814,
   Elder of Queen Anne's, later Centreville, Circuit, Q. A.
   Co.; 1820 to 1821 in Tal. Co.

SMITH, Rev. Purnell Fletcher; Prot. Ep.; native of Wor. Co., ordained
   in 1813; 1813, St. James' Par., A. A. Co.; 1817, All Saint's,
   Cal. Co.; 1818, All Hallow's and Worcester Par., Wor. Co.;
   1821, South Sassafras Par., Kent Co.; 1826, resigned; d.
   1843, age 59.

STEELE, Rev. David; Meth. Ep.; entered the ministry in 1820; d. May
   4, 1852, in Wash., D. C., age 60.

STONE, Rev.; fl.1816; possibly Joseph Stone; Meth. Ep.; entered the
   ministry in 1796; d. Oct. 7, 1819, at Fauquier Co., Va.,
   age 76.

STORKS, Rev. Levi; fl.1833; Meth.; in a Tal. Co. Circuit from 1832
   to 1833, and again from 1844 to 1845.

SWAN, Rev. John; Prot. Ep.; native of Scotland, ordained in 1829;
   1831, Trinity Par., Upper Marlboro; 1837, went to Ohio.

THORNTON, Rev.; fl.1836, in Balto.; possibly Thomas C. Thornton;
   Meth.; Secretary of the Baltimore Conference in 1820.

TIPPETT, Rev.; fl.1838, in Balto.; possibly Charles Tippett, Meth.
   Ep.; entered the ministry in 1820, died Feb. 25, 1867, in
   Arlington, Va., age 66.

TYDINGS, Rev.; fl.1820; probably Richard Tydings; Meth. Ep.; name
   found as minister in Records of the First Methodist Episcopal Church in Balto.

TYNG, Rev. Stephen Higginson; Prot. Ep.; native of Mass., ordained in 1821; 1821, George-Town Par., George-Town, D. C.; 1823, Queen Anne Par., P. G. Co.; 1828, moved to Phila.

UHLHORN, Rev. Mr. Jonathan, Lutheran; 1823, engaged as a second pastor at Zion Lutheran Church; d. 1834, age about 38 years.

VALIANT, Rev. John; fl.1825, Balto.; Meth. Prot.

VANDEN [VARDEN], Rev. Josiah; Meth.; 1831, assistant on Eastern Shore; 1836, George-Town, D. C.; 1837, at Alexandria, Va.; 1838, Westminster; 1839, Tal. Co. Circuit; 1840, Q. A. Co.; 1840/1, East Balto.

VAN QUICKENBORNE, Rev.; fl.1823, P. G. Co.; prob. Rev. Charles Van Quickenborne, S. J., died Aug. 17, 1837, at Portage des Sious, St. Charles Co., Mo.

VINTON, Rev. Robert S.; Meth. Ep.; entered in the ministry in 1818, d. July 31, 1870, in Balto.

WALKER, Rev. T. S.; fl.1834; prob. Rev. Sater Thomas Walker; Baptist; b. 1789; d. 1849; buried in Greenmount Cemetery, Balto.

WATERS, Rev. Richard J. Henry; Prot. Ep.; native of Chas. Co., ordained 1837; 1837, Somerset Par., Som. Co.; 1840, Queen Caroline Par., A. A. Co.; 1855, St. Philip's Par., P. G. and How. Co.; 1859, Trinity Par., Cecil Co.

WATERS, Rev. Thomas G.; denomination not determined; d. Jan. 21, 1845, in his 44th year.

WATKINS, Rev. Nicholas; Meth. Ep.; d. Aug. 1, 1858, formerly of Annap.; a Meth. Ep. minister for over 50 years.

WEEMS, Rev.; fl.1810, 1811; prob. Rev. John Weems; Prot. Ep.; d. Nov. 2, 1821, in his 57th year, having been rector of Port Tobacco Par. for more than 30 years. Rev. John Weems was a native of A. A. Co., and was ordained in 1787. Port Tobacco Par. was his first and only charge.

WELCH, Rev. Robert; Meth. Ep.; d. July 2, 1826, age 55 at his residence in A. A. Co.

WELLER, Rev. Mr. George; Prot. Ep.; native of Boston, ordained in 1816; 1818, Great Choptank Par., Dor. Co.; 1819, Dorchester Par., Dor. Co.; 1823, North Sassafras Par., Cecil Co.; 1826, moved to Penna.; d. 1841, age 50, in Mass.

WEYLIE, Rev. John V.; Prot. Ep.; d. 1817.

WHITEHEAD, Rev. James; Prot. Ep.; native of Va., ordained in 1787;

1806, he was an Associate Pastor of St. Paul's Church, Balto.;
d. 1808 in Balto.

WILMER, Rev.; fl.1774; prob. Rev. James Jones Wilmer; Prot. Ep.,
and later Swedenborgian (New Jerusalem); b. 1749/50, Kent
Co., Md.

WOART, Rev. John Loring; Prot. Ep.; native of Mass., ordained 1831;
1835, St. John's Par., P. G. Co.; 1836, moved to N. J.; d.
1838 when the Pulaski sank.

WOODLY, Rev.; fl.1834; not further identified.

WRIGHT, Mr. Lucien Bonaparte; Prot. Ep.; native of Ohio, ordained
in 1833; 1833, All Hallows Par., A. A. Co.; 1835, moved to
Alabama; 1847 to 1849, returned to Md.

WYATT, Rev. Mr. Joseph; fl.1812; not further identified.

ZOOCHEY, Rev.; fl.1806, Frederick Town; prob. Nicholas Zocchey.

SOURCES OF INFORMATION FOR

NOTES ON MARYLAND CLERGY

Ethan Allen. Clergy in Maryland of the Protestant Episcopal Church,
Since the Independence of 1783. Baltimore: James S. Waters,
1860.

Raymond B. Clark, Jr., and Sara Seth Clark. Talbot County, Maryland,
Marriages, 1794-1824. Washington, 1965.

Raymond B. Clark, Jr., and Sara Seth Clark. Talbot County, Maryland,
Marriage Licenses, 1825-1850. St. Michael's, Md., 1967.

Dielman File, Maryland Historical Society, Baltimore.

Frederic Emory. Queen Anne's County, Maryland, Its Early History
and Development. Baltimore: Maryland Historical Society,
1950.

History of the Baptist Churches in Maryland Connected with the Maryland Baptist Union Association. Baltimore: J. F. Weishampel,
Jr., 1855.

Thomas Hamilton Lewis. Historical Record of the Maryland Annual
Conference of the Methodist Protestant Church from the First
Session, 1829 - to the One Hundred and Eleventh, Concluding
Session, 1939; 5th Revised Edition. No place: no pub., no
date.

Minutes of the Baltimore Annual Conference, Methodist Episcopal
    Church: Official Journal, One Hundred and Forty-Fourth
    Session. No place: no pub., 1928.

Official Minutes, Maryland Annual Conference, Methodist Protestant
    Church, One Hundred and Sixth Session, 1934.

Joseph T. Watts. The Rise and Progress of Maryland Baptists Issued
    by the State Mission Board of the Maryland Baptist Union
    Association. No place: no pub., no date.

Frederick L. Weis. The Colonial Clergy of Maryland, Delaware, and
    Georgia. Lancaster, Mass.: Society of the Descendants of
    Colonial Clergy, 1950.

Abdel Ross Wentz. History of the Evangelical Lutheran Synod of
    Maryland of the United Lutheran Church in America, 1820-1920.
    Harrisburg: The Evangelical Press, 1920.

* * * * *

INDEX

McElhiney (cont'd),
140,173,175,194,
197,210
M'Feeley, 183
McGill, 159
M'Keehan, 60
Mackenheimer, 15,110,
122,125,189
McKenny, 210
McKim, 123
Mackubin, 5,22,40,54,
63,178
McLaughlin, 27,49
McMechen, 70
McMullin, 16
McPherson, 128

Mace, 103,166,186
Madison, 105
Maggs, 113
Magruder, 41,160,162
Mahaffy, 29
Malcolm, 28
Malonee, 49,109
Mann, 37,177
Marle, 157
Marr, 106
Marriott, 31,103,194
Marsh, 16,156
Marshall, 200
Martin, 33,105,106,
108
Mason, 123
Matthews, 12
Maud, 104
Maxcy, 96
Maxwell, 102
Maybury, 99
Maynadier, 60,107
Maynard, 136
Mayo, 199,205
Medairy, 17
Meriwether, 104
Merriken, 98,119,154,
194,196
Mewburn, 78,79
Middleton, 2,62
Millard, 20
Miller, 97,108,128,
141,148,174
Mills, 53,56,86,102

Mitchell, 42
Moreau, 114
Morgan, 175
Morrell, 163
Morris, 165
Morton, 50
Moss, 81
Muenscher, 20
Mullinix, 40
Munn, 13
Munroe, 32,150,173
Murdoch, 36,162,212
Murdock, 78,167
Murphy, 17
Murray, 27,159,173,
182
Muse, 210

Neth, 120
Nevins, 41
Nevitt, 135
Newbern, 192
Nicholls, 122
Nichols, 196,202
Nicholson, 58,94,
164,189,200
Nicols, 99
Nind, 15,40,98,106,
119,155,176
Nixon, 155
Norman, 47,109,189
Norris, 127
North, 27,130

O'Bryan, 152
Ogle, 11,62
Orme, 46
Orr, 170
Owen, 70,126
Owings, 79,155

Parker, 46
Parkinson, 55,180
Parran, 163
Parrott, 51
Pascault, 104
Patterson, 23
Peach, 78
Peaco, 31
Peacock, 133
Pearce, 5,43

Penn, 191
Pennington, 138
Phelps, 71,98
Philips, 62,75,186
Phillips, 140,202
Philpott, 12
Pierce, 66
Pilmore, 196
Pinckney, 69,79,86,
171
Pindell, 12
Pitcher, 113
Pitts, 199
Plain, 98,208
Plater, 180
Pleasants, 90
Poe, 142
Poisal, 17,22,24,31,
99,129,157,188,208
Pollard, 94
Pompey, 57
Popnam, 92
Pothain, 129
Pottenger, 77
Potter, 21
Powell, 57
Poyntell, 25
Price, 49
Prout, 30
Purdy, 17,130,141
Pursle, 211

Quynn, 128

Rackliffe, 134
Rafferty, 19,47,55,57,
61,76,123,163,198,
199
Raitt, 36,58
Ralph, 32,209
Randall, 75,121
Rankin, 163
Rattoone, 193
Rawlings, 15,16,17,181
Ray, 15
Read, 33,40,103
Reaney, 6
Reid, 150
Reiner, 78
Reis, 42
Reitzel, 61

CPSIA information can be obtained
at www.ICGtesting.com
Printed in the USA
FSHW011613170819
61137FS